Contents

Introduction   Robert S. Dombroski   1

Boccaccio   Ugo Foscolo   15

Boccaccio's Human Comedy   Francesco De Sanctis   26

The Epic of the Italian Merchant   Vittore Branca   38

The Place of the *Decameron*   Giuseppe Petronio   48

Some Reflections on the *Decameron*   Victor Šhklovskij   61

Frate Alberto   Erich Auerbach   69

The Legendary Style of the *Decameron*   Enrico de' Negri   82

Boccaccio   Alberto Moravia   99

Forms of Accommodation in the *Decameron*   Thomas M. Greene   113

The *Decameron*: the Marginality of Literature   Giuseppe Mazzotta   129

Selected Bibliography   145

Notes on the Contributors   147

Critical Perspectives
on the
Decameron

Critical Perspectives
on the
Decameron

Edited by

Robert S. Dombroski

BARNES & NOBLE
BOOKS
10 East 53d St., New York 10022
(a division of Harper & Row Publishers, inc.)

ISBN 0–06–491735–5

LCC 76–24068

First published 1976 by Hodder and Stoughton Educational
Published in the U.S.A. 1977 by
HARPER & ROW PUBLISHERS, INC.
BARNES & NOBLE IMPORT DIVISION

Printed and bound in Great Britain

For Stanislaus

Introduction

In his introductory essay to the Rigg translation of the *Decameron*,[1] John Addington Symonds pays eloquent tribute to Boccaccio's work, underscoring its elemental and narrative force as one of the great masterpieces of European fiction; his judgement remains, I believe, indisputable: 'It is impossible to imagine an age in which the *Decameron* will fail of general recognition as, in point alike of invention as of style, one of the most notable creations of human genius. Of few books are the sources so recondite, insomuch that it seems to be certain that in the main they must have been merely oral tradition, and few have exercised so wide and mighty an influence. The profound, many-sided and intimate knowledge of human nature which it evinces, its vast variety of incident, its wealth of tears and laughter, its copious and felicitous diction, inevitably apt for every occasion, and, notwithstanding the frequent harshness, and occasional obscurity of its at times tangled, at times laboured periods, its sustained energy and animation of style must ever ensure for this human comedy unchallenged rank among the literary masterpieces that are truly immortal.' Yet among those not professionally concerned with the Italian Trecento, the *Decameron* is still virtually unknown in the complexity of its artistic structure and meaning. The number of readers who have actually read the entire work may tend to be influenced by what has become its rather oversimplified image as a collection of witty and salacious tales aimed at comforting idle ladies in love (Boccaccio's proposed reason for writing the work), which – in the words of one modern critic – constitute the 'battle cry' of literary naturalism.[2] To encapsulate the *Decameron* in a formula, however true or suggestive, serves only to diminish the total value of its stimulus and runs the risk of obstructing a mature reading of the work. This is not to say that judgements of this sort are false in

---

[1] Florence: The Medici Press, 1947, p. xxi.
[2] Aldo D. Scaglione, *Nature and Love in the Late Middle Ages* (Berkeley and Los Angeles: University of California Press, 1963), p. 68.

substance. On the contrary, they may be wholly correct. Their sin is one of omission: in their resolve to classify, they tend to neglect the *means* and *manner* by which Boccaccio carries out his intention, that is, the strategy of form that makes the *Decameron* the masterpiece it is.

Like the *Divina Commedia*, the *Decameron* is in form a 'comedy'. The word 'comedy', in the terminology of medieval poetics, refers to a composition beginning in sadness and ending in joy: 'a principio horribilis et fetidus, in fine prosperus desiderabilis et gratus.'[3] The term well explains the purpose of Boccaccio's design, establishing an ideal relationship between the vices criticized in the First Day and the brilliant examples of generosity, friendship, and patience of the Tenth. But the comic scheme of the tales reveals only partially the work's moral structure and the point of view from which it was written. In order to understand the genesis, plan, and strategy of the *Decameron* we must turn to the Proem and Introduction to the First Day: the so-called 'double frame'.

In the Proem, Boccaccio stresses the reality of personal experience as the motive force behind the stories he is about to tell. The tone of truth or verisimilitude and the vitality of situations in the work depend on this declared autobiographical origin of his inspiration, however stylized it may appear. Secondly, Boccaccio states that his work is dedicated to the ladies, a fact which verifies his acceptance of the convention according to which love poetry and prose romances were written in the vernacular so that they might be understood by women who were unfamiliar with Latin. But it would be to over-simplify to take Boccaccio's words only at their face value, for he is more concerned with an ideal reading public, made up of those who share the interests and ambitions of the operative burgher class to which he belonged, than with the woes of a restricted audience. His dedication of the *Decameron* to the ladies should be viewed as a means for indicating the naturalistic origin of the work. The ladies, in fact – as we learn from the Introduction to the Fourth Day – are the symbol of a new poetic literature concerned exclusively with the affairs of this life: 'Le Muse son donne . . . [le donne] hanno nel primo aspetto

---

[3] See Vittore Branca, *Boccaccio medievale* (Florence: Sansoni, 1956), p. 14. Also, as attested by Dante in the Second Book of the *De Vulgari Eloquentia*, the term 'comedy' had important stylistic connotations: tragedy was considered the most elevated style in prose or poetry; elegy the most humble; comedy, a mixture of the two.

somiglianza di quelle.' (The Muses are ladies ... [the ladies] have
their outward semblance.) The Proem concludes with a passage of
great relevance that has the value of an *incipit*:

> Adunque, accio che per me in parte s'ammendi il peccato della
> Fortuna ... in soccorso e rifugio di quelle che amano ...
> intendo di raccontare cento novelle, o favole o parabole o
> istorie che dire le vogliamo, raccontate in dieci giorni ... da
> una onesta brigata di sette donne e di tre giovani, nel pistilen-
> zioso tempo della passata mortalità fatta, e alcune canzonette
> delle predette donne cantate a lor diletto. Nelle quali novelle,
> piacevoli e aspri casi d'amore e altri fortunosi avvenimenti si
> vedranno, così ne' moderni tempi avvenuti come negli antichi...
>
> Wherefore, in order that in some measure the injustice of For-
> tune be corrected ... I, for the succour and relief of those
> [ladies] in love, ... intend to recount one hundred novellas, or
> fables, or parables, or histories, as we may please to call them,
> told in ten days ... by an honourable company of seven ladies
> and three men, in the time of the late mortal pestilence, and
> some canzonets sung by the said ladies for their pleasure. In
> which novellas will be seen felicitous and bitter instances of
> love and other eventful happenings of times both modern and
> ancient....[4]

Besides defending the scope of his work and alluding to its multiple
and various forms, Boccaccio expresses here the point of view which
gives ideological unity to his work, namely his faith in man's
capacity to rule over the multiform reality of social life; a faith
characteristic of the merchant class of his time and rooted in his
conception of the natural and universal forces of Love. Boccaccio
goes on to employ the grand architecture of the Introduction to
exemplify his viewpoint.

The structure of the Introduction consists of two parts: the
description of the plague and the formation of the group of storytellers; the first indicates the moment of tragedy, the latter the
moment of escape. The contrast between the horrid beginning and
the final delight transcends the limits of rhetorical convention. The

---

[4] Translation mine. Unless stated otherwise, the passages translated
from the *Decameron* have been taken from G. H. McWilliam's new translation: *The Decameron* (Harmondsworth: Penguin Books, 1972).

breakdown of civic laws and norms caused by the plague is superseded by the storytellers through the composure and moderation of
their 'onesto vivere'; the company overcomes the obstacle of bad
fortune by turning to reason and common sense. Its decision to flee
the disaster of pestilence signifies, on the one hand, a reaction to the
collapse of the social order, on the other, the possible domination
of man over Fortune. In contrast to the majority of the population,
the courteous and noble storytellers retain their respect for religious
and societal norms (we find them in church, dressed in black as a
sign of mourning) and thus function as a counterpoint to the new
reality brought about by the plague; they seek to re-establish order
in a time of chaos by means of reason. Their ideal of moderation and
respect for convention is further reflected in their life of temporary
exile and precisely in the ordered and harmonious way they structure their interpersonal relationships and activities: to cite one
example, their assigning the rule of the First Day to Pampinea, the
oldest and maturest of the ladies, and the rule of the last day to
Panfilo, the oldest and maturest of the men. Therefore through
recourse to the literary *topos* of the 'plague' and to the difficult rhetorical exercise of the *imitatio* or competition with an authoritative
text (in the case of the *Decameron*, the *Historia Langobardorum* of Paolo
Diacono),[5] Boccaccio expresses a specific social outlook, a means of
approaching reality, which in various forms appears in the tales. The
novellas themselves – as some of the essays collected in this volume
will show – are the work of a narrative genius who reaches his goal
of delight through the artful construction of naturalistic situations;
these are conceived with a strategy of form attuned to the 'onesto
vivere' characteristic of the storytellers who represent the ideal
human condition as envisaged by Boccaccio.

Concerning Boccaccio's life, contemporary scholarship has reduced
the portrait of the author from what had become a romantic legend
replete with exceptional occurrences to more modest but certainly
more humanly comprehensible dimensions. The myth of Fiammetta,
for instance, is now recognized as simply the product of Boccaccio's
desire to conventionalize the love experiences of his youth. For
many, Fiammetta had been the *senhal* of a certain Maria d'Aquino, the
supposed illegitimate daughter of King Robert of Naples. But, as

---

[5] See V. Branca, *op. cit.*, pp. 209–13.

Branca and others have shown,[6] besides the fact that the extant
genealogies and documents belonging to the Aquino family make
no mention at all of such a woman, it is clear that the charming and
seductive image of Fiammetta, so dear to past criticism, is constructed according to the standard modes and rules of the love
literature of the high Middle Ages.

A bare minimum of factual data is necessary to acquaint one
with Boccaccio's life and works. He was born in Florence (less
probably at Certaldo) in the summer of 1313, the natural son of
Boccaccino di Chellino, a successful Florentine merchant. He undertook his early studies in his native city under the tutelage of the
Florentine grammarian Giovanni Mazzuoli da Strada, father of the
poet Zanobi da Strada. Towards the middle of 1327, Boccaccio's
father moved to Naples as an agent of the Bardi company. Boccaccio,
who had unwillingly followed his father, learned there the rudi-
ments of commerce and law and mixed with the local aristocracy
and the refined society of the court of Robert of Anjou. Naples also
provided the young Boccaccio with coteries of scholars and learned
men who contributed to the formation and the direction his studies
were to take. There he became familiar with, among others, the
humanist Paolo da Perugia; the jurist and poet Cino da Pistoia who,
with Graziolo de' Bambaglioli, introduced him to Dante's works;
and the Augustine friar Dionigi da Borgo San Sepolcro from whom
he learned about Petrarch.

It is also in Naples that Boccaccio begins his literary apprenticeship. In the period 1330–40, he composes a number of lyric poems
and the works *Elegia di Costanza*, *Allegoria mitologica*, *Caccia di Diana* (c.
1334), *Filostrato* (c. 1335) and *Filocolo* (c. 1336), in addition to a good
part of the *Teseida*, which he was to complete later in Florence. In
1338 he terminates his association with the Bardi company and two
years later he is forced to return to Florence. From the splendour and
refinement of the court of Anjou, Boccaccio now experiences the
harsh reality of a city troubled by political and economic problems;
a change which was to affect his outlook, directing him towards a
literature of greater contemporary relevance. The *Comedia della ninfe*
(1341–2) and the *Amorosa visione*, written in *terza rima*, mark a move
from the subject matter of legendary adventures characteristic of his

---

[6] Cf. Giovanni Boccaccio, *Tutte le opere*, Vittore Branca ed. (Milano:
Mondadori, 1967), vol. I, pp. 67–70.

Neapolitan production to the representation of events and people
known to the Florence of his day. These works are followed by the
prose romance *Elegia di Madonna Fiammetta* (1343–4) and the *Ninfale
fiesolano* (1344–6), a poem that celebrates the mythical founding of
Florence.

From 1345 to the beginning of 1348 there is evidence of
Boccaccio's being first in Ravenna and then in Forlì at the courts of
Ostasio da Polenta and Francesco degli Ordelaffi. Early in 1348 he
returns to Florence to see the city in the grips of the Black Plague,
which takes the lives of his father and stepmother. It is in this period
(1348–51) that he gives form to his *Decameron*. The plague having
provided the necessary impetus and suggestion for the frame, he
begins reworking, assembling and editing rough copies of the tales
written beforehand, as well as composing new ones. In 1350 he
meets Petrarch in Florence, thus starting a deep friendship which
was to produce one of the most fecund exchanges of letters known
to European literature.

From 1348 Boccaccio is deeply involved in Florentine public
life, accepting various assignments and diplomatic missions. Early in
1351 he is appointed Chamberlain of the Camera del Commune and
in this capacity discusses the annexation of Prato with the House of
Anjou. Later that year we find him in Tyrol at the court of Ludwig
of Bavaria with overtures for an alliance against the Visconti;
towards the end of 1352 he goes to Padua on behalf of the Signoria
to announce to Petrarch his restitution to citizenship and to offer
him a chair at the newly founded University of Florence; and in the
spring of 1354 he is sent to Avignon to discuss with Pope Innocent
VI the approaching visit of Charles IV to Italy. At this time he is at
work at what is known as *Zibaldone Magliabechiano*, a notebook containing themes and topics which he was to employ in his future
writings. Between 1350 and 1355 he composes some of the works
which were to bring him fame as a scholar: *Genealogia deorum gentilium*,
De casibus, *De montibus*, and *De claris mulieribus*, in addition to the first
draft of the *Trattatello in laude di Dante*.

In 1360 Boccaccio helps institute at the University of Florence
the first chair of Greek outside Byzantine Europe. Now, disillusioned
with political intrigue and desirous of reconciling his literary and
cultural ambitions with his religious aspirations, he takes minor
orders and retreats to Certaldo, where he writes the provoking
Epistola consolatoria a Pino de' Rossi (1361–2). Later at Ravenna, having

been asked by Petrarch to furnish him with material on St Peter Damian for his *De vita solitaria*, Boccaccio transcribes and completes the unfinished life of the saint written by his disciple Giovanni da Lodi. Then, after brief visits to Naples and to the home of Petrarch in Venice, he returns to Certaldo to work at the *Trattatello* and *Corbaccio* (c. 1365), as well as at the noted defence of poetry contained in the final books of the *Genealogia*. During the years 1367–71 he is busy revising and recopying his *Decameron* into what is known as the autograph codex Hamilton 90 of Berlin. Between 1373 and 1374 it is possible that he met Chaucer, who was in Italy from December 1372 to March 1374 in occasion of some commercial arrangements between England and the Republic of Genoa. Recent criticism, however, is sceptical of any would-be meeting between the two.

For many years already a cultural leader whose influence and example extended throughout Europe, Boccaccio spends his remaining years in the solitude of Certaldo, commenting on Dante's *Commedia* and ordering the thoughts on the divine origin of poetry which are contained in the *Genealogia*, a work that remains with him until his death. In 1374 he is informed of the death of Petrarch, and about a year and a half later, on 21 December 1375, he himself dies, bequeathing his magnificent library to the Augustine fathers of the Church of Santo Spirito in Florence.

The extent of Boccaccio's influence on European literature may be measured by the vast number of imitations and adaptations his stories have undergone. Among the earliest of printed books, of which four editions appeared between 1471 and 1492, the tales of the *Decameron* extended in many directions and affected a variety of literary modes. Poets and dramatists of all European countries drew continuously from their wealth of plots and situations. Some novellas, in fact, such as those of Griselda (X, 10), Ghismonda (VI, 1), and Federigo degli Alberighi (V, 9), attained through the centuries a popularity matching only that of certain biblical stories.

In the fourteenth century, Ser Giovanni Fiorentino, Giovanni Sercambi, and Francesco Sacchetti were among the first to retell Boccaccio's stories, thus initiating a vogue which was to determine the course of Italian novelistic and dramatic literature for centuries to come. The fortunes of the *Decameron* in France were also immediate and lasting. The tale of Griselda, translated by Philippe de Mézières (c. 1384–9) from Petrarch's Latin version, was widely circulated

before Laurent de Premierfait's translation of the entire work in
1414. And within seventy years of Antoine le Maçon's version in
1545, nineteen editions appeared in Paris, Lyons, Amsterdam, and
Rotterdam. Boccaccio's impact on French renaissance culture may
be gauged by the remarks with which Queen Margaret of Navarre,
sister of Francis I, prefaces her *Heptaméron*, an unfinished collection of
stories inspired by the *Decameron*: 'Le roi Francois, premier de son
nom, Monseigneur le dauphin, madame la dauphine, madame
Marguerite font tant de cas que si Boccace, du lieu où il était les
eût pu ouïr, il devait ressusciter à la louange de telles personnes . . .'
And in 1663, La Fontaine, who retold twenty or more of Boccaccio's
stories, entitled his collection of tales *Nouvelles en vers tirées de Bocace et
de l'Arioste*. Germany was no less responsive to Boccaccio's narratives.
A German version of the *Decameron*, printed in 1473, left a deep mark
on Hans Sachs who drew from it ample material for his *Schwänke*.
Luther too adapted several of Boccaccio's stories for his *Tischreden*.
The question of whether Chaucer had actually read the *Decameron* in
Italian still remains unsolved. However, in view of his familiarity
with the language, his knowledge of the *Teseida* and the *Filostrato*, and
the fact that six of the *Canterbury Tales* resemble stories of the *Decameron*,
it is natural to assume that he must have read, if not the original in
its entirety, at least certain tales which were in circulation during
his visit to Italy. In any case, it was – to recall the words of Herbert
Wright – 'the wonderful good fortune for English literature that its
first great poet was sent on missions in the course of which he could
hear the tongue of Boccaccio.'[7] The English writers who were
influenced by the *Decameron* are too numerous to mention and include
such illustrious names as Shakespeare, Jonson, Dryden, Coleridge,
Keats and Shelley. To these may be added those of Lope de Vega in
Spain, Goethe and Lessing in Germany, Goldoni in Italy, and Molière
and Musset in France.

The reason for the popularity of the *Decameron* lies mainly in its
being a veritable treasury of masterfully written tales depicting a vast
range of human experience. Boccaccio did not only rewrite the
hundred and one best stories of his time, but in doing so offered an
unparalleled example of story-telling, designed to give the reader
the greatest possible delight. In narrative structure, he achieved a

---

[7] *Boccaccio in England from Chaucer to Tennyson* (London: The Athlone Press,
1957), p. 480.

blend of classicism and medievalism in the vernacular which was never equalled in the short story, and set the norms, formulated by Bembo, for renaissance prose style. His firm yet flexible narrative perspective and his diversity of moral attitude ensured following generations of writers absolute freedom in imitation and adaptation of his stories.

From the standpoint of critical interpretation, the *Decameron*, like every other classic of world literature, has undergone throughout the centuries a complete process of evaluation and re-evaluation. In every age men have viewed the *Decameron* from the perspective of their own times and through the lenses of contemporary interests and pre-suppositions. In our times the work's image is relatively felicitous, for the most part unblemished by the cultural snares and moral obstructions which in the past served to diminish its value. A brief chronicle of the fortunes of the *Decameron* will acquaint us with many of the problems discussed in the following essays.

The story of *Decameron* criticism begins with Boccaccio himself, who within the limits of his own experience as a writer establishes two divergent tendencies of judgement which were to reappear in the study of his work for at least three centuries. On the one hand, he defends his *Decameron* against real or would-be detractors (cf. Introduction to the Fourth Day and Conclusion), arguing in support of both the form and subject matter of his tales: although composed in the vernacular, in prose, and in 'istile umilissimo', the stories constitute a work of art and continue the Italian poetic tradition begun by Dante and Cavalcante; and the occasional licentiousness of the tales should not divert attention from their essential sobriety and sincerity of purpose. Later, in a different frame of mind, influenced by new cultural forces, Boccaccio was to reject his work precisely on the grounds of its lack of moral restraint, judging it from the humanistic viewpoint, that is, from the ideal of *latinitas* which postulated the elegance of Latin style and the gravity of subject matter as the essential criteria of great writing.[8] The humanist position on the *Decameron* is best summed up by Petrarch in the letter he sent Boccaccio accompanying his translation of the Griselda tale: 'I received – I am not sure how, nor who might have brought it to me – the book that in your youth you wrote in your native

---

[8] Cf. Giuseppe Petronio, 'Giovanni Boccaccio', *I classici italiani nella storia della critica,* Walter Binni ed. (Florence: La Nuova Italia, 1954), vol. I, p. 170.

tongue. I would lie if I were to say that I read it; the bulk of the volume and the fact that it is written in prose and for popular consumption were reasons enough not to have it distract me from more important business. ... But glancing at your book, I was pleased and, although offended by certain licentious and immoderate passages, I felt that your age at the time you wrote it, its language, style, levity of subject matter, and above all the type of reader it was addressed to would serve as your apology.'[9] Petrarch's view, whereby the *Decameron* is seen as limited by its very nature, yet pleasant and valid in itself, is restated with slight variations by the humanists for most of the fifteenth century.

In the early sixteenth century the image of the *Decameron* is fundamentally reshaped, as the work meets the interest of scholars whose goal it was to put the vernacular on equal footing with Latin as a literary medium and to establish the primacy of Tuscan over the other Italian dialects. In his *Prose della volgar lingua*, Pietro Bembo cites the *Decameron* as an illustrious example of Tuscan prose, underscoring the stylistic qualities which make it a model to be imitated. In spite of the particular slant of Bembo's view, his tendency to judge the work solely in terms of language and style, its importance consists in having removed the *Decameron* from the category of *letteratura amena* and having attributed to it the status of poetry.

From the Renaissance to the nineteenth century the terms and criteria of critical evaluation expounded by Bembo remain unaltered, conditioned only by variations in taste and culture. In the second half of the sixteenth century the Accademia della Crusca praises Boccaccio's work for its linguistic purity and its importance as a treasury of good grammar. But theoreticians and *literati* of the following century, motivated by the new poetics of 'novelty' and contemptuous of the linguistic and rhetorical precepts of the purists, began to oppose the standardized image of the *Decameron* as an exclusively linguistic model.

With the Enlightenment, Boccaccio's fortunes fared no better. Still utilized as an instrument of cultural debate, the *Decameron* received the ministrations of literary reformers, such as Saverio Bettinelli and Giuseppe Baretti, who reacted strongly against its classical

---

9 *Seniles*, Giuseppe Fracassetti ed. (Florence: Le Monnier, 1869–70), vol. II, pp. 541–2. Cited by G. Petronio, *op. cit.* p. 173.

elements: its use of Latin periods and its rhetorical excesses;[10] others who remained loyal to the classical ideal of literary prose, Giuseppe Parini for example, expressed moderate admiration for Boccaccio's language and style, while voicing disaffection with the 'frivolous' and 'indecent' subject matter of certain tales.[11] At the same time, the *Decameron* summoned the attention of critics interested in the sources and historicity of the tales. In 1742 Domenico Maria Manni published his notable *Istoria del Decamerone*, while between the years 1725 and 1764 Giovanni Bottari read to the Accademia della Crusca commentaries (published as a book in 1818) on each of the one hundred stories.

Although at times suggestive, the views and tendencies described so far are of little use in understanding Boccaccio's art and the complex world of his novellas. The body of true literary criticism on the *Decameron* which we possess today begins slowly to accumulate in the nineteenth century, when the investigation of literature becomes a discipline in itself, distinguished from the art of rhetoric.

The 'Discorso storico sul testo del *Decamerone*' by Ugo Foscolo (1825) marks an important change in the standpoint from which the *Decameron* was viewed. Although sharing in many ways the literary tastes of the previous century, Foscolo's essay postulated the need, characteristic of Romantic criticism, to combine philology and history in the evaluation of literature. He realized that any attempt to trace the history of the *Decameron* as a text meant tracing the development of the Italian language, which in turn meant shifting the focus from the work as a rhetorical and stylistic unity to the work as an integral part of the literary and civic history of the Italian people.[12]

With Romantic criticism, we have the total rejection of that mode of evaluation which judged a writer according to fixed rules and models. Boccaccio's work, now viewed as a moment in the development of Italian literature, becomes subject to the moralistic

---

[10] Saverio Bettinelli, *Lettere virgiliane e inglesi e altri scritti critici*, Vittorio Enzo Alfieri ed. (Bari: Laterza, 1930), p. 125; Giuseppe Baretti, *La Frusta letteraria*, Luigi Piccioni ed. (Bari: Laterza, 1932), vol. I, p. 342.

[11] Giuseppe Parini, *Tutte le opere*, Guido Mazzoni ed. (Florence: G. Barbera, 1925), pp. 815–16.

[12] 'Discorso storico sul testo del *Decamerone*', in *Saggi e discorsi critici*, Edizione Nationale delle Opere di Ugo Foscolo (Florence: Le Monnier, 1953), C. Foligno ed., vol. X, pp. 303–75. The principal ideas of the 'Discorso storico' are to be found in 'Boccaccio', an article written in English, and published in the *London Magazine*, vol. V, no. XVIII (June 1826), pp. 145–57. (Reprinted below, pp. 15–25.)

severity of readers concerned with the civic, religious, and social import of literature. Villemain, Gioberti, and Quinet – to mention the most provocative of anticlerical historians who wrote before De Sanctis – recognized Boccaccio as a ruthless critic of medieval society whose work, considered poor in inspiration and spirituality compared to Dante, marks the initial triumph of the Renaissance ideal of l'art pour l'art.[13]

The first thoroughly historical and critical systematization of Boccaccio's work is contained in Francesco De Sanctis' monumental Storia della letteratura italiana (published in 1870–1). De Sanctis developed the views of his immediate predecessors into a new synthesis which defined the structure and inspiration of the Decameron, as well as its historical significance. He sees Boccaccio as the voice of the Italian spirit in the age of the Renaissance: an age which was bourgeois, secular, and individualistic in the sense of caring little for public life or communal welfare; indifferent to religion, morality or patriotism, devoted to art and giving artistic form to every aspect of life. As a reflex of its age the world of the Decameron is superficially brilliant: a world whose only law is nature which thrives on a sensuous love of beauty and is regulated by a serenely comic spirit.

After De Sanctis, Burckhardt and Carducci celebrate Boccaccio as the first champion of antiquity, while the positivist critics, in their search for direct literary sources, insert the Decameron into the antimedieval and irreligious tradition of the fabliaux. A turning point in Boccaccio's fortunes is marked by the reaction of Croce and his followers to the Romantic and positivistic literary historiography. From the standpoint of method, it consists in the denial of the validity of any history of literature which is not a collection of successive monographs focusing on the intrinsic value of a work of art. From here we return to the problem of the aesthetic unity of the Decameron, originally posed by De Sanctis, an inquiry which gives rise to a variety of formulas mostly centred around the acceptance of Love, Nobility, or Intelligence as the unifying element or theme.[14]

In more recent times the pendulum has swung back from the

---

[13] See, Abel François Villemain, Cours de littérature française (Paris: Pichon et Didier, 1830), vol. II, pp. 32–51; Gustavo Balsamo Crivelli ed. (Turin: UTET, 1946), vol. II, p. 34; Edgardo Quinet, Rivoluzioni d'Italia, Carlo Muscetta ed. (Bari: Laterza, 1935), pp. 110 f.

[14] For an extensive treatment of these views and a bibliography, see G. Petronio, op. cit., pp. 209–22.

'impressionistic' methods of Crocean and neo-Crocean aestheticism to attempts at creating a more veritable historical picture of the *Decameron*. With a blend of traditional philology, textual criticism, and socio-historical inquiry, Vittore Branca has corrected the Romantic thesis, in which the work is seen as the antithesis of the Middle Ages. For Branca, on the contrary, Boccaccio's 'human comedy' reflects the glorious autumn of the medieval world; it is the direct voice of the burgher merchant class of the late Middle Ages, and should be understood, not in contrast, but as a complement or counterpart to Dante's *Divina Commedia*. Giuseppe Petronio, on the other hand, in an attempt to temper Branca's revindication of Boccaccio's medieval heritage, shows that the society of and for which Boccaccio writes has neither the ideals nor the mentality of medieval society; at the same time it is not the new Renaissance burgher class, but rather a society of transition, characterised by the secular and burgher ideals of the *popolo grasso* of the Florentine Commune. Thus for Petronio, the *Decameron* is a document reflecting the dynamics of an 'intermediate' age, which he acutely analyses through the evolution of the social virtues of 'liberalità' and 'masserizia'.

Instead of approaching the *Decameron* from the standpoint of poetic unity or as a historical document, the trend of much contemporary criticism has been to examine the work as an artefact, that is, to define not so much what the *Decameron* is – as how, in the utilization of particular linguistic and thematic structures, it becomes what it is; or, put another way, how its principal semantic categories reveal its ideological dimension. To this end a number of recent efforts in structural and semiotic analysis have been devoted

The criticism reprinted here represents a variety of methods and perspectives aimed at understanding the *Decameron* both as a historical document and as an artistic entity. My objective in collecting and editing these writings is simply to introduce Boccaccio's great art to students of literature, most of whom will read the *Decameron* in translation. The views collected here, although among the most excellent, are meant not to be exhaustive, but rather to form a complex of authoritative viewpoints in the light of which one may begin to comprehend a great masterpiece of world literature.

In conclusion, I wish to thank the University of Connecticut Research Foundation for granting me funds to cover the permission fees for the material reprinted in this book.

Robert S. Dombroski

Boccaccio

[Boccaccio] died not only without the hope, but without the desire, that his *Decameron* should outlive him. His autograph copy has never been found, and from what we shall presently have occasion to observe about his handwriting, we derive very strong presumptive evidence that he destroyed it himself. A young friend of his,[1] eight or ten years after his death, transcribed it with the most scrupulous exactness, frankly confessing that the copy he used was full of errors. After the introduction of printing, copies and editions were multiplied with mistakes, which, it was clear, were partly accumulated by the negligence of printers, while their art was yet in its infancy. But from the age of Boccaccio to that of Lorenzo de Medici and the pontificate of Leo X, the Italian language was so barbarised that it seemed lost to the learned men of Italy; for more than a century they wrote in Latin, which had fixed rules and was common to all Europe. The critics of that illustrious epoch strove by every means to form the language spoken by Italians into a literary language, well adapted for written composition and for being understood by the whole nation, and in the penury of authors who could furnish observations, and examples, and principles, from which a right method might be derived, they had recourse, with common consent, to the tales of Boccaccio; they found words at once vernacular and perfectly elegant, distinct and expressive; skilful construction, musical periods, and diversity of style; nor perhaps could any expedient at that time have been found better adapted for obviating numerous difficulties which presented themselves. But the maxims and the practice of the literary men of that age consisted not so much in constructing rules from observations as in imitating punctually, servilely, and childishly the most admired writers. In poetry they were implicit copiers of Petrarch, and sang of pure and

---

'Boccaccio' by Ugo Foscolo; abridged by Robert S. Dombroski from *Edizione nazionale delle opere di Ugo Foscolo*, vol. X: *Saggi e discorsi critici*, Cesare Foligno ed. (Firenze: Le Monnier, 1953), pp. 384–96.

[1] [Francesco Mannelli].

sacred love. In Latin they imitated Virgil and Cicero, and treated sacred things in profane words. Thus the system of restricting a whole dead language to the works of a few writers was still more absurdly applied to the living tongue of Italy, and the critics were almost unanimous in decreeing that no example was to be adduced from any poem except the Canzoniere Amoroso of Petrarch.

From this circumstance, the Protestants took occasion to impute to the literary men of that time very small regard to manners, and no sense of religion. The first accusation is exaggerated, and was common to them with all orders of society in Europe; the other is most absurd, but has prevailed in Protestant universities from that day, and has been handed down by long tradition, on the testimony of the first religious reformers, who, in order to open every possible way for the reception of their doctrines, imputed infidelity to all the learned men of the court of Leo X. But most, if not all of these men believed the faith they possessed, and which was then attacked by hostile superstition. Some made a vow never to read a profane book, but being unable long to observe it, got absolution from the Pope; others, that they might not contaminate Christian things with the impure latinity of monks and friars, tried to translate the Bible into the language of the age of Augustus. This system of servilely imitating excellent authors did not prevent some men of genius, particularly historians, from attempting to relate in a style at once original, dignified, and energetic, the events of their country. But they were living writers, nor had long celebrity and prescriptive authority yet stamped them as models. To this reason, which holds good of every age and country, was added, that the liberty of the numerous republics of Italy which had sprung up in the barbarism of the Middle Ages, declined in the most fertile and splendid period of her literature, and the historians who were witnesses of the misfortunes and degradation of their country, wrote in a manner which was not agreeable to her tyrants. Hence Machiavelli, Guicciardini, Segni, and others who are now studied as masters of style, were not then read, except by a few; their works were hardly known in manuscript, and if published they were mutilated; nor were any complete editions of their histories printed until two centuries after they were written. Thus the Novelle of Boccaccio held the field, and their popularity was greatly increased by the abhorrence and contempt which they inspired against the wickedness of the monks.

Certain young men of Florence conspired against Duke Alex-

ander, bastard of Clement VII, with the design of driving him from
their country, and re-establishing the republic. They held meetings
under the colour of amending the text of Boccaccio by the collation
of manuscripts, and by critical examination. Such was the source,
and such the authors, of the celebrated edition of Giunti, in 1527, now
regarded as one of the rarest curiosities of bibliography, and preserved from that time as a record of the Florentine republic, almost
all these young men having fought against the house of Medici, and
died at the siege of Florence or in exile. The work subsequently became more scarce, because it was constantly exposed to the danger
of being mutilated or prohibited through the interest of the monks.
Leo X made a jest of those things, and crowned the abbot of Gaeta,
seated on an elephant, with laurel and cabbage-leaves. Adrian VI, who
succeeded him, had been immured in a cloister, and the cardinals of
his school shortly after proposed that the Colloquies of Erasmus, and
every popular book injurious to the clergy, should be prohibited.
Paul III was of the opinion that the threat was sufficient, nor was it
at that time put in execution; but when the Decameron, which had
already been translated into several languages, was quoted by the
Anti-Papists, the Church ceased to confine herself to threats, and
began actually to prohibit the reprinting and the reading of Boccaccio's tales; nor could any one have a copy in his possession without
a licence from his confessor. The Protestant Reformation provoked a
reform in the Catholic Church, which though less apparent was
perhaps greater and more solid. The Protestants took as the basis of
theirs the liberty of interpreting the oracles of the Holy Spirit by
the aid of human reason; while the Catholics admitted no interpretations but those inspired by God as represented by the Popes.
Which of these two was the most beneficial to the interest of religion is a difficult question. Perhaps every religion which is subjected
to the scrutiny of reason ceases to be faith; while every creed
inculcated without the concurrence of the reason degenerates into
blind superstition. But, as far as literature was concerned, liberty of
conscience, in many countries, prepared the way for civil liberty, and
for the free expression of thoughts and opinions; while in Italy,
passive obedience to the religious power strengthened political
tyranny, and increased the debasement and long servitude of the
public mind. The Protestant Reformation was principally confined to
dogmas – the Catholic wholly to discipline; and, therefore, all
speculations on the lives and manners of ecclesiastics were then

repressed as leading to new heresies. The Council of Trent saw that the people of Germany did not stop short at complaining that the monks were traders in Indulgences, but went on to deny the sacrament of confession, the celibacy of the clergy, and the infallibility and spiritual power of the Pope. It therefore decreed that any attack upon, or insinuations against, the clergy, should be followed by immediate registration of the book containing them in the index of prohibited works; and that the reading or the possession of any such book, without licence from a bishop, should be regarded both as a sin and as an offence punishable in virtue of the anathema. These laws, of ecclesiastical origin, were thenceforth interpreted and administered by civil tribunals subjected to the presidency of inquisitors of the order of St Dominic; who, moreover, by the consent of the Italian governments, were invested with authority to examine, alter, mutilate and suppress every book, whether ancient or modern, previously to its being printed.

The Spanish domination in Italy, the long reign of Philip II (the most tyrannical of the tyrants), and the Council of Trent, had imposed silence upon genius. Cosmo I, Grand Duke of Tuscany, kept in his pay one or two historians of the house of Medici; he caused all books of a less servile character to be collected together from every part and burnt. The Decameron was, therefore, by an absolute political necessity, resorted to by literary men as the sole rule and standard of the written prose language. To cancel every memorial of freedom, Cosmo I suppressed all the academies instituted in Tuscany during the republican government of its cities; the only indulgence he showed was to an assembly of grammarians, who afterwards became famous rather than illustrious under the name of the Accademia della Crusca; and then, when the indolence of slavery deadened and chilled the passions; when education, committed to the Jesuits, had enfeebled all intellect; when men of letters became the furniture of courts, often of foreign courts; when universities were in the pay of kings, and under the direction of inquisitors – then did the Accademia della Crusca begin to claim supremacy over Italian literature, and to establish the tales of Boccaccio as the sole text and rule for every dictionary of grammar, and the basis of every philosophical theory regarding the language.

Nevertheless the academicians found that the Decameron had never been printed in a genuine and correct form, fitted to serve as the ground-work of language. After many years spent in consulting,

correcting, and collating manuscripts, they prepared an edition
which they hoped to consecrate as the oracle in all grammatical
questions: but the Holy Office interposed in the most furious
manner, and did not allow it to be printed. They therefore consen-
ted, as they could do no better, to publish a mutilated edition. The
grand dukes of Tuscany, in order to put an end to these difficulties,
deputed certain learned men to negotiate with the Master of the
Sacred Palace in the Vatican, of whom one was a bishop, and nearly
all dignified ecclesiastics. The Master of the Sacred Palace, a Dominican friar and a Spaniard, attended their meetings in his own right.
Writing his opinions in a bastard language, he gave his advice as an
official grammarian: they did not, however, come to any conclusion.

At length an Italian Dominican, of a more facile character, was
added to the council, and having been confessor to Pius V he prevailed on Gregory XIII to allow the *Decameron* to be printed without
any other alteration than what was necessary for the good fame of
the ecclesiastics. Thus, abbesses and nuns in love with their gar-
deners were transformed into matrons and young ladies; friars who
got up impostures and miracles into necromancers; and priests who
intrigued with their parishioners' wives into soldiers; and by dint of
a hundred other inevitable transformations and mutilations, the
academy, after four years' labour, succeeded in publishing the
Decameron in Florence, illustrated by their researches. But Sextus V
ordered that even this edition, though approved by his predecessor,
should be infamized in the Index. It was therefore necessary to have
recourse to fresh mangling and interpolation, and of texts so fabri-
cated, therefore, the academicians of La Crusca weighed every word
and every syllable of the *Novelle*, exaggerated every minute detail, and
described every thing under the high-sounding names of the richness, propriety, grace, elegance, the figures, laws, and principles of
language. . . .

This singular destiny of a work composed as a mere pastime,
threw into comparative oblivion its other literary merits, which were
more useful to the civilisation of Europe, and stamped upon the
name of its author an infamous celebrity, which has always hidden
from the world the true character of his mind. . . . It is unquestionable, that if Petrarch had expended on writing Italian prose the
tenth part of the labour which he bestowed on his poetry, he would
not have been able to write so much as he did. This reason, among
many others, contributed to induce him to write in Latin: the chief

motive, however, was the glory which then attached to the Latin poets, and which, in the universities and the courts of the princes, was scarcely granted to those who write in Italian. Few however, if any, had any real conception of the spirit and merits of the Latin tongue. Coluccio Salutato was a man of great learning and enjoyed a high reputation among the scholars of that age; yet he pronounced that the pastoral poems of Boccaccio, written in Latin, were only inferior to Petrarch, and that Petrarch was superior to Virgil![2] Erasmus, a critic of another age, and of a different turn of mind, when commenting on the literature of the fourteenth century, detracts a little from the praises bestowed upon Petrarch, and enhances those of Boccaccio, whose Latinity he esteems the less barbarous of the two.[3]

The injury which Petrarch did to his native tongue, by his ambition of writing in Latin, was compensated by his indefatigable and generous perseverance in restoring to Europe the most noble remains of human intellect. No monument of antiquity, no series of medals, or manuscript of Roman literature was neglected by him wherever he had the least hope of rescuing the one from oblivion, or of multiplying copies of the other. He acquired a claim to the gratitude of all Europe, and is still deservedly called the first restorer of classical literature. Boccaccio, however, is entitled not only to a share, but to an equal share, to say the least, of this honour. We are perfectly aware that our opinion on this subject will be at first regarded as a paradox put forth from a mere ambition of novelty; the proofs, however, which we shall briefly adduce, will convert the surprise of our readers at our temerity into wonder at the scanty recompense which Boccaccio has hitherto received, in spite of his gigantic and successful endeavours to dispel the ignorance of the Middle Ages.

The allegorical mythology, together with the theology and metaphysics of the ancients, the events of the history of ages less remote, and even geography, were illustrated by Boccaccio in his voluminous Latin Treatises, now little read, but at that time studied by all as the chiefest and best works of solid learning. Petrarch knew nothing of Greek; and whatever acquaintance, in Tuscany or Italy, they had with the writers of that language, they owed entirely to

---

[2] *Colutius Salutatus Epis. ad Bocc.*
[3] *Ciceronianus.*

Boccaccio. He went to Sicily, where there were still some remains of
a Greek dialect, and masters who taught the language, and put himself under two preceptors of the greatest merit, Barlaamus and
Leontius. Under them he studied several years; he afterwards prevailed on the republic of Florence to establish a chair of Greek
literature for Leontius. Had it not been for Boccaccio, the poems of
Homer would have remained long undiscovered. The story of the
Trojan War was read in the celebrated romance called the History
of Guido delle Colonne, from which also were derived many wild
inventions and apocryphal records of Homeric times, and various
dramas, like Shakespeare's *Troilus and Cressida*, containing not a single
circumstance to be met with in the *Iliad* or *Odyssey*. Nor should it be
forgotten, that undertakings like these demanded affluence, which
Petrarch possessed; while Boccaccio's whole life was passed in the
midst of difficulties and privations. He compensated for the want of
pecuniary resources by indefatigable industry; he submitted to
mechanical labours, wholly unsuited to the bent of his character and
genius, and copied manuscripts with his own hand. Leonardo Bruni,
who was born before the death of Boccaccio, was astonished when he
saw the multitude of authors' copies transcribed by him.[4] Benvenuto
da Imola, who was a disciple of Boccaccio, relates a curious anecdote
on this subject, which as we do not recollect that it is anywhere
to be met with, except in the great collection of the writers of the
Middle Ages, by Muratori, a work inaccessible to the greater number
of our readers, we shall insert.[5] – Going once to the abbey of Monte
Cassino, celebrated for the number of manuscripts which lay there,
unknown and neglected, Boccaccio humbly requested to be shown
into the library of the monastery. A monk dryly replied, 'Go, it
stands open', and pointed to a very high staircase. The good
Boccaccio found every book he opened torn and mutilated; lament-
ing that all these fruits of the labours of the great men of antiquity
had fallen into the hands of such masters, he went away weeping.
Coming down the staircase he met another monk, and asked him
'How those books could possibly have been so mutilated?' – 'We
make covers for little Prayer-books out of the parchment leaves of
those volumes', said he, coolly, 'and sell them for twopence,
threepence and sometimes fivepence each'. – 'And now go'.

---

[4] Leonardo Aretino, *Vita del Petrarca*, in fine.
[5] *Benvenutus Imolensis apud Muratorium Script. Rer. Ital.*

concludes the pupil of Boccaccio, 'go, you unfortunate author, and distract your brain in composing more books.' Such were the obstacles [imposed] by the imperfect civilisation of his age which this admirable man, together with Petrarch, had to surmount; and it is an act of tardy and religious justice to show that the tribute of grateful recollection which they were both entitled to receive from posterity was almost [only] awarded to his more fortunate contemporary. We cannot conclude our remarks, without paying another debt to the memory of Boccaccio. The indecency of the *Novelle*, and their immoral tendency, can neither be justified nor extenuated; but from the herd of writers in England, who confidently repeat this merited censure of Boccaccio, year after year, it appears but too much as if the study of the language and of the style had been made a pretext for feeding the imaginations of the readers with ideas which all are prone to indulge, but compelled to conceal; and that the tales of Boccaccio would not have predominated so much over all other literature, if they had been more chaste. The art of suggesting thoughts, at once desired and forbidden, flatters while it irritates the passions, and is an efficacious instrument for governing the consciences of boys, and of the most discreet old men. The Jesuits, therefore, no sooner made themselves masters of the schools of Italy, than they adopted this book, mutilated in the same manner as some of the licentious Latin poets, well knowing that the expunged passages are the most coveted, precisely because they *are* expunged, and that the imaginations of youth supply ideas worse than they would have formed had the books been left entire.

In order to excuse the use they made of the *Decameron* in their colleges, the Jesuits succeeded in persuading Bellarmine to justify, in his controversies, the intentions of the author. Perhaps, indeed, they interpolated these arguments as they did soon many others, in the edition of Bellarmine, wherever the doctrines did not accord with the interests of their order.[6] It is, moreover, probable that they favoured a book famous for its invectives against the rules of the cloister, and written long before their order had arisen to acquire a jurisdiction over all. Bellarmine was much less indulgent than Boccaccio to the reputations of the old congregations; and although some writers who have undertaken their defence have called his *Gemitus Columbae* apocryphal, it was, at all events, printed among his

---

[6] Fuligatus, in *Vita Bellarmini*.

works during his life. To return to Boccaccio. Before he died he had
atoned for his want of respect for decorum; he felt that men thought
him culpable, and he expiated his tales by a punishment heavier,
perhaps, than the offence. There is some reason to believe that he
wrote them when under the influence of a lady whom he abjured
just before, and whom he defames in his *Laberinto d'Amore*. However
this may be, he conjured fathers of families not to suffer the
Decameron to go into the hands of any who had not already lost the
modesty of youth. – 'Do not let that book be read; and if it is true
that you love me, and weep for my afflictions, have pity, were it
only for my honour's sake.'

With remorse of conscience which does more honour to the
excellence of his intentions than to the strength of his mind, he even
tried to atone for the ridicule he had poured upon the priests and
their infamous superstitions. No writer, perhaps, since Aristophanes,
has so bitterly satirised the effrontery of ignorant preachers, and the
credulity of their ignorant hearers, as Boccaccio in the *Novelle*, which
are written in a spirit of implacable hostility to monks. In one of
them[7] he introduces one of these vagabonds boasting from the
pulpit, that he had wandered through all the countries in the terr-
aqueous globe, and even beyond it, in search of relics of saints, and
making the people in the church pay to adore them. And yet, in
spite of this, he said, on his death-bed, that he had been long in
search of holy relics through various parts of the world, and he left
them, for the devotion of the people, to a convent of friars. This
desire was found expressed in a will, written in Italian in his own
hand; and in another in Latin, drawn up many years afterwards by
a notary, and signed and approved by Boccaccio a short time before
he died. In both these wills he bequeathed all his books and manuscripts to his confessor and to the convent of Santo Spirito, in order
that the monks might pray to God for his soul, and that his fellow-
citizens might read and copy them for their instruction. It is therefore more than probable, that there was among these books no copy
of the *Decameron*; and from the following anecdote, which being
found in books which are read by very few is little known, it appears
that the original manuscript of the *Novelle* was destroyed long before
by the author; it is, in fact, as we have already remarked, impossible
to find it.

---

[7] [VI, 10].

Towards the end of his life, poverty, which is rendered more grievous by old age, and the turbulent state of Florence, made social life a burden to him, so that he fled to solitude; but his generous and amiable soul was debased and depressed by religious terrors. There lived at that time two Sienese, who were afterwards canonised. One of them was a man of letters and a Carthusian monk, mentioned by Fabricius as Sanctus Petrus Petronus; the other was Giovanni Colombini, who founded another order of monks, and wrote the life of St Pietro Petroni by divine inspiration. The Bollandists allege that the manuscript of the new saint, after having been lost for two centuries and a half, miraculously fell into the hands of a Carthusian, who translated it from Italian into Latin, and in 1619 dedicated it to a Cardinal de Medici. It is possible that Colombini never wrote, and that the biographer of the saints, who wrote in the seventeenth century, drew his descriptions of miracles from those recorded in the chronicles and other documents of the fourteenth century; and in order to exaggerate the miraculous conversion of Boccaccio, he perverted a letter of Petrarch, entitled 'De Vaticinio Morientium', which is to be found in his Latin works. The blessed Petroni, at his death, which happened about the year 1360, charged a monk to advise Boccaccio to desist from his studies and to prepare for death. Boccaccio wrote in terror to Petrarch, who replied: 'My brother, your letter filled my mind with horrible fantasies, and I read it assailed by great wonder and great affliction. And how could I, without fearful eyes, behold you weeping and calling to mind your near-approaching death; whilst I, not well informed of the fact, most anxiously explored the meaning of your words? But now that I have discovered the cause of your terrors, and have reflected somewhat upon them, I have no longer either sadness or surprise. You write that an – I know not what – Pietro di Siena, celebrated for his piety, and also for his miracles, predicted to us two, many future occurrences; and in the witness of the truth of them, sent to signify to us certain past things which you and I have kept secret from all men, and which he, who never knew us, nor was known by us, knew as if he had seen them with his mind's eye. This is a great thing, if indeed it be true. But the art of covering and adorning impostures with the veil of religion and of sanctity, is most common and old. Those who use it explore the age, the countenance, the eyes, the manners of the man; his daily customs, his motions, his standing, his sitting, his voice, his speech, and above all, his intentions and affections; and draw predictions which they ascribe to divine inspiration. Now if he, dying, foretold your death, so also did Hector in former times to Achilles; and Orodes to Mezentius, in Virgil; and Cheramenes to Eritia, in Cicero; and Calamus to Alexander; and Posidonius, the illustrious philosopher, when dying, named six of his contemporaries who were soon to follow him, and told who should die first, and who afterwards. It matters not to dispute now concerning the truth or the origin of such-like predictions; nor to you, if even this your alarmer [terrificator hic tuus] had told the truth, would it avail any thing to afflict yourself. How then? If this man had not sent to let you know, would you have been ignorant that there remains not to you a long space of life? and even if you were young, is death any respector of age?'[8] But neither these, nor all the other arguments in Petrarch's letter, which is very long, nor the eloquence with which he combines the consolations of the Christian religion with the manly philosophy of the ancients, could deliver his friend from superstitious terrors.

Boccaccio survived the prediction more than twelve years, and the older he grew the more did he feel the seeds scattered in his mind by his grandmother and his nurse, spring up like thorns. He died in 1375, aged sixty-two, and not more than twelve or fourteen months after Petrarch. Nor did Petrarch himself always contemplate death with a steadfast eye. Such was the character of those times; and such, under varied appearances, will always be the nature of man.

Ugo Foscolo

---

[8] [Ep. Sen., I, 5, June 1362].

Boccaccio's
Human Comedy

Boccaccio is not a superior soul, a writer who looks at society from
a lofty height, sees the good and bad in it, exposes it impartially,
and is perfectly conscious of it all; he is an artist who feels himself
one with the society in which he lives, and he writes with that sort
of semi-consciousness of men who are swayed by the shifting
impressions of life without stopping to analyse them. And this is
really the quality that divides him substantially from the ecstatic
Dante and the ecstatic Petrarch. Boccaccio is all on the surface of
life, among the pleasures and idlenesses and vicissitudes of everyday
existence, and these are enough for him, he is busy and satisfied. He
is not the type to turn his soul into himself and think deeply with
knotted brow and pensive gaze; it was not for nothing that they
called him 'Giovanni the Tranquil'. Intimacy, raptness, ecstasy, the
unquiet deeps of thought, the living in one's own spirit with
phantasms and mysteries, disappear from Italian literature when
Boccaccio enters it. Life rises to the surface, and is smoothed down,
made attractive. The world of the spirit makes its exit; the world of
Nature comes in.

This world of Nature, empty and superficial, devoid of all the
inner powers of the spirit, has no seriousness at all of means or of
end. The thing that moves it is instinct – natural inclination; no
longer God or science, and no longer the unifying love of intellect
and act, the great basis of the Middle Ages: it is a real and violent
reaction against mysticism. The author introduces us to a merry
gathering of men and women who are trying to forget the ills and
tedium of life by passing the warm hours of the day in pleasant
story-telling. It was the time of the plague, and men faced by death

[Title mine – ed.] From *History of Italian Literature* by Francesco De
Sanctis, translated by Joan Redfern (London: Oxford University Press,
1930), vol. I, pp. 335–49. Copyright, 1931, 1959, by Harcourt Brace
Jovanovich, Inc. Reprinted by permission of Harcourt Brace Jovanovich, Inc.

on every side felt that all the restraints of life were loosened, and gave themselves up to the carnival of the imagination. Boccaccio had had experience of carnivals at the court where the happiest days of his life were spent, and his imagination had taken its colour from that dungheap on which the Muses and the Graces had lavished so many flowers. In the *Ameto*, the pastoral *Decameron*, we have a similar gathering of people. But the stories in the *Ameto* are allegorical, so are preordained to an abstract ending. Though the poem has nothing of the spirit of the *Divine Comedy*, it is built on its skeleton. Here, on the contrary, the sole aim of the stories is to make the time pass pleasantly; they are real panders to pleasure and to love, the Greek title of the book being only a modest veil of the author's Italian title, which was that of the Prince Galeotto. And the characters, evoked from so many different people and so many different epochs, here are all of the same world, the external world of tranquil thoughtlessness.

In this care-free world of the *Decameron* events are left to take care of themselves, the results being decided by chance. God and Providence are acknowledged by name, almost by a sort of tacit agreement, in the words of people who have sunk into complete religious, political, and moral indifference. Nor is there even that intimate force of things which endows the events with a sort of logic and necessity; the book, indeed, is charming for exactly the opposite quality; it is charming for its completely unexpected *dénouements*, which are utterly different from anything we could reasonably have foreseen, and this by the whim of chance. It is a new form of the marvellous, no longer caused by the penetration into human life of ultra-natural forces, such as visions and miracles, but by a curious conflux of fortuitous events that no one could have possibly foreseen or controlled. We are left with the feeling that the ruler of the world, the *deus ex machina*, is chance; we see it in the varied play of the inclinations of these people, all of them ruled by the changing chances of life.

Since the machinery, the moving force of the stories, is the marvellous, the fortuitous, the unexpected, it follows that their interest does not lie in the morality of the actions, but in the strangeness of their causes and effects. Not that Boccaccio rejects morality or alters the ordinary ideas of right and wrong; it is only that questions of morality do not happen to be the questions that interest him. But the thing that does interest him is his power to stimulate his readers'

interest by strangeness of character and events. Virtue is used as a
means of impressing the imagination, an instrument of the marvellous like the rest, so ceases to be simple and proportionate; in
fact, it is exaggerated to such a degree as to show clearly the emptiness
of the author's conscience and his want of moral feeling. A famous
instance is the story of the patient Griselda, the most virtuous of all
the characters of the book. To prove that she is a good and faithful
wife she suffocates every natural feeling of a woman, and her own
personality, and her free will. The author, in trying to show an
extraordinary example of virtue that will strike the imagination of
his readers, has fallen into the very mysticism he dislikes, and makes
use of it by placing the ideal of feminine virtue in the abnegation
of self, exactly like the theologians, who teach that flesh is absorbed
by spirit, and spirit by God. It is a sort of sacrifice of Abraham,
except that here it is the husband who puts Nature so cruelly to the
test. And the virtue in the stories of Tito and Gisippo is proved by
such strange and out-of-the-way happenings that instead of charming us as an example it only amazes us as a miracle. But extraordinary and spectacular virtue is rare in the tales; the virtue is generally
the traditional virtue of chivalric and feudal times – a certain
generosity and kindliness of kings and princes and marquises,
reminiscences of chivalric and heroic tales in bourgeois times. A
prince's virtue lies in his using his power to protect the people
below him, and especially to protect the men of high intelligence
and culture who happen to be poor, as did the Abbot of Cluny and
Can Grande della Scala, who treated Primasso and Bergamino with
magnificence. A much-praised person is Charles I of Anjou who,
instead of seizing and raping two beautiful girls, daughters of a
Ghibelline, who had fallen into his power, preferred to dower them
magnificently and find them husbands. These powerful nobles were
virtuous because they did not misuse their power, but behaved
instead in a liberal and courteous manner. And already a class of
literati was arising who lived at the expense of this virtue, feeding on
its bounty and extolling it in fair exchange. The lofty soul of Dante
had bent itself with difficulty to this patronage; not the least of his
causes of bitterness was the begging of bread from strangers, crust
by crust, and the treading of other people's stairs. But the heroic age
was past. Petrarch allowed his Maecenas to provide for him and
support him, and Boccaccio lived on the refuse of the court of
Naples, comically enraged when the provision struck him as not up

to standard, and disposed to panegryic or satire according to whether the food was good or bad. In Boccaccio's world 'virtue' as a rule means liberality or courtesy of soul, which had spread from the castle to the city, and even into the woods where the outlaws had taken refuge – men like Natan, and Saladino, and Alfonso, and Ghino di Tacco, and the wizard of Ansaldo. Strictly speaking, of course, this virtue is not morality; but at least it is a sense of nice behaviour, which makes the habits of the day more agreeable, takes from virtue that theological and mystical character connected with abstinence and suffering, and gives it a pleasing appearance, in keeping with a cultured and gay society. It is true that the chance which ruled the lives of these people played them many a trick, and the pervading gaiety, the charming serenity, were often disturbed by some sad event. But the clouds came suddenly, without warning, were soon scattered, and gave an added value to the sun when it shone again; in Fiammetta's words, sorrow was 'a fine material for tempering gladness'.

If we look more deeply into these questions of joy and sorrow, we shall see that the joy has very few chords; the joy would be level and dull, and no longer joyous (as is often the case with idyllic poems), except that pain pierces into it – pain with its richer and more varied harmonies, and its living passions of love, jealousy, contempt, indignation. Pain is here not for its own sake, but as a seasoner of joy; it is here to enliven the spirit, to keep it in suspense, to excite it – until kindly fortune, or chance, shall suddenly make the sun to shine again. And even when the story has a sad ending (as in all of the tales of the Third Day) the sadness is only superficial; it is relieved and softened by descriptions, dissertations, and musings, and is never so strong as to be torment, like Dante's proud suffering. In that world of Nature and love pain is a tragic apparition that flits past. It is not caused by a moral purpose, but by the 'point of honour', the chivalric virtue – by honour in collision with Nature and love. A case in point is the lovely story of Gerbino; and also the story of Tancredi, who is a witness to his daughter's shame, and kills the lover, and sends the lover's heart to his daughter in a golden cup; his daughter puts poison in the cup, and drinks it, and dies. The tragedy turns on the point of honour. Tancredi feels more dishonoured by his daughter's having loved a man beneath her in rank than by the fact that she has loved illicitly. But his daughter justifies her love by quoting the laws of Nature, and says that true

nobility comes from worth and not from blood. When we take
leave of the father weeping vainly and remorsefully over his daughter's body, we see him not as a man who has avenged his tarnished
honour, but as a traitor to the laws of Nature and of love. But
indeed, we pity the father and daughter equally – the high-souled
father and the human and tender-hearted daughter; both are victims
of the society they belong to, and neither has sinned. Our last
impression is that Nature and love have taken their revenge. So the
tragic motive is in keeping with Boccaccio's world; and the fugitive,
vanishing pain is shown most tenderly and gently, almost with
compassion. Pain gives a flavour to joy, for joy would end by
being insipid if pain were not there to season it. Tragedy is changed
at its root. There is no longer the terror of a mysterious fate, shown
in catastrophe, as with the Greeks, nor of a punishment falling on
man for breaking the laws of a higher justice, as in Dante; tragedy
here is the fact that the world is at the mercy of its own blind and
natural forces, and the higher law in this struggle is love – whoever
opposes love is in the wrong. With Dante Nature was sin: with
Boccaccio Nature is law. And it is not opposed by religion or morality (of which nothing remains at all, though both are believed in
theoretically, and quoted), but by society as arranged in that complex system of laws and customs called 'honour'. But the struggle is
all external; it is shown in the events that arise from these various
forces brought into conflict, and is ended by the kindness or the
spite of chance or fortune. And the struggle stops short at that inner
conflict which leads to passion and makes character. Boccaccio has no
idea of rebelling against society, and certainly is nothing of a
reformer; he takes life as he finds it. And though his sympathies are
entirely with the victims of love, he is not biased for that reason
against the characters who are driven to cruel actions through love;
they too are worthy of respect, for they are victims of love like the
others. Though he glorifies Gerbino, who breaks his pledge to the
King, his grandfather, rather than break the laws of love and be
thought a coward, he has no word of blame for the King, who
orders the death of his grandson, 'choosing to be without a grandson
rather than be thought a king wanting in honour'. In the midst of
the outer conflict of events an inner calm, a sort of equilibrium, is
born, an inner calm quite empty of emotion, except the degree of
emotion that is necessary for varying its life. And so this bourgeois,
indifferent world of tragedy, whose only ruler is Nature, is external

and superficial, is a piece of wreckage adrift on the immensity of the ocean. The action is developed from strong passions provoked by the conflict of events, not by conscious thought; and it melts away into a game of the imagination, becomes an artistic contemplation of the different events of life that arrest our attention and surprise us. Virtue and vice are meaningless except in so far as they lead to 'adventures', to strange events governed by the caprices of chance. To the audience they are only a means for making the time pass pleasantly; virtue and pain are procedures of pleasure.

A world ruled by pleasure and guided by chance is heedless and gay, but is comic too. This taking of events without seriousness, this capricious interweaving of chance happenings, this inner equilibrium undisturbed by the most cruel vicissitudes, are the natural breeding-ground of the comic. When laughter is empty and meaningless it is nothing but the mirth of fools; laughter to be intelligent and malicious must have a point and a meaning, must be comic. And the comic gives this world its physiognomy and its seriousness.

Boccaccio's world is material for comedy by its very nature; for nothing is more comic than a thoughtless and sensual society, which gives rise to types like Don Juan and Sancho Panza. But it represented the extreme of culture and intellect that was known at that time, and was aware of the fact. It had the advantage of being taken seriously by all the world, and at the same time of making fun of the world. In fact, these tales have two sides to them that are serious: the glorification of intelligence (the most powerful nobles are shown as respecting it) and a certain pride of the burgher who is taking his due position in the world and is setting himself up as the equal of the barons and the counts. This bourgeois class was Boccaccio's own; it was a class of educated, intelligent people who thought that they were the only people who were civilized, and that all the others were barbarians. And the comedy springs from the caricature by the intelligent man of the things and people in a lower stratum of intellectual life than his own. Side by side with cultured society were the friars and priests, or, in Boccaccio's words, 'the Catholic things' – prayers, confessions, sermons, fasts, mortifications of the flesh, visions, and miracles. And behind the Catholic things were the people, with their stupidity and their credulity. These are the two orders of things and people round whom he cracks his whip.

Prayers like the Lord's Prayer of St Julian, the serving of God in the desert, the everyday life of the friars and priests and nuns, which belied their teachings, the art of sanctification taught to Fra Puccio, the miracles of saints and their visions, such as the apparition of the Angel Gabriel; and the stupidity of the people made game of by the clever – these are comic material. Most clear of all in the *Decameron* is the reaction of the flesh against the inordinate rigour of the clergy, who had forbidden the theatres and romances, and had preached that Paradise was only to be won through fasting and the wearing of hair shirts. The natural form of expression of the reaction is licence and cynicism. The flesh avenges its curse, turns on its enemies, and calls them 'mechanists' – meaning people who judge stupidly, who follow vulgar opinion. So the exaggerated world of the spirit has become 'vulgar'. We can well picture all the voluptuousness of the flesh as it stretches itself after its long subjection; with what relish it unfolds its joys one by one, choosing just those ways and expressions which of all others have been most forbidden, and often giving obscene double meanings to holy words and sayings. The profane world is in open rebellion, has broken its bonds, and is mocking its former master. This is the basis of the comedy; a great variety of intertwined chance events are built on it. We have the two eternal protagonists of all comedies: the person who makes fun and the person made fun of, the clever man and the simpleton; and of all the simpletons the most cruelly treated, and the most innocent, are the husbands. And amid the many fortuitous events are born a great variety of comic characters, of which some have remained as real types, such as the *cativello*, the naughty one, of Calandrino and the revengeful scholar who knows where the Devil keeps his tail. The serious characters are rather singularities than types; individuals lost in the minute description and the eccentricity of their natures, like Griselda, Tito, the Count of Anguersa, Madama Beritola, Ginevra, Salvestra, Isabetta, and Tancredi's daughter. But the poignant and intimate part of the book is in the comic characters; these are the universal types which we meet with every day, like Compar Pietro, and Maestro Simone, and Fra Puccio, the friar who was sheep-like, and the judge who was *squasimodeo* (of no account), and Monna Belcolore, and Tofano, and Gianni Lotteringhi, and all the others, for 'the number of the stupid is infinite'. And this gay and thoughtless world unfolds itself, gains an outline and a character, and becomes the 'human comedy'.

And so, within a short distance of each other we get the comedy

and the anti-comedy – we get the 'divine comedy' and its parody,
the 'human comedy'. On the same threshold and in the same times
we have Passavanti, Cavalca, Catherine of Siena – voices of the other
world – and Giovanni Boccaccio drowning them with his loud and
profane laugh. The Gay Science[1] has arisen from its grave with its
laughter as fresh as ever; the troubadours and the story-tellers, whom
the priests had silenced, have come back to life and are dancing as
merrily as before and are singing their profane *canzoni* in the
Florence of the Guelfs. The forbidden tale and romance are ruling
in the realm of literature. Naturally the change is not quite un-
announced, does not come like an earthquake. As we have seen, the
lay spirit has kept an unbroken tradition through the whole of
literature, until in the *Divine Comedy* it takes its place with boldness,
and declares that it too is sacred and of divine right, and Dante, a
layman, speaks like a priest and an apostle. But Dante is so careful
that his building shall stand, that its foundation shall be firm.
Dante's *Divine Comedy* is a reformation; Boccaccio's is a revolution,
which throws the whole edifice to the ground and erects another in
its ruins.

   The *Divine Comedy* ceased to be a living book; it was expounded
as a classical work, but was little read, or understood or enjoyed,
though it was always admired. It was divine, but no longer alive.
And sinking into its grave it drew along with it all those kinds of
literature whose germs appear so strongly and vigorously in its
immortal sketches: tragedy, drama, the hymn, the laud, the legend,
the mystery. There feeling died with them for the family, for Nature,
for country, the belief in a better world, rapture and ecstasy and
inwardness, the pure joys of friendship and love, the seriousness of
life, and ideality. Of all this immense world which collapsed before
it came to fruition, all that remained was Malebolge, the realm of
malice, the seat of the 'human comedy'; Malebolge, which Dante
had thrown into filth, the place where laughter was choked by disgust
and indignation. Here is Malebolge, but on the earth, laughing
infernally, adorned by the Graces, and announcing that it alone is
truly Paradise – as Don Felice understood very well, but not poor
Fra Puccio. The world in fact is upside down. To Dante the *Divine
Comedy* is heavenly bliss; to Boccaccio the 'comedy' is earthly bliss,
and one of the pleasures of this earthly bliss is the driving away of

---

[1] [Science of Love].

sadness by making jokes about Heaven. The flesh is out to enjoy itself; the spirit is paying the bill.

The flesh was reacting against a spirituality that was over-strained and out of touch with real life. And if the reaction had taken the form of an active struggle in the lofty regions of the spirit, as happened in other countries, the change would have come more gradually, or have been more opposed, but would have borne more fruit. Faith and conviction would have been strengthened by the struggle, and would have generated a literature full of vigour and substance, with something of the passion of Luther, the eloquence of Bossuet, the doubts of Pascal, and with those literary forms which are found only when the inner life is strong and healthy. The move-ment would have been at the same time negative and positive, destructive and constructive. But audacity of thought had been punished without mercy, the Ghibelline faction had been crushed with bloodshed, and the papacy was near at hand, watchful and suspicious. The world of religion, as corrupt in its habits as it was absolute in its doctrine and grotesque in its forms, collided with the new culture that had grown so fast, with the spirit that was so adult and matured by the study of the classics. These cultured people were unable to take the religious world seriously, and so were cut from the rest of society, from the greater part of the people, who remained as they were, passive and inert in the hands of the priest of Varlungo, of Donno Gianni, of Frate Rinaldo, of Frate Cipolla. Educated people came to look on that world as stupid and mechanical, and to laugh at it became the hallmark of the cultured person; even the priests themselves laughed at it, those priests who aspired to being cultured.

And so there were two separate and distinct societies, living side by side, and on the whole without bothering each other too much. Men were forbidden to think for themselves, or to question abstract doctrines, but their everyday lives were another thing entirely – they lived and let live, squeezed amusement out of everything, and eased their feelings by calling on the names of God and Mary. Even the preachers amused their congregations with mottoes, jokes, banter-ing, a habit which Dante thought obnoxious in the highest degree, but which drew a laugh from Boccaccio. At the end of his *Novelliere* he says: 'If the sermons of the friars, preached to make men remorse-ful for their sins, are full of jokes and nonsense and mockery, it seemed to me that these same things would not be unbecoming in my tales, which are written to drive away melancholy from women.'

Dante's indignation has gone, and in its place has come laughter, as though at the expense of things become common. Anger is the sign of saints and of men of conscience everywhere; to be angry a man must first believe, must feel his beliefs to be outraged. But the cultured society of that day had no notion of losing its temper over the sinfulness of mankind. In the *Decameron* the 'unblushing dames of Florence' are charmers and seducers of men and are grouped into 'living pictures', as they would be called today. The traffic in holy things, which drove believing Germany into schism, which Dante in his noble wrath called 'adultery', here is only a matter for amiable quibbling, without rancour or malice. The confessional is the centre of ambiguities that are very amusing; the laity, both men and women, play tricks on the priests – on 'the round fat men' – as we see from the confessor of Ser Ciappelletto and from Frate Bestia, excellent comic characters. Sham miracles, like that of Masetto, the market-gardener, or of Martellino in difficulty, or of Frate Alberto, or of Frate Cipolla, and the faking of saints and making them into miracle-workers, as in the tale of Ser Ciappelletto – these are shown with the gay sense of the comic of a cultured and sceptical people. Profanations like these make people laugh, because the things profaned no longer inspire any reverence.

This society was taken bodily, just as it was, warm, palpitating, vividly alive, and was put into the *Decameron*. The book is an immense picture of life in all its variety of the characters and the events most calculated to make people marvel. Here is Malebolge, the sensual and profligate world of cunning and ignorance, taken out of hell and staged on the earth; and within Malebolge, but not amalgamating with it, is the cultured and civilized world, the world of courtesy, the echo of chivalric times – just a trifle bourgeois, perhaps, but witty, elegant, clever, pleasing; its finest type is Federigo degli Alberighi. The priests and friars and peasants and artisans and lowly burghers and small merchants, with their women, are the natives of the country; and the loud plebeian laughter of these people in their perpetual carnival is all around the ladies and the knights of the world of spirit, culture, wit, and elegance, with its courtesies and habits of chivalry – a world gay like the other, but with a polite and measured gaiety, with a large way of doing things, pleasant modes of speaking, and decorum in its customs. These two worlds, different, but living cheek by jowl, are fused together in the background of the picture, producing an effect of harmony that is unique; they are fused into a single world that is thoughtless and superficial, living externally in the enjoyment of life, and led hither and thither just as fortune decrees.

This twofold world, whose varied notes are so excellently harmonized, takes its tone from the author and from the merry company he puts on the stage. The author and the characters who tell the tales belong to the cultured class: the name of God is often in their mouths, they speak respectfully of the Church, conform to the customs of religion, take a holiday on Friday, because Friday was the day on which Our Lord 'died that we might live', sing allegorical and Platonic *canzoni*, and live a life of gaiety, but one arranged in a manner befitting civilized persons. This society had culture, wit, elegance, poetry, to make it pleasant – was, in fact, like the high society of today. It reflected the feudal world of courtesy, which the cultured and wealthy burgher-class was taking as its model, but dressing up with new adornment of culture and wit. Just as the feudal world had had its buffoons and jugglers, this society had the people who made it merry; its buffoons and jugglers were the people about it – the numberless crowd of priests, friars, peasants, and artisans; amusement was drawn from everything, from the stupid as well as from the clever. The comedy is utterly lacking in any high or serious intention, either to break down prejudice, or to attack institutions, or to fight ignorance, or to moralise, or to reform – as was true with Rabelais or Montaigne, whose comic art is the reaction of good sense from the superficial and the conventional. The laughter of those writers is serious because it leaves something behind it in the consciousness. But Boccaccio's laughter is an end in itself. Its aim is to drive away melancholy and prevent tedium, and that is all. Boccaccio looks at the plebeian world with the eye of an artist studying his model; he is bent on mastering its curves and features and placing it in the light best calculated to please his noble company. From all the immense shipwreck of conscience there still survives a sense of literary integrity, of artistic feeling, strengthened by wit and culture. The masterpieces of the *Decameron* are the fruit of this literary conscience; types are idealised to suit and please the intelligent and sensual society of our genial artist, the idol of the young women to whom he dedicates his stories.

The special quality that makes these models immortal is the comic idea of showing that society at close quarters and exactly as it is, with all its ignorance and malice, and as seen through the eyes of intelligent people who are there merely to enjoy the spectacle and clap their hands. The motive of the comedy does not come from the moral world, but from the intellectual world; much more humorous. What makes the picture so lively is chiefly a certain simplicity of mind that we find in uncultured people, thrown into relief by that cunning which is the basis of a fool's character; besides being stupid, the fool is often credulous, vain, boastful, vulgarly ambitious. So cunning gives vanity to character and throws its ridiculous side into relief. But cunning is comic too – not, of course, to the fool himself, but to the clever people who understand him. So the two types of actor play into each other's hands, each doing his best towards getting the laughs. And here we have the foundation of Boccaccio's 'comedy': culture blossoming for the first time, and conscious of itself, and turning the ignorance and malice of the lower classes into a joke. And the comic element is most highly flavoured of all when it happens that the people made game of are those who have the habit of victimising others – the cunning people who vicitimise the simpletons made game of in their turn by the intelligent, as when women make game of their confessors.

Francesco De Sanctis

The Epic of
the Italian Merchant

In Dante's works, mercantile society was still confined to a sphere of aristocratic contempt for 'la gente nova e i subiti guadagni'. Petrarch ignored it as inferior or alien to his refined experience, and in Compagni's historical works or in the stylized prose of the *Novellino*, its presence was marginal. With Boccaccio, this society bursts into the 'human comedy' of the *Decameron*, dominating it with exuberant vitality. I am not referring simply to the host of themes, settings, characters, mores, and the various allusions that lend the rich colours of this world to more than half the stories. Rather it is the central position occupied by this society in the *Decameron*'s ideal scheme, its exemplary meaning in a humanistic and artistic sense, that makes the presence of the merchant class a characteristic feature, almost essential for the work's development.

The representation of the use man makes of his talents and capacities when confronted with the great powers of Fortune, Love, and Human Ingenuity that seem to rule over mankind – the principal theme of Boccaccio's 'human comedy of the Middle Ages' – could not find in that age more forceful and overwhelming examples of eloquence. After the legendary feats of the knights of the sword, cherished now only by memory or delicate nostalgia, the thirteenth-century world of our merchants offers the liveliest and most aggressive champions in the struggle against these superhuman forces. In this world, the 'human plant' – to use Stendhal's expression – grew ever more vigorous, amid people who roamed the world forever battling against the snares of Fortune, always prepared to overcome with their Ingenuity the ambitions and deceits of others,

This essay was originally entitled 'L'epopea mercantile', and appeared in *Boccaccio Medievale* (Florence: Sansoni, 1956), pp. 71–84. It has been translated and abridged by Robert S. Dombroski, and is reprinted here by permission of Sansoni. The reader is referred to the Italian original for elaborate footnotes in which the author expands certain points.

and forever ready to prove their elegant human quickness in the most diverse of Love's adventures. These men were the true pioneers of late medieval civilization. . . .

Italian society of that time resounded with this grand and eventful mercantile enterprise that had its centre in Florence and its universal might in the florin, which had replaced the Byzantine hyperpyrs and the Muslim dinars. Yet it was in the very heart of his family, in his youthful experiences, that Boccaccio lived the brightest and most impassioned moments of his life. As independent merchants and, above all, as agents and 'factors' of the most powerful Bardi Company – which, together with its associates the Peruzzi and the Acciauoli, constituted the 'pillars of Christian trade' (Villani) – his father and uncles had travelled for more than forty years the great trade routes of Europe between Florence, Naples, Paris, and the French fairs. In his Latin works, Boccaccio nostalgically recalls his father's stories about adventurous and, at times, fearful experiences. And he himself, as a boy a capable 'abacist', grew up in Naples in the shadow of the Bardi bank, next to the Frescobaldi warehouse, in the business district he was to summon most vividly from memory as the magical setting for the picaresque night of Andreuccio. In those years at the bench, receiving clients, managing the till, keeping the books of inventory, assignments, cash, withdrawals, acquisitions and sales, and preparing statements which would help his partners arrive at a final balancing of the books (and exercising all the other functions common to the 'pupil' he was), Boccaccio underwent for hours on end the toil and risks of a refined, venturesome, and precarious existence. He practised his business daily with the zeal of one who has cautiously to count and weigh coins and balance the various entries, making ever new contacts with people from different lands who assembled in the warehouse not only to carry out business, but to await messages and dispatches from the various 'piazzas' and to appraise and compare them. In the reality of his trade the bright lights and legends about relatives and friends were nourished and confirmed by hard, direct experience, by a solid truth that made these stories imaginatively sound and exact.

The extreme sharpness of contours and the unfailing clarity of references, derived from Boccaccio's long experience of hardship, determine the fascination of the Decameron's mercantile tales and their capacity to develop and gravitate around the representation of a milieu, which, at times, appears as the work's true protagonist. The crescendo of Ciappelletto's cold, calculated impiety stands out against the texture of mercantile impartiality and ruthlessness that regulates, according to historically documented customs and needs, the actions of Musciatto Franzesi and the Florentine usurers. The light-headed naivety of Andreuccio, which starts the phantasmagoric sequence of ever more romantic adventures, is captured in the impudent but customary act of bargaining in the Neopolitan 'Piazza del Mercato', one of the most lively and renowned centres for horse trading. The rapid alternation of Landolfo's and Martuccio's fortunes appears more sudden and tempestuous against the background of the commercial galley fleets (the convoys) and of the ease with which the most fly-by-night and venturesome merchants gave themselves to piracy. . . . The poetry of the theme of love and death is found in the figures of Simona and Silvestra in all its chaste fragrance because it rises from a humble world of work and love, depicted and defined imaginatively in the coherent exactness of gestures with which the 'masters', 'factors', 'apprentices', . . . 'artisans', and 'spinners' (Simona is the first elegiac spinner of our literature!) are made to act. The light knavish rhythm of the story in which Salaebetto and the beautiful Sicilian try to dupe each other can only be securely developed through detailed knowledge, or better through direct experience, of the port apparatus for consignments, guarantees, and deposits. . . .

Boccaccio's mercantile experience furnished him with a perspective for observing contemporary life through which he could see beyond communal, regional, and national confines, throughout civilised Europe and the eventful Mediterranean: throughout the entire boundless arena open to the enterprise of those heroes of trade and continuously covered by their swift and wonderful messengers. In addition to the Tuscan cities of Florence, Siena, and Pisa, always at the centre of the *Decameron*'s ideal geography (as they were in the real world of trade and finance), the other regions are defined with singular precision and animated with rich colours in the rapidly traced but sharply outlined settings of the various novellas.

On Italy's borders, Piedmont (with the exception of Asti) still enclosed in its archaic feudal life and mountain austerity, is depicted almost as in a fairy tale (I, 6; X, 10); while at the other extreme of the Alpine chain Friuli, 'a somewhat cold country, enlivened with noble mountains and a wealth of running streams and clear springs', returns to life, coloured entirely with the activities of Boccaccio's fellow citizens . . . Lapo and Lodaringo da Certaldo (X, 5). And the

lines and perspectives become sharper as we descend into the
regions where the local merchants participate more actively in
European trade, at times in direct and bitter competition with the
Florentine and Sienese companies. Naturally the echoes of this
rivalry and of the contrasting alliances (often extended to the political sphere) lend light and shade to the settings. Venice, resounding
with trade, suspicious and jealous of the Florentines, is sketched
through a veil of scornful animosity with its customary 'escutcheon'
of corruption, disloyalty, and garrulous frivolity, which was well
known in Tuscan business circles and surely confirmed by Boccaccio's
friends from Romagna (IV, 2; VI, 4; also II, 1); while its great rival
(whose friendship, on account of the age-long struggles with Pisa,
was one of the mainstays of Florentine politics in the fourteenth
century) is presented through a gallery of industrious and tenacious
merchants, obstinate to the point of meanness, but open to the most
liberal of impulses and loyal to the ancient, unconquerable ideal of
decorum to which corresponds the highly praised modesty of their
women (I, 8; II, 8, 9; II, 10). Around the two great republics the
landscape is enlarged: on the one hand, the courtly life of the
refined cities of the Venetian terra firma, from Treviso to Verona
(II, 1; I, 4); on the other, the harsh beauty of the eastern and
western Rivieras, studded with castles, hard-working citizens, and
lands put to use by the merchants themselves (Mulazzo, Lerici,
Finale, Albenga, Monaco: I, 4; II, 6, 8, 9, 10; VIII, 10). Lombardy
and Milan were more isolated and remote from Boccaccio's narrative
sympathies, perhaps because their commercial and financial activities
were not yet vigorously developed, and because they directed themselves to lands, like Switzerland and Germany, somewhat distant
from the principal interests of the Tuscan companies; but also
because Florence, in those years, was especially distrustful of, and
downright hostile towards, that region and its lords. Nevertheless,
Milan ... does serve as the background for the plot dealing with a
German and one of those Lombard money lenders, famous in all of
Europe (VIII, 1); and at Pavia (in addition to the great portrait of
Lombard life contained in the tale of Teodolinda), in the gilded
memory of what three centuries earlier was one of the greatest
emporia between East and West, Boccaccio gives us the loftiest and
most refined idealisation of mercantile life and of the encounters
between Christian kindness and Arab liberality (X, 9: the Brescian
background in the tale of Andreuola is of another origin). And still

in the *Padania* appear the enterprising Emilian 'companies' ... and
their wealthy industrial cities, each so alive with its own characteristic way of life. Piacenza, which had sent its men to France to resist
the Florentines, is portrayed in its sanguine vitality through the
unscrupulous boldness of Ambrogiuolo (II, 9) ; Modena and Bologna,
rich in trade, cultured and refined (I, 10; II, 2; VII, 7; VIII, 9; X, 4);
Ferrara, in the eleventh century the centre for the marketing of silks
imported from the Orient and now the point of departure to the
Venetian lands, notwithstanding the torments of war and the unsafe
trade routes (II, 2; VIII, 10); further south we have Faenza, Forlì,
Ravenna, Imola, Rimini, and other minor towns, then the lands of
Romagna so dear to the Florentines and so much a part of Boccaccio's
direct experience (IV, 2; V, 4, 5, 8; VII, 5; and even III, 7).

Even the regions less known in the history and life of the times
do not escape Boccaccio's careful observation, just as they did not
escape the tenacious penetration of the Florentine companies: the
Marches and the Abruzzi, main points of support for the Acciaiuoli,
Peruzzi, and Bardi Companies (who had branches at Ancona and
Aquila; cf. II, 7; IX, 4) and for all mercantile operations between
Florence and Naples, appear shaded with semi-fantastic and semi-
mocking tones in the speeches of Maso del Seggio and Frate Cipolla,
who are the farcical caricatures of commercial echoes (VIII, 3;
VI, 10; III, 7; V, 5; VII, 5; IX, 4). But more directly bound to
Boccaccio's mercantile practice are the references he makes to the
other areas of central Italy. Perugia, a city which furnished messengers and horse dealers to the kingdom of Naples (Perugia incidentally is the home of Andreuccio, 'a horse dealer by trade'), is
depicted with its unforgettable piazza as the background for the unbelievable adventures of the Vinciolos, governors in Terra d'Abruzzo
by appointment of the Acciaiuoli (II, 5; V, 10); while Rome and
Lazio, shaken and abandoned during the Babylonian captivity,
return to life in sad glimpses with the tale of Agnolella and in the
vivid description of the Roman countryside, abundant with snares
and surprises for the Florentine merchants who travelled through it
on the way to Naples (V, 2; the references to papal Rome are to be
considered apart, from I, 2 to X, 2).

In light of the Neapolitan activity of the Florentine companies
and of the importance of Naples in Boccaccio's life, it is fitting that
the kingdom of Naples, after Tuscany, should be that part of Italy
most present and most vividly represented in the *Decameron*. Naturally

Boccaccio reserves for the 'Kingdom' too a scintillating and fantastic show of princes and knights, as a sign of his literary yearnings for a radiant and legendary past, forever in decline. But the vital and concrete aspects of the Neapolitan settings derive instead from his usual, impassioned experience of mercantile life. The Puglie, rich in wines and bustling fairs, wholly oriented towards the Byzantine Empire, are reflected in the tales of Landolfo Rudolfo and Donno Gianni (II, 4; IX, 10) through landscapes and settings known and experienced by the 'apprentice' of the Bardi company which had branches in that area; while from Calabria, poor and deserted, arises only the fearful echo of the terror instilled by pirates (V, 6). But as is fitting, the two pivotal centres – in mercantile life as well as in the tales – are Naples and the Campagna on the one hand, and Sicily on the other. Besides the precise (almost magical) reconstruction of commerce in the port area of Naples, described in the tale of Andreuccio (and under other aspects in that of Catella and Peronella) in an aura of past commercial prosperity, it is the entire 'Amalfi coast, a place full of little towns, gardens and fountains, and wealthy men as bustling in commerce as any in the world' (II, 4), the forgetful gulfs of Salerno, Naples, and Gaeta with their islands (Ischia, Procida, Ponza), fairs (...), and sprightly citizens ..., that unfolds itself in an entire series of tales (II, 4, 6; IV, 1, 10; V, 6; VIII, 10; X, 5 etc.). And Sicily, controlled by the Tuscan merchants at Palermo, Messina, Trapani, and Catania, appears ... as a rich, intimate land, stretching out towards the dreaded legendary barbarous countries (II, 5; IV, 4, 5; V, 2, 6, 7; VIII, 10; X, 7 etc.) Also the other great Italian island of Sardinia, where the Bardi had special agents and factors for the grain trade, is portrayed in a certain vague and imaginary light, as a necessary stopping point in the navigation of the Mediterranean between Africa and the Provençal and Catalan ports (II, 7; IV, 4; also III, 8; VI, 10).

The horizons of the landscapes and environments depicted expand, as never before in our literature, against the vast European and Mediterranean background in which are set the adventures, or rather the heroic quest, of our merchants. Beyond the Alps the expanse of lands and the wealth of the cities of France, Provence, Burgundy, and Flanders disclose itself; and over the Channel, the cities of England, Scotland, and Ireland; that is, all the cities that represented targets of conquest for our companies. .... The ruthless greed of the French and the calculating indifference of Ciappelletto

and the usurers cast a pale light on these settings; the bold and
jocular chatting of the merchants in the smoke-filled Parisian inn or
the vicissitudes of Lamberti lend a rhythm of open-minded and forever new enterprise to them; and the politeness of the young
Alessandro or the dreamy Lodovico suddenly illuminates this
bustling and severe world with the light of that magnanimity and
courtesy which were the leaven of a great civic and artistic renaissance, rooted in a prodigious economic vitality (II, 3; VII, 7). On
the periphery of this more familiar Europe lie Spain and Catalonia,
compulsory stops both in trade and in the undertaking of dangerous
sea itineraries (here the Peruzzi were especially powerful); and
Germany, even more isolated and violent like its mercenaries who,
incidentally, were good clients of our money lenders (VIII, 1;
also II, 1).

But the true spacious arena, opened up to Boccaccio by his Neapolitan experiences and by a celebrated voyage of the Acciaiuoli
company, was the sea of Greece with its famous ports of Morea and
the eastern Mediterranean, studded with islands, ravaged by winds,
wars, pirates, and by diverse fortune and violence, ruled by Con-
stantinople, the clearing station for all eastern trade directed towards
the Black Sea and the rich port of Caffa; and the western Mediterranean, more limited in its narrative geography on account of its
commercial ties with Provence, Catalonia and the Balearic Islands
(where the Bardi had branches and the Angevins great interests).
Beyond the European waters lies the mysterious and dreaded continent of Africa, from which emerge clearly Tunisia and Alexandria,
the real Meccas of our companies (IV, 4; V, 2; I, 3; II, 6, 7, 9;
VIII, 2; X, 9). Further to the east lay the legendary Orient of the
Crusades and of Saladin: the much desired but often illusory target
of our trade which, having developed on the still fresh and forever
renewed tracks of the Crusades, held on, more tenaciously than the
Crusaders themselves, to those valuable outposts of a vast and
immensely rich Asia . . .

In sum, there is no land, marked by the feats of these daring
and tenacious conquistadores of the late Middle Ages, that does not
evoke precise acknowledgement and colourful fictional transfigura-
tion in the Decameron: this marvellous 'libro del navigar mercantesco'.

To this new and unlimited broadening of geographic horizons
corresponds an equally rich and original enlargement of human
perspectives. In the brilliant series of frescoes, in which Boccaccio

chose to exemplify the design or the ideal thematics of his 'comedy', intrepid figures of merchants always occupy a central position as protagonists. For in order to present live, authoritative witnesses – both in a negative as well as in a positive sense – to the great human truths underlying the *Decameron*, it was natural that the writer should turn to the representatives of that same humanity which, in the words of Renan, gave 'la plus grande leçon d'énergie et de volonté de l'histoire'.

In the harsh reproof of human vices which constitutes the theme of the First Day, the ruthless greed of the French, the calculated impiety of Ciappelletto, and the mean avarice of Ermino Grimaldi deepen with pale light and sinister shadows the bitterly polemical representation of the great men of the century; while the subtle and quick sagacity of Melchisedech or Abraham, and the simple wisdom of Giannotto or of the merchant pursued by the Inquisitor are in contrast to the cupidity of the powerful. . . . And after this semi-prelude, in which the most defined and unforgettable characters come from the mercantile sectors, we then have the brightly animated diptych on the two sides of Fortune[1] (Second and Third Days), thronged, especially with these pioneers of Italian economic sovereignty. From the free-living Sandro Agolanti, who has a tight grip on commerce in Treviso, to the circle of Italian merchants so lightly yet so brilliantly sketched in their jovial and salacious after-supper chats amid the smoke and wine around a tavern fireplace, we have a whole gallery of vivid portraits, of settings, first minutely studied, then impressionistically drawn, which create in the Second Day a grandiose and highly animated succession of mercantile scenes. Rinaldo d'Esti, the somewhat naïve but pious trader of the regions between Emilia and Veneto, who, after the most unexpected misfortunes, receives from his Saint Julian the grace of delightful hospitality; the rapid alternation between the failures and unforeseen fortunes of the Lamberti, forever on horseback between Florence and England; the foolish adventures with happy endings of imprudent and light-headed youths, such as Landolfo and Andreuccio; the gay, astute sagacity of the merchants who wisely bring to a term the unbelievable, sorrowful wanderings of Alatiel; and finally the quick and light sketch of Monaco, the Frankish port for pirates and a Calvary for traders (cf. VIII, 10).

---

[1] [sc. Fortune dominated and dominating].

As all the tales of the Second Day (with the exception of the eighth) bear the mercantile seal, so in the Third Day the epic of the Italian merchant is further developed. We have, among other stories, the subtle, contemptuous contrast between the lady of noble ancestry and the rich wool-seller to whom she is given as a wife (II, 3), the cautious prudence of Il Zima who profits from the stinginess of the noble Vergellesi, and the oriental adventure in which a Florentine patrician, Tedaldo Elisei, strives to forget love. It seems that here Boccaccio chooses to contrast Human Ingenuity and Fortune, alluding to the juxtaposition of fortuitous nobility and the nobility earned through the continuous struggle of a life forever prone to risk and bound to responsibilities. His choice of protagonists from the burgher and merchant class, in the drama between man and Fortune, reveals a new impassioned attention given to that society. . . .

The force with which the world of Boccaccio's youth imposes itself on his fantasy is clearly disclosed in the diptych dedicated to Love, considered as the supreme proof of man's gentleness or baseness (Fourth and Fifth Days). If with the preceding theme . . . recourse to examples taken from the eventful life of the merchants would seem natural in itself, with respect to the theme of Love, it is, abstractly, totally gratuitous. Yet families or persons belonging to the middle class almost always occupy the forefront in these two days: the Balducci, agents for the Bardi company, protagonists of the famous apologue contained in the Introduction to the Fourth Day; the great Venetian merchants of 'ca' Quirino' who have trade relations with Flanders; the loyal Provençal 'Civada' who travel the trade routes of Spain; even the Florentine Sighieri or the Liparoli, devoted to piracy, and the Sicilians and Genovese of the tales of Gianni and Teodoro. Moreover, in the grand symphony of love and death of the Fourth Day, as well as in the merry flightiness of the musical comedies of the Fifth, the gentlest and warmest women, the ones most caressed by Boccaccio's fantasy, belong precisely to the world that the Stil Novo and Petrarch chose to ignore . . . These unforgettable figures of love radiate with timid charm as they stand out meek and fragile against the dark background of a world dominated by money, greed, and the implacable ruthlessness of financial expediency. Unadorned and somewhat withered, their beauty is more seductive than that of the bejewelled and proud feudal ladies; and they are certainly not inferior in nobility and heroic sentiments.

To be sure, the mercantile symphony, varied but always well

harmonised, reaches full orchestration as we move to the vast trip-
tych dedicated to Ingenuity (Sixth, Seventh and Eighth Days). Here
too, from the very first retort that, through a tempered sharpness of
intellect, elevates the humble merchant Cisti above noble and great
men, to the last that elicits around Salaebetto and Canigiani an
entire unscrupulous and knavish world, the Decameron gives its
preference to the figures, environment and concerns of the new
ruling class.

So after the pause of the Ninth Day . . ., dedicated to magnificent
economic portraits of the great men of the past, Boccaccio makes
room for the supremely noble examples taken from the world to
which he was the first to give literary dignity. After the urbane
prudence and sagacity of Gilberto, and the stricken, inflamed profile
of Lisa, in the tale of Torello there stands out the most aristocratic
visualisation of the sage and eloquent figure of the Italian merchant.

Thus throughout the precise and well calibrated structure of the
Decameron, along the great double or triple arches which give it
organic development and logical consistency, the mercantile 'constant' of the dynamics and value of this intricate architecture reveals
itself continuously and necessarily. Without the urgency for a new
world of literature and without the original life of a class depicted
in its own technical and expressive idiom, the Decameron would
possess neither its striking 'exemplary' force, nor its eloquent and
multiform human richness. It would not be the poem of the waning
of the Middle Ages in Italy, if it were not also the epic of the men
who most forcefully characterised this society, leading it as they did
into the centre of European life.

                                                    Vittore Branca

The Place of
the *Decameron*

Feudal society was founded on personal relationships. By restraining man with the bonds of subjection and vassallage, it shattered the social unity of the previous times into a myriad of small societies each built around a leader. In the small, self-contained world of the castle, a whole court lived around a count or a baron. Warriors, pages, unmarried vassals, nobles and indentured servants fulfilled their apprenticeship in arms and courtly manners, while into the castle came guests of every sort: pilgrims travelling to important holy places, merchants on their way to the seasonal fairs, monks, beggars, and minstrels. Every so often the lord threw open the gates of the castle and held 'open court'. Everyone, the rich and the poor, the great and the humble, was able to spend several days there; the castle became a place for meetings and banquets, and, when it was over, no one was granted permission either 'to remain or to depart' without having received one or more gifts. Thus, feudal economy, entirely based on the indirect exploitation of land, assembled around a lord a mass of parasites who, together with him, derisively exploited the villein, the only one who actually produced goods. The life of these parasites was moreover conditioned by the generosity of the lord who needed their number and devotion as testimony of his power and nobility.

'Magnanimity', or 'liberality' as it was also called, was therefore, at a certain moment in feudal society, a necessary virtue, bound to the conditions of castle life as an essential part of courtesy (cf. *Convivio*, II, X, 7). It is natural that later, when art began to idealize this life, it also idealized the virtue, and prescribed it to the lords as an essential condition of valour or excellence. A liberal man is one who

---

This essay was originally entitled 'La posizione del *Decameron*', and appeared in *La Rassegna della Letteratura Italiana*, VII, 2 (1957), pp. 189–206. It has been translated and abridged by Robert S. Dombroski.

gives freely, without being asked or obliged, who gives to someone
according to his merit, who avoids any sort of stinginess and actually
squanders his money to display his unselfishness. Obviously, avarice
is characteristic of a mean and common spirit, *villano*: 'Avaritiam
sicut nocivam pestem effugias' instructs Andreas Capellanus (*Trattato
d'amore*, S. Battaglia ed., Rome, 1947, p. 100). 'Be generous in
spending and have beautiful houses without doors or keys' recommends a Provençal nobleman Arnaut Guilhem of Marsan in his
Ensenhamen; and an Italian lord, the marquis Malaspina, having been
reproached for acts of brigandage, replies that he stole in order to
give, not to hoard, and the justification appeared to be good. The
French chronicler Geoffroi de Vigeois tells us about a knight who
had a piece of ploughed land sown with silver coins, and another
who, 'out of vaingloriousness', had thirty of his own horses burned
alive. . . .

Meanwhile, during the thirteenth and fourteenth centuries, the
new social and political organisation of the Commune was being
developed. The Commune, at least at the height of its development,
was composed of bankers, merchants, and artisans who assembled in
the city and made their living from small industries and trade,
rather than from the exploitation of the land. Money takes on a new
meaning: earned through work, it is used to make money. A self-
subsistent economy, which aimed only at fiscal balance, is replaced
by a barter economy whose goal is the creation of a surplus wealth.
The change in the social structure brings about a change in the
philosophy of life and in moral judgement. One still talks about and
celebrates the ideals of liberality and courtesy, because when a new
social class begins to rule, it tends to ennoble itself by taking on the
customs and philosophy of life of the former ruling class. But the
words acquire new connotations in their attempt to express a new
way of perceiving reality; while at the same time, other concepts
and words arise and become diffused. Hence the bourgeois writers
of treatises begin to celebrate a new virtue: temperance (or moderation) which no longer complements the courtesy of old, but replaces
it. . . .

It would be wrong, however, to think that the process I have
briefly described came about in a simple and linear way through a
steady and continuous evolution. Reality is always complex, never
simple and uniform, and the evolution of systems and ideologies is
never steady or linear. We find in every moment of social reality an

intermixture of at least three currents: institutions and philosophies that have been already superseded, yet whose spirit remains; the dominant institutions and philosophies that give an age its colour and tone; new institutions and philosophies that arise confusedly and toil along with difficulty. Social reality is thus riddled with contradictions, and the men of an historical epoch reflect the divergent institutions and philosophies in their own particular way; they too suffer internal conflicts of which they are not entirely aware and which they are not capable of solving.

In the thirteenth and fourteenth centuries, the flow of life and ideas in Florence was therefore divergent and complex. Writers emerging from the new merchant and artisan classes expressed, more or less consciously, the new social reality of the Commune; while other writers, belonging to the noble cliques and educated in the previous culture, cherished the antique ideals. Since they did not see these ideals as a part of the people and customs, they clothed them in a seductive light of regret; and being contemptuous of a vile present, they idolised a chivalric past of refinement and courtesy. Thus the life styles and the ideals of the nobility continued in part to inform society, even now that the social world in which they arose had disappeared. . . .

Boccaccio came from a family of merchants, but his refined humanistic culture had kindled in him a strong desire to set himself apart from the masses who were devoted only to trade and profit. He considered the vile 'mechanics' (men who, incapable of raising themselves to free and impartial cultural activity, were given to manual labour and mercenary work) with the same aristocratic contempt that Dante had for the 'genti nove'; while he yearned for the courtly times of Saladin and past generations. Boccaccio's cultural ideal was therefore chivalric and courtly; but living in the middle of the fourteenth century, he was forced to push his ideal back in time, for his age was truly 'mechanical'. The feudal courts were no longer in existence, and the great princely courts of the Renaissance had yet to be created. Like Dante's Romagna, all of Italy was divided between 'tyranny' and the 'Frankish state', between the Communes made up of proud, quarrelsome merchants and signorie of tyrants, preoccupied with the future, not yet softened by time and by the security of dominion. Patronage was a thing of the past and would rise again in the future: the magnanimous feudal barons were dead and the magnificent lords of the Renaissance had yet to be born.

Contemporary knights were gross and tyrannical, like those who composed the 'courts' and the 'families' of the podestas, such as the judge of the Marches of *Decameron* VIII, 5, whose breeches are taken by three young men while he is on the bench. Thus the world of chivalry belongs to the past; but by celebrating chivalric times and men, Boccaccio naturally expresses an ideal present to him and sets in not so distant times the aspirations he would have liked to see realised in his own age. For this reason, he exalts with reverent wonder the knightly loyalty of the Norman king William II, who in order to keep his word has his most beloved young nephew killed, and casts in such an ideal light the chivalric magnanimity of anyone who consumes all his wealth for love, while remaining faithful to the lady and her cult (V, 8, 9); for this reason, in the Tenth Day, he varies and repeats his praise for magnanimity and for all the aspects of courtesy, even up to the point of renouncing love and life itself; for this reason, when appropriate, he continually inveighs against the great enemy: avarice, the gross cupidity that extinguishes in man's spirit every spark of generosity; this is why he often rages against the 'corrupt and vile habits of those who today wish to be considered gentlemen and lords', but who instead should be called 'asses, bred in the filth of all the wickedness of the vilest men' (I, 8).

Nevertheless, Boccaccio does not limit himself to representing and exalting only the cultural ideals of the past, ignoring or not acknowledging the present. Like every great writer, he is capable of acutely observing and objectively representing the real world around him, and the representation of contemporary social reality is, in the *Decameron*, vaster and more animated than it would seem from the above quotations. The deep meaning of the communal revolution lies in its having given way to a new culture that has inserted lay and earthly themes into the context of the religious and clerical culture of the past, preparing the way for Humanism and the Renaissance. . . .

In its renewal of life and culture, the Commune had not only politically destroyed the old feudal nobility (in the sense of replacing it as a ruling class), but it had also destroyed a particular way of viewing man, his virtues, and his work. Money acquires a new value that derives from the activity of men, not from its intrinsic worth; nobility is no longer a matter of blood and heredity, but rather an individual matter based on intimate refinement and personal valour. . . .

Boccaccio is the poet of this new burgher communal aristocracy. It is true that he often assails the movement of people from the country to the city, which he feels is responsible for the introduction of base feelings and customs into Florence (cf. *Letter to Pino dei Rossi*, in *L'Ameto*, N. Bruscoli ed., Bari, 1940, p. 164). It is true that he seems to yearn for and regret the passing of the antique chivalric world; but in reality, he is the poet of the most elevated classes of the new fourteenth-century society, of those classes that, mercantile by interest and birth, tended to set themselves apart from the less wealthy and refined in order to institute an aristocracy of the intellect, of feeling, of taste. Thus we have Federigo degli Alberighi, 'renowned above all other *donzele* of Tuscany for his prowess in arms and in courtesy'. Here the word '*donzela*' appears somewhat abstract and literary, because if *donzela* in the sense of 'young aspiring knight' was common in Provençal literature, it was rare in Tuscany, where chivalric traditions were always rather weak. In fact, Federigo, of noble family and courtly manners, puts into practice his politeness according to traditional chivalric rules: in loving, in the handling of arms, and in giving beyond measure. Yet there is something more modern, more 'bourgeois' in his story, and the novella ends, in a bourgeois way, against all norms of courtly tradition, with marriage. Andreas Capellanus, the great theoretician of courtly love, had taught that love and marriage were mutually exclusive; in fact, the concept of marriage had been alien to all Italian and Provençal love poetry, as well as to all chivalric literature; but here Monna Giovanna marries Federigo in a bourgeois way and Federigo, instructed by his difficult experience, 'having become more prudent with his money', lives happily with her. The noble and courtly *donzela* is transformed into an advocate of economy and moderation, virtues characteristic of the merchant Paolo da Certaldo and of Leon Battista Alberti. An age has definitely ended and Boccaccio has faithfully registered its demise.

With the end of the world of old, Boccaccio documents the birth of the new, in the tale of Cisti the baker. Naturally, the story should be read together with the introduction that precedes it, because only in this way is it possible to view the contrast between Boccaccio's ideological convictions and his zest for realism. Boccaccio the ideologue cannot understand how Cisti, a man whose polite and courtly discretion he greatly admires, could only be a baker. For him, nobility of spirit should be bound, if not exactly to nobility of blood, at least to social rank, to economic independence which permits the education of the mind and the long practice of refined customs. But the new social reality is in contrast to these traditional biases which still persist. And there are many examples (. . .) of how Fortune gives 'a base occupation to a body endowed with a noble soul'. Boccaccio cannot help noticing this new social reality. Among the common people working in the minor trades who take part in the councils of the Commune, there are not only the base 'mechanics' seeking vile earnings, but courteous, unselfish men, endowed with minds sharpened through participation in the political process, and instinctively magnificent spirits. With frank realism, Boccaccio can only attribute to this strange phenomenon an imaginative and mythical explanation: 'And so the two ministers of this world – Nature and Fortune – often hide their most valuable possession under the shadow of the occupations reputed base, so that when they are drawn forth at the fitting moment, their splendour will be the more apparent.' (VI, 2) But it is precisely the mythical character of this explanation that reveals Boccaccio's embarrassment and clarifies the contradictions present in him while he writes and the triumph of his realism over the prejudices stemming from his upbringing and social class. . . .

Moreover, in order to understand the seriousness with which Boccaccio grasps and expresses the character of his age, let us reconstruct the picture that the Decameron gives us of fourteenth-century Florence. The novellas of courtesy and tragedy, the rhetorical and abstract novellas, are never set in Florence. The great (too great!) heroes of courtesy are sovereigns (King Charles and King Peter), who reside in the lands of Lombardy – understood in its widest medieval meaning – rich in feuds and in lords (Messer Torello, the Marquis of Saluzzo); they are foreigners, imaginary characters of old. The Florentines, even when they are noble, courteous, cultured, are always, so to speak, concrete, endowed with a courtesy that is realistically human and earthly: Federigo degli Alberighi, whose wholly fourteenth-century character we have underscored; Guido Cavalcanti, philosopher, logician, who as poet seems abstract, yet so brilliant a product of society, so typically Florentine; polite men and women gifted with sharp wit, so able to fling back witticisms and jibes; Chichibio's master, for example, so lordly, yet so realistically represented; quick-witted and clever minds, like Giotto and Messer Forese da Rabatta; artisans like Cisti, the baker, and artists of the populace, like Bruno, Buffalmacco, and Calandrino; burgher physicians like Maestro Simone; rich merchants like the characters in the tale of Gerlamo; plebeians like Simona and Pasquino, merry fellows like Scalza, half 'men of court', that is, outright parasites such as Ciacco and Biondello, empty heads such as the young men who take the breeches off the judge of the Marches. And surrounding these characters, there is the country with its 'earnest gentlemen' (the man who is playing court to Belcolore, or the accomplice to the practical jokes of Bruno and Buffalmacco), its innkeepers and their families, peasant women ready to lie in the hay, merry, open-minded monks, and crude farmers. All of fourteenth-century Florence is present with its diverse social levels, yet by now completely Guelf and burgher; and the ten young men and women of the graceful and honourable company of story-tellers, in whom Boccaccio has pictured himself, his ideals and taste, represent the new Florentine burgher aristocracy: rich, cultured, honourable, and free living, yet already idealised and stylised, as the symbol and idealisation of their class. They represent a new aristocracy of wealth which also seeks to be an aristocracy of the spirit, but which has nothing in common with the ancient feudal world. Yet it feels itself different from the vile customs of the 'mechanics' and is contemptuous of baseness and avarice, yearns for the courtly companies of old (VI, 9), and has nostalgia for the ladies and the knights, the troubles and the comforts of the past. But it does so in its own way, within the limits we have drawn – which are the same limits that set apart the new century from the preceding ones and made this second or third generation of fourteenth-century citizenry fundamentally different from the first generation of thirteenth-century citizenry.

Thus the Decameron appears conceived on the divide that sets apart two worlds and two ages, in years abundant in sharp contrasts that are reflected somewhat subtly and harmoniously in the work. They are the years in which the Commune, incapable of becoming a people's government, already anticipates the Signoria; years in which a new intellectual caste begins to separate itself from the populace with which it is unable to merge. On the surface, the courteous, liberal, magnanimous tales appear only as a weary continuation of feudal literature; and, in a certain sense, this is true. But there is more. If at times liberality and courtesy appear as literary themes, at other times they are vital elements of the fourteenth-century world that the Decameron reflects in all its complex structure.

Moreover, we have evidence of this diversity in inspiration in the artistic diversity among the various tales: the abstract ones, even though great literature, are rhetorical, wholly literary, replete with superhuman heroes, unrelated to the fourteenth-century society; in the other tales we have great, powerful, realistic art filled with modern and practical courtesy. Having read the Decameron, one tends to remember Mitridanes and Natan or Tito and Gisippo, while forgetting Cisti the baker, or Federigo degli Alberighi and Monna Giovanna. The actuality of Boccaccio's art is an index of the actuality of his inspiration, which depends on the possibility of adhering to life: to real life and to the vital forces at work in it. . . .

It is very difficult to assign a place to Boccaccio and to the Decameron in the evolution of the concept of culture and art, because among his contemporaries the conceptions of the meaning and value of culture were varied, complex, and contrasting. The ideas of past epochs linger on, kept alive by tradition and by the schools, while newer ideas forge ahead with difficulty.

At the beginning of the thirteenth century a great cultural tradition was about to reach its fullest maturity. The culture is in the hands of clerics; it is learned and discussed in Latin, in a language no longer spoken or understood except by the scholae. Its object is the rational understanding and systematisation of revealed truths; it utilizes all of the cultural patrimony handed down from Greek and Roman antiquity, but evaluated against a rigorous criterion of judgement that establishes whether or not its assertions correspond to those of the Holy Scriptures. The 'masters of the sentences' had already promoted this culture, and soon the great authors of the summae, Albertus Magnus and Saint Thomas Aquinas, would brilliantly systematise it.

But at that very moment, a clamorous rebellion erupts alongside and against this orderly work of systematisation. The wave of mysticism moving from the Franciscan Umbria threatens to overthrow even the fortress of scholasticism, while the Friars Minor, in their impassioned reinterpretation of all human values, also give a new interpretation to learning. We have, in a certain sense, the return of the Christian position which countered the pagan docta sapientia with the docta ignorantia or the indocta sapientia. . . .

Thus Saint Francis and the Franciscan literature take a clear stand against all vacuous and worldly learning. For Saint Francis, as for his early followers, at least until 1230, the only learning accepted was Christian learning. The *scientia graeca*, the *quaestiones curiosae et aridae*, that is, liberal arts, philosophy, and law, were prohibited. And theological studies themselves, although necessary, were allowed only to those who had entered the order already skilled in them. . . .

Similar polemics recur in all of Franciscan literature, throughout the century and beyond. In the thirteenth and fourteenth centuries, while Saint Thomas was assembling his *Summa*, while Dante was composing the *Divine Comedy*, and Petrarch and Boccaccio were laying the foundations of Humanism, many friars, Franciscan and others, continued to contrast the wisdom of the faithful with the knowledge drawn from books . . . Jacopone da Todi was continually to contrast holy madness with systematic knowledge, stressing the antithesis between Assisi and Paris, between infused and acquired knowledge, and between the feeling for God and the knowledge of Him. . . .

The devaluation of learning, pursued in the middle of the fourteenth century, has no longer a positive historical significance, but is only the sign of the inert survival of old themes or the mystical withdrawal from the new values that in the meantime were being advanced. Attitudes like those of Jacopo Passavanti, Saint Catherine of Siena, Giovanni delle Celle, and Saint Bernadine, taken individually could have a highly positive value, as signs of religious experiences lived with absolute fullness; socially, however, they had a negative value, inasmuch as they were no longer in harmony with the course of social-cultural institutions already under way. Instead, the devaluation of learning in the early thirteenth century was a sign of that youthful fervour which animated the whole of Italian society in those years when the common people were deeply moved by a force that was at the same time political, social, and spiritual.

In that particular moment of Italian history, when the new Communes were being created everywhere, to deny scholastic and juridical learning, to evoke feeling and faith, meant to deny the culture on which the feudal society was structured, even if, as often happens, the ideals and the goals of the rising communal society presented themselves in the guise of a return to the past: to a mythical, apostolic, and evangelical age. . . .

But for this very reason the cultural revolution conquered only certain restricted circles. These were years of social, political, and economic development, years of intense cultural life; years, in Dante's words, that were followed not by *etadi grosse*, but by steadily more refined ages, and the new human values affirmed themselves not against the culture, but within it. . . .

Therefore soon even the new religious orders became learned. The following decades witnessed the fierce battle waged by the mendicant orders for the conquest of the Sorbonne, and the early ascetic spirit that celebrated the *docta ignorantia* remained alive only among the heretical groups, or among the Friars Minor and spiritual groups banished by the Church and persecuted as heretics. The Church recognized itself not in Fra Jacopone but in Saint Thomas Aquinas.

On the other hand, even though the Commune did not express the interests of the magnates, neither did it express those of the common people. It became more and more the organization of the bourgeoisie, of the *popolo grasso*, the *buoni popolani*, who, having immediately understood the value of learning as a powerful instrument of freedom and domination of civilization and progress, wanted to make it its own. The evolution of the schools in the thirteenth and fourteenth centuries, the development of lay schools in addition to the clerical schools, the ever increasing diffusion of learning, . . . the gradual predominance of technical over, say, humanistic studies are both the signs and the consequences of the transformation of thirteenth-century society.

We have thus a rapid development of learning and literature, and the intelligentsia of the new ruling class, the judges, and notaries, seek in many ways to adapt the old culture to the demands of a new public. . . .

The Commune had also become the social and political organization of the *popolo grasso*, that is, of a class that inserted itself between the feudal nobility, with which it eventually merged, and the common people. The *popolo grasso* (the 'good and dear citizens', as they were called), which quickly became a class in itself, were the true masters of the Commune and the protagonists of a new history. . . . For them, learning was the property of the public and not of a caste. They felt that it should be transmitted in the vernacular, because the new generation of merchants, financiers, and artisans were unacquainted with Latin; that it should be both popular and national and, besides restating old theses and theories, reflect – which in effect it did – the new social, economic, and spiritual interests of the new classes to which it addressed itself and from which came its writers. However, it was not a universally democratic culture that represented the spirit and the interests of all the citizens in the Commune. . . . Nevertheless, the literature of the thirteenth century within certain limits does have a national and popular character that perhaps is not equalled in Italian literature at least until the Risorgimento: Dante's *Divine Comedy* is the highest expression of this character. . . . But after the *Divine Comedy* the unity of culture with popular tradition, of personal inspiration and collective spirit, is shattered . . . [and] it becomes easy to distinguish clearly between a cultured and petty bourgeois literary tradition, between works that are intentionally 'rhetorical' such as Petrarch's *Canzoniere* and the *Decameron*, and those of medium tonality based on a more modest and less ambitious form of culture: this is a literature, created by base and crude men, that addresses itself to the common people. Thus we are headed towards Humanism, where literature and culture become once again the patrimony of a closed caste, a caste this time made up of the laity. . . .

During the fourteenth century a new type of intellectual was being formed. He was no longer a man among men, citizen of the Commune: notary, judge, prior, merchant, magnate, dedicated to politics, one who worked and administered by day, and translated and composed by night. The new intellectual was on the contrary a man of letters who made a profession out of learning and an occupation out of poetry. The greatest example, almost the model and symbol, of this type of intellectual was Petrarch, who already in the fourteenth century anticipated better than anyone else the character of the humanist, completely dedicated to learning. . . .

Boccaccio, as a man, is halfway between the old and the new *literato*; but as a theoretician, at a certain point in his life, it is he who, along with Petrarch, depicts, in his *Trattatello in lode di Dante*, the figure of the new intellectual. No longer a *fabuloso parlare*, poetry is now theology. . . . and the poets and *literati* are the saints of this new secular theology, saints whose lives are to be narrated according to the hagiographic schemes of old. . . .

The *Decameron* is situated at the height of the parabola, at a halfway point between the two ages, when the cult of literature had assumed in Boccaccio a character that was no longer medieval; but, at the same time, not having met Petrarch, Boccaccio had yet to detach himself from literature and still shared Dante's hope in the maturity and in the expressive possibilities of the vernacular. . . . The *Decameron*, therefore, is written in the vernacular, in prose; and [its stories] 'bear no title' [and are written] in 'the most homely and unassuming style it is possible to imagine', dedicated to the gentlest and dearest ladies; that is to say, it is intentionally conceived and addressed not to the new caste of intellectuals then being formed, but to the middle class Florentine reading public. Thus, as Branca's studies have shown, the book circulated in mercantile and burgher circles, and Boccaccio later, when he was converted to Humanism, repudiated it together with all his other early works. In other words, for Boccaccio himself the *Decameron* belonged to the literature and the culture of the Communes; in it we find no trace – with respect to themes, style, and tonality – of any link with the poetics of Humanism of which the *Trattatello in lode di Dante* some years later draws the essential characteristics. On the other hand, the poetics of the *Decameron* are altogether different from those of the folk literature of the common people; it is a work pervaded by an aristocratic spirit and by a conscious desire to go beyond the naturalism of the subject matter through the medium of literary re-elaboration, in an attempt to sublimate the crudeness of reality into literary schemes.

Whoever in fact picks up the *Decameron*, after reading the minor writers of the fourteenth century, is immediately aware of passing from one world to another. Those writers of prose were capable of reaching a certain degree of art, but the *Decameron* is something else. It not only contains a greater knowledge of man, and a greater power of art which is lacking in the others; but there is a different conception of art based on the faith that writing even in prose, in the common vernacular, recounting tales, is a task to which the Muses give assistance; the conviction that poetry is a world by itself, an art that independently of its content sustains itself by its own rules and aspires to its own effects.

Hence the character of the book, which is never the reproduction of the vocabulary or the syntax of the spoken idiom, but rather, even in the most earthy of situations, the transposition of the vocabulary and the syntax to another system, possessing its own rules and cadences, its own forms: the inversion of words and phrases so that they may answer the demands of rhetoric and music.

Thus the impression that the reader receives is one of a greater artfulness than that to which Boccaccio aspired. For upon careful examination and viewed within the perspective of the language of the times, the *Decameron* appears more vivid and 'modern' than we are generally accustomed to think; it issues from the emerging of two equally dominant tendencies in Boccaccio: the aspiration towards art understood as rhetoric and his propensity toward realism. . . . In a word, the vocabulary of the *Decameron* may be described as 'urbane', the Florentine idiom of the wealthy and cultured classes of the fourteenth century: the language which the seven young women and their three young knights would more or less have spoken if, having met during the plague, they really had fled to the country hills to tell each other stories in a refined manner.

Quintilian has defined 'urbanity' as a quality having nothing dissonant, rustic, or alien in meaning, expression, gesture, or sound, consisting not so much in the singular terms as in the general tone of the discourse. And earlier, he had even been more precise, calling it a discourse in which there is a flavour of the language of the cultured citizenry; in sum, the very opposite of a rustic tone.[1] Now it is precisely this urbaneness, this flavour of the city and of its learning that makes up the linguistic fabric of the *Decameron*, in which are present words of diverse tonality: even rustic, base, or plebeian, but seen as such, employed from time to time in the service of particular artistic effects. . . .

The vocabulary that Boccaccio calls *volgare* and *umile* is cast in a sentence structure accurately studied and elaborated according to precise rules, belonging to a long tradition and subjected, when necessary, to the refined and complex norms of medieval and artistic prose and of the *cursus*. To be sure, the language of the *Decameron* – its words and its grammar – is not that of the models of Guido Faba or of Guittone d'Arezzo, nor of Dante's *Convivio*, nor even of Boccaccio's early romances. Having been the fruit of a long linguistic elaboration, it marks the moment in which the ideal of thirteenth-century artistic prose reaches its dignity as art, equally distant from naturalistic immediacy and academic composure.

Giuseppe Petronio

---

[1] [*Institutio Oratoria*, VI, III, 16–19.]

Some Reflections on
the *Decameron*

The very first tale of the *Decameron* leads us into a world full of conflict, irony, and contradictions. The novella's content is anticipated in its title: 'Ser Cepperello deceives a holy friar with a false confession, then he dies; and although in life he was a most wicked man, in death he is reputed to be a saint, and is called Saint Ciappelletto.'

Boccaccio presents the time and the story's entire band of circumstances with the utmost precision. He tells us that a certain Musciatto Franzesi, compelled to journey into Tuscany with Carlo Senzaterra, brother to the King of France, and discovering that his affairs are in disarray, dispatched a man called Cepperello da Prato to collect the repayment of money he had lent to some Burgundians. Ser Franzesi was a wealthy merchant. The information given about him confers a business-like tone to the prose.

Ciappelletto is small in stature, dresses nicely, is by profession a notary, by nature a false witness, sodomite, glutton, drunk, cheat, and conspirer. He goes to Burgundy and stays at the house of two Florentine usurers. The brothers are not simply usurers, but representatives of the new profession of bankers. Such people were called Lombards, from the place of their origin. They were, so to speak, among the founders of banking, which now flourishes in many countries.

The Lombard gentlemen and Ser Ciappelletto are people of a new age, not patriarchal merchants; in their hands financial operations begin to take on an abstract, almost algebraic character. The collection of pledges, which today is handled by pawn shops, had

---

[Title mine – ed.] From Victor Šhklovskij, *Chudožestuennaja Proza* (Moscow, 1959), pp. 168–74, 184–8: translated and abridged by Ronald Walter and Robert S. Dombroski. A major part of *Chudožestuennaja Proza* has been rendered into Italian: V. Šhklovskij, *Lettura del Decameron* (Bologna, 1969). The translation is by Alessandro Ivanov.

been practised for some time, but the banking activity in the strict sense was recent. . . . The Lombards of the first tale were disliked by everyone and still recognized themselves as evildoers. One of the world's most perfect scoundrels is destined to die in their home. After hearing Ciappelletto's confession, the priest would have surely denied him communion and holy burial. The disgrace that the guest would have incurred would have certainly increased the people's contempt for the bankers. To allow the guest to die without confession would have been impossible and would have served to dishonour them. Such is the situation. But the old scoundrel comforts his hosts: 'I don't want you to worry in the slightest on my account, nor to fear that I will cause you to suffer any harm.'

Ser Ciappelletto willingly prepares his great deception; his last conversation must be a fraud. He deceives the monk who absolves him by confessing sins of no consequence and by showing impassioned repentance for them. The monk accepts the confession with veneration, and, after the villain's death, he proclaims him a saint.

Such is the plot. Let us now examine the tale's composition. The entire fraudulent confession and the story of Ciappelletto's succeeding canonization is related by Panfilo in the manner used in describing the lives of the saints.

The tale begins with a pious reflection: 'It is proper, dearest ladies, that everything done by man should begin with the sacred and admirable name of Him that was the maker of all things.' Thus at the outset of his Decameron Boccaccio invokes God and mentions the absolute necessity of His glorification. On the following pages the notion of the mortality of all existing things is developed. Later we are told that divine grace does not descend upon us through any merit of our own, rather through the intercession of the saints who were mortal men but who, by carrying out God's will, became the eternal mediators of all who pray. All of this reasoning seems to be leading to a story about saints.

Then there is a religiously motivated digression. It is possible that a priest has not lived a righteous life, but the sacraments he administers, according to the Church, are none the less valid, for he possesses the grace transferred to him by means of the holy oils of ordination. Boccaccio continues to elaborate this concept, taking it to the absurd: 'And our regard for Him, who is so compassionate and generous towards us, is all the greater when, the human eye being quite unable to penetrate the secrets of divine intelligence, common opinion deceives us and perhaps we appoint as our advocate in His majestic presence one who has been cast by Him into eternal exile. Yet He from whom nothing is hidden, paying more attention to the purity of the supplicant's motives than to his ignorance or to the banishment of the intercessor, answers those who pray to Him exactly as if the advocate were blessed in His sight.'

The conclusion suggested by the narrator seems to consist in the fact that God, without concerning Himself with the boorishness of whoever prays, listens only to the prayers and does not consider the errors they contain; and not only the priest, but the saint too can be an immoral person and even a criminal.

The tale of this extraordinary scoundrel who swindles the populace before dying is developed in a tone characteristic of hagiographic prose. ... The story's hagiographic form underscores the perception of difference, questions the accuracy of the other Lives, and, through the juxtaposition of the villain's story with the Lives of the Saints, negates the very idea of saintly intercession on behalf of a sinner, notwithstanding the pious tone of the conversation.

Ingenuity leads to the discovery of the essence of superstition. Certain slips of the tongue, concise as they are, do not exceed the tonal limits of the hagiographic narrative. The tension in plot is maintained by our sensing that the storyteller might, at any time, say too much and that he wants to say something which is totally impermissible; but, within the limits of what is allowed, he develops his story ironically in the terms of the orthodox faith. For example, he says at the last moment that the usurer could have actually repented: 'Nor would I wish to deny that perhaps God has blessed and admitted him to His presence. For albeit he led a wicked, sinful life, it is possible that at the eleventh hour he was so sincerely repentant that God had mercy upon him and received him into His kingdom.' But Boccaccio mentioned before that Ciappelletto had not only confessed, but had received communion, after which he was given extreme unction; and shortly after vespers he was dead. Therefore, although there is some talk about the possibility of repentance, the novella's temporal dimension is already complete. Panfilo ends his story with these words: 'And therefore, so that we, the members of this joyful company, may be guided safely and securely by His grace through these present adversities, let us praise the name of Him with whom we began our storytelling, let us hold

Him in reverence, and let us commend ourselves to Him in the hour of our need, in the certain knowledge that we shall be heard.' It is as if a man, intending to write to God, reveals beforehand that the mailbox where the letter is to be deposited offers little hope that it will reach its destination. The saint is a cheat and his miracles happen by mistake or through God's indulgence. Rome and the Roman Church are corrupt; they do a business in the faith unequalled even by the cloth business of Parisian merchants. Many doubts may arise about the merchandise, for there can be various qualities of cloth, but faith for the believer is one or does not exist.

Only after having eliminated with the first three tales the standard religious beliefs does Boccaccio go on to tell about the life of the Italians, the true foundations of their morality, and the sins of the clerics; in general, he considers them amusing and for the most part the conclusions are happy ones.

The laws of reason, based on rhetoric, are for Boccaccio logical, incontrovertible and necessary. In the tales, they are often presented to us in a naïve and tedious way, but for the reader of Boccaccio's day they appeared daring on account of their unsuspected application. The precepts of religious morality having been rejected, what remains are the rules of everyday, common sense behaviour, which are justified in detail through the use of rhetoric.

The plot structure is usually based on the juxtaposition of meaning, on the various ways of understanding one and the same phenomenon; the perception of this diversity in the ways of understanding comes about at times by casting the story in a style and a genre which do not correspond to it.

The introductory tale is not the only one with a religious theme. There follows a second in which Boccaccio tells of how a rich Jew, Abraham, merchant and expert in the Jewish law, agrees under the influence of his Christian friend to become a convert, but first decides to go to Rome: 'and there observe the man whom you call the vicar of God on earth, and examine his life and habits together with those of his fellow cardinals; and if they seem to me such that, added to your own arguments, they lead me to the conclusion that your faith is superior to mine, as you have taken such pains to show me, then I shall do as I have promised; but if things turn out differently, I shall remain a Jew as I am at present.' His Christian friend was somewhat troubled, knowing what Rome was like. But the Jew departed for Rome and saw there a corrupt city:

the selling of the sacraments and, in general, of all that was sellable; he witnessed cupidity, lust, hypocrisy, simony, 'together with many other things of which it is more prudent to remain silent'. On the sins of the Roman curia, Boccaccio expresses himself generically, as if it were an obvious matter.

From the standpoint of art, the tale sustains itself through an unexpected denouement constructed with paradoxical *calembours*. Having seen so much corruption, Abraham suddenly decides to become a Christian. He justifies his choice in the following way: 'I regard the place as a hotbed of diabolical rather than divine activities.' But he reasons that if all these diabolical vices have not succeeded in putting an end to the Christian faith which continues to exist and grow, 'I can only conclude that, being a more holy and genuine religion than any of the others, it deservedly has the Holy Ghost as its foundation and support.'

The novella appears to pacify religious censorship. In reality, however, it denies, while pretending to affirm by means of negation. Rome is sinful and immersed in the bartering of sacred things, yet Christianity continues to flourish, while it seems destined to perish. The fact that it withstands even these conditions can only be explained by a miracle. To accept the existence of the Christian faith is a sign of devotion, but as proof of its existence only its 'growth' is cited. Such a rhetorical device can only be called irony.

The third tale is the famous story of the 'three rings'. The sultan Saladin, desirous of obtaining money from a Jew named Melchisedech, decides to ask him which of the three faiths, Islam, Judaism, or Christianity, is the true one. But the person to whom the question was put was a man of sharp wits. Islam, Christianity, and Judaism constituted the traditional religious complex 'possessing scriptures'. The Moslems believed their religion to be the true one and Judaism and Christianity to be tolerable because genetically bound to the Koran.

The choice of the three rings was a historical fact. The tale circulated for some time among weak peoples: it was an attempt on the part of the infidels to defend before the representatives of the dominant religions their right to worship another cult. At the same time, this novella expresses a tolerance *sui generis*, that is to say, a sort of diplomatic and commercial indulgence for unorthodox belief. Tolerance of this sort could be found only in the Italian mercantile republics. . . .

The first three, more or less religious, tales, consciously placed at the beginning of the entire work, reject religion as a norm that gives man a definite moral foundation and certain moral precepts by which he governs his behaviour. The old faith is burned, like rags during the plague for the purpose of disinfection.

In the *Decameron* there are many novellas that employ devices common to the Greek romances. These stories tell about unjustly slandered wives, lost children, and how they are finally recognised by certain marks, just when the hero is about to be burned at the stake or when he is being led to his death under the lashes of a whip. In that very moment, the hero is not only pardoned, but is allowed to marry the woman he has seduced; for some time marriages of this kind were the dream of parents who had lost their betrothed children.

The greatest number of such tales is found in the Second Day. The topic itself of the Second Day seems to formulate the fundamental principle of the Greek romances: 'those who after suffering a series of misfortunes are brought to a state of unexpected happiness'. Here particularly important is the expression 'of unexpected happiness', which underscores the traditional surprise of the romantic denouement. . . .

We can ascertain the sources of many of the novellas; critics endowed with greater erudition than mine can determine the sources of all the tales. But even in this kind of research errors can be made. For the echoes of the past, the so-called borrowings, change their meaning when they enter into new relationships. The historian of literature often follows the repetition in diversity of the same element; but he often fails to observe that a thing is not repeated; rather its meaning is changed.

What in the Greek romances was explained by the wrath of the gods, in Boccaccio is explained by the thirst for profit. The shores and destinations are changed even though they seem to be the same stories about shipwrecked persons and pirates.

In the *Aethiopica*, the Greek romance of Heliodorus, the world is noted but not understood. A Greek who happens among the Ethiopians defeats a giant, but remains fascinated by the magic, religion, and customs of these barbarians; he is amazed by their life. Thus we have before us the first rough draft of a sense for the communality of human kind.

In the *Decameron* the objectives are more vital; the hero is not weighed down by historical analogies and prejudices. Although he finds himself in situations that are repeated and that have a millenary past, at the end he shows his awareness of new goals, of a new conception of human accomplishment and morality.

In the Second Day, Panfilo recounts a tale (the seventh), the content of which Boccaccio presents with these words: 'The Sultan of Babylon sends his daughter off to marry the King of Algarve. Owing to a series of mishaps, she passes through the hands of nine men in various places within the space of four years. Finally, having been restored to her father as a virgin, she sets off, as before, to become the King of Algarve's wife.'

The interest shown by the Greek historians in the kidnapping of some beautiful maiden who has fallen under the wrath of the gods (often that of the envious Venus), and in her passing from one suitor to another, is always based on the fact that the maiden remains pure. ... Even in the above mentioned tale the lovely Alatiel is shipwrecked and ends up in the hands of a gentleman who obtains her love without much resistance. A little later, she passes on to the suitor's brother, escapes with him, but is taken from her new lover by some shipowners. The author hardly has time to name her suitors who, one after another, wildly possess her. The beautiful maiden reacts to them all with forced consent, but the events are not really unpleasant for her. ... Finally some people who were in the service of the heroine's father recognize her and bring her back to him.

A. Veselovskij became interested in the origins of this tale. As a possible source he suggested one of the fables of A Thousand and One Nights; but there the heroine remains virtuous. The critic wonders at this, stating: 'The theme of the innocent beauty pursued by a series of misfortunes, had to be re-elaborated somewhat in order to arrive at a radical transformation of this sort; but it is quite probable that Boccaccio had in mind, rather than a story of this type, another in which a fatal lack of virtue constituted the main situation.'[1] He then proposes as the source the Hindu story of a woman who was too vain about her beauty. On account of this, in the successive versions of the story, she had little fortune in marriage.

---

[1] A. N. Veselovskij, Sobraniesocinenij [Works] (Saint Petersburg [Leningrad], 1913), vol. V, p. 495. Aleksandr Veselovskij (1833–1906) was a Russian philologist and historian.

Veselovskij believes that the story could have reached Boccaccio through a Moslem adaptation. It is hardly likely. The fact is that not only does the heroine pass through numerous love adventures, but that she is also insolent, and, after having enjoyed the love of many suitors, talks ironically about her fidelity. Having returned to her father's house, the lovely prisoner relates that immediately after she was kidnapped she was taken from the bandits by some admirable people who escorted her to a convent. The description of the religious services in this convent belongs to the category of the salacious and erotic *calembours* with which the Moslem Alatiel succeeds in parodying the Christian veneration of the saints and of their names. Boccaccio himself, on behalf of the narrator, refers to what consoled the maiden during the time of her second kidnapping from the home of Pericone by employing an analogous Christian phraseology with an equally parodistic function. Alatiel does not hide her passion. It is not a case of forced abduction, rather one of pleasure with many.

The new unity of the collection of tales consists in a new relationship and a different morality. . . . The tradition of the inviolability of the heroine was maintained in the romances for millennia. At the dawn of a new century, Dioneo[2] happily and persuasively breaks it, stirring up sighs of envy in the ladies.

Victor Šhklovskij

---

[2] [Dioneo tells the story of Alatiel.]

Frate Alberto

In a famous novella of the *Decameron* (IV, 2), Boccaccio tells of a man from Imola whose vice and dishonesty had made him a social outcast in his native town, so that he preferred to leave it. He went to Venice, there became a Franciscan monk and even a priest, called himself Frate Alberto, and managed to attract so much attention by striking penances and pious acts and sermons that he was generally regarded as a godly and trustworthy man. Then one day he tells one of his penitents – a particularly stupid and conceited creature, the wife of a merchant away on a journey – that the angel Gabriel has fallen in love with her beauty and would like to visit her at night. He visits her himself as Gabriel and has his fun with her. This goes on for a while, but in the end it turns out badly. This is what happens:

> Pure avenne un giorno che, essendo madonna Lisetta con una sua comare, et insieme di bellezze quistionando, per porre la sua inanzi ad ogni altra, si come colei che poco sale aveva in zucca, disse: Se voi sapeste a cui la mia bellezza piace, in verità voi tacereste dell'altre. La comare vaga d'udire, si come colei che ben la conoscea, disse: Madonna, voi potreste dir vero, ma tuttavia non sapendo chi questo si sia, altri non si rivolgerebbe così leggiero. Allora la donna, che piccola levatura avea, disse: Comare, egli non si vuol dire, ma l'intendimento mio è l'agnolo Gabriello, il quale più che sè m'ama, si come la più bella donna, per quello che egli mi dica, che sia nel mondo o in maremma. La comare allora ebbe voglia di ridere, ma pur si tenne per farla più avanti parlare, e disse: In fè di Dio, Madonna, se l'agnolo Gabriello è il vostro intendimento, e dicevi questo, egli dee ben

This essay has been abridged by Robert S. Dombroski from Erich Auerbach's *Mimesis: the Representation of Reality in Western Literature*, translated by Willard Trask (Princeton: Princeton University Press, 1953; Doubleday Anchor Book), pp. 177–82, 186–93, 195–6. It is reprinted here by permission of Princeton University Press.

esser così; ma io non credeva che gli agnoli facesson queste cose.
Disse la donna: Comare, voi siete errata; per le piaghe di Dio
egli fa meglio che mio marido; e dicemi che egli si fa anche
colassù; ma perciocchè io gli paio più bella che niuna che ne
sia in cielo, s'è egli innamorato di me, e viensene a star meco
ben spesso: mo vedi vu? La comare partita da madonna Lisetta,
le parve mille anni che ella fosse in parte ove ella potesse queste
cose ridire; e ragunatasi ad una festa con una gran brigata di
donne, loro ordinatamente raccontò la novella. Queste donne il
dissero a' mariti ed ad altre donne; e quelle a quell'altre, e così
in meno di due dì ne fu tutta ripiena Vinegia. Ma tra gli altri,
a' quali questa cosa venne agli orecchi, furono i cognati di lei, li
quali, senza alcuna cosa dirle, si posero in cuore di trovare questo
agnolo, e di sapere se egli sapesse volare; e più notti stettero in
posta. Avvenne che di questo fatto alcuna novelluzza ne vanne
a frate Alberto agli orecchi, il quale, per riprender la donna, una
notte andatovi, appena spogliato s'era, che i cognati di lei, che
veduto l'avean venire, furono all'uscio della sua camera per
aprirlo. Il che frate Alberto sentendo, e avvisato ciò che era,
levatosi, non avendo altro rifugio, aperse una finestra, la qual
sopra il maggior canal rispondea, e quindi si gittò nell'aqua. Il
fondo v'era grande, ed egli sapeva ben notare, si che male alcun
non si fece: e notato dall'altra parte del canale, in una casa, che
aperta v'era, prestamente se n'entrò, pregando un buon uomo,
che dentro v'era, che per l'amor di Dio gli scampasse la vita, sue
favole dicendo, perchè quivi a quella ora et ignudo fosse. Il buon
uomo mosso a pietà, convenendogli andare a fare sue bisogne,
nel suo letto il mise, e dissegli che quivi infino alla sua tornata si
stesse; e dentro serratolo, andò a fare i fatti suoi. I cognati della
donna entrati nella camera trovarono che l'agnolo Gabriello,
quivi avendo lasciate l'ali, se n'era volato: di che quasi scornati,
grandissima villania dissero alla donna, e lei ultimamente scon-
solata lasciarono stare, et a casa lor tornarsi con gli arnesi
dell'agnolo.

[However, it chanced one day that Madam Lisetta, being in dispute with a gossip of hers upon the question of female charms,
to set her own above all other said, like a woman who had little
wit in her noodle, 'An you but knew whom my beauty pleaseth,
in truth you would hold your peace of other women.' The other,

longing to hear, said, as one who knew her well, 'Madam, maybe
you sooth; but knowing not who this may be, one cannot turn
about so lightly.' Thereupon quoth Lisetta, who was eath enough
to draw, 'Gossip, it must go no farther; but he I mean is the
angel Gabriel, who loveth me more than himself, as the fairest
lady (for that which he telleth me) who is in the world or the
Maremma.' The other had a mind to laugh, but contained herself, so she might make Lisetta speak further, and said, 'Faith,
madam, an the angel Gabriel be your lover and tell you this,
needs must it be so; but methought not the angels did these
things.' 'Gossip', answered the lady, 'you are mistaken; zounds,
he doth what you wot of better than my husband and telleth me
they do it also up yonder; but, for that I seem to him fairer than
any she in heaven, he hath fallen in love with me and cometh
full oft to lie with me; seestow now?' The gossip, to whom it
seemed a thousand years till she would be whereas she might
repeat these things, took leave of Madam Lisetta, and fore-
gathering at an entertainment with a great company of ladies,
orderly recounted to them the whole story. They told it again to
their husbands and other ladies, and these to yet others, and so
in less than two days Venice was all full of it. Among others to
whose ears the thing came were Lisetta's brothers-in-law, who,
without saying aught to her, bethought themselves to find the
angel in question and see if he knew how to fly, and to this end
lay several nights in wait for him. As chance would have it, some
inkling of the matter came to the ears of Fra Alberto, who
accordingly repaired one night to the lady's house, to reprove
her, but hardly had he put off his clothes ere her brothers-in-
law, who had seen him come, were at the door of her chamber
to open it. Fra Alberto, hearing this and guessing what was to
do, started up and having no other resource, opened a window,
which gave on the Grand Canal, and cast himself thence into
the water. The canal was deep there and he could swim well, so
that he did himself no hurt, but made his way to the opposite
bank and hastily entering a house that stood open there, besought
a poor man, whom he found within, to save his life for the love
of God, telling him a tale of his own fashion, to explain how he
came there at that hour and naked. The good man was moved
to pity and it behoving him to go do his occasions, he put him
in his own bed and bade him abide there against his return;

then, locking him in, he went about his affairs. Meanwhile, the lady's brothers-in-law entered her chamber and found that the angel Gabriel had flown, leaving his wings there; whereupon, seeing themselves baffled, they gave her all manner of hard words and ultimately made off to their own house with the angel's trappings, leaving her disconsolate.][1]

As I have said, the story ends very badly for Frate Alberto. His host hears on the Rialto what happened that night at Madonna Lisetta's and infers who the man he took in is. He exorts a large sum of money from Frate Alberto and then betrays him nevertheless; and he does it in so disgusting a way that the frate becomes the object of a public scandal with moral and practical consequences from which he never recovers. We feel almost sorry for him, especially if we consider with what delight and indulgence Boccaccio relates the erotic escapades of other clerics no better than Frate Alberto (for instance III, 4, the story of the monk Don Felice who induces his lady love's husband to perform a ridiculous penance which keeps him away from home nights; or III, 8, the story of an abbot who takes the husband to Purgatory for a while and even makes him do penance there).

The passage reprinted above contains the crisis of the novella. It consists of Madonna Lisetta's conversation with her confidante and the consequences of their conversation: the strange rumour spreading through the town; the relatives hearing it and deciding to catch the angel; the nocturnal scene in which the frate escapes for the time being by boldly jumping into the canal. The conversation between the two women is psychologically and stylistically a masterly treatment of a vivid everyday scene. Both the confidante who, suppressing her laughter, voices some doubt with simulated politeness to get Lisetta to go on talking, as well as the heroine herself who, in her vaingloriousness, lets herself be lured even beyond the limits of her innate stupidity, impress us as true to life and natural. Yet the stylistic devices which Boccaccio employs are anything but purely popular. His prose, which has often been analysed, reflects the schooling it received from antique models and the precepts of medieval rhetoric, and it displays all its arts. It summarises complex situations in a single period and puts a shifting word order at the service of emphasising what is important, of re-

---

[1] *Decameron*, translated by John Payne (Macy Library Edition).

tarding or accelerating the tempo of the action, of rhythmic and
melodic effect.

The introductory sentence itself is a rich period, and the two
gerunds *essendo* and *quistionando* – one in initial, the other in final
position, with a leisurely interval between them – are as well calculated as the syntactic stress on *la sua* which concludes the first of two
rhythmically quite similar cadences, the second of which ends with
ogni altra. And when the actual conversations begins, our good
Lisetta is so enthusiastic about herself that she fairly bursts into
song: *se voi sapeste a cui la mia bellezza piace* . . . Still more delightful is
her second speech with its many brief and almost equisyllabic units
in which the so-called *cursus velox* predominates. The most beautiful
of them, *ma l'intendimento mio / è l'agnolo Gabriello*, is echoed in her confidante's reply, *se l'agnolo Gabriello / è vostro intendimento*. In this second
speech we find the first colloquialisms: *intendimento*, presumably of
social rather than local colour, can hardly have been in polite usage
in this particular acceptation (roughly, *desiderium*, English 'sweet-
heart'), nor yet the expression *nel mondo o in maremma* (which gives us
another charming cadence). The more excited she grows, the more
numerous are the colloquial and now even dialectical forms; the
Venetian *marido* in the enchanting sentence which stresses the praises
of Gabriel's erotic prowess by the adjurational formula, *per le piaghe
di Dio*, and the climactic effect (again Venetian), *mo vedi vu*, whose
note of vulgar triumph is more humorous as, just before, she has
again been singing sweetly, *ma perciocchè io gli paio più bella che niuna che
ne sia in cielo, s'è egli innamorato di me* . . .

The next two periods comprise the spreading of the rumour
throughout the town, in two stages. The first leads from *la comare* to
the *brigata di donne*, the second from *queste donne* to *Vinegia*. Each has its
own source of motion: the first, in the confidante's impatience to
unburden herself of her story, an impatience whose urgency and
subsequent appeasement come out remarkably well in a correspond-
ing movement of the verbs (*partita* . . . *le parve mille anni che ella fosse* . . .
ove potesse . . . *e ragunatasi* . . . *ordinatamente raccontò*); the second, in the
progressive expansion, paratactically expressed, of the field covered.
From here on the narration becomes more rapid and more dramatic.
The very next sentence reaches all the way from the moment when
the relatives hear the rumour to the nocturnal ambush, although
there is room in it for a few additional details of fact and psychological description. Yet it seems relatively empty and calm compared

with the two which follow, in which the entire night scene in Lisetta's house, down to Frate Alberto's bold leap, takes its course in two periods which, however, together constitute but a single movement. This is done by interlacing hypotactic forms, with participial constructions (generally a favourite device with Boccaccio) playing the most important part. The first sentence begins quietly enough with the principal verb *avenne* and the corresponding subject clause *che . . . venne . . .*; but in the attached relative clause, *il quale* (a secondary subordinate clause, that is), the catastrophe bursts: *. . . andatovi, appena spogliato s'era, che i cognati . . . furono all'uscio.* And then comes a tempest of verb forms: *sentendo, e avvisato, levatosi, non avendo, aperse, e si gittò.* If only by reason of the brevity of the crowding units, the effect is one of extraordinary speed and dramatic precipitation. And for the same reason — despite the learned and classical origin of the stylistic devices employed — it is not at all literary; the tone is not that of written language but of oral narrative, the more so because the position of the verbs, and hence the length and tempo of the intervening sections of greater calm, is constantly varied in an artistically spontaneous fashion: *sentendo* and *avvisato* are placed close together, as are *levatosi* and *non avendo*; *aperse* soon follows, but the concluding *si gittò* appears only after the relative clause referring to the window. I do not quite see, by the way, why Boccaccio has the frate hear of the rumour which is going the rounds. So shrewd a knave would hardly put his head in such a trap, in order to give Lisetta a piece of his mind, if he were at all aware that there was any risk. The whole thing, it seems to me, would be more natural if he had no inkling that something was afoot. His quick and bold escape requires no special motivation in the form of a previously crystallised suspicion. Or did Boccaccio have some other reason for making the statement? I see none.

While the frate swims the canal, the narrative becomes momentarily quieter, more relaxed, slower: we have principal verbs in an imperfect of description, arranged paratactically. But no sooner has he reached the other side than the verbs begin jostling each other again, especially when he enters the strange house: *prestamente se n'entrò, pregando . . . che per l'amor di Dio gli scampasse la vita, sue favole dicendo, perchè . . . fosse.* The intervals between the verbs are likewise brief or urgent. Exceedingly condensed or hurried is *quivi a quella ora e ignudo.* Then the tide begins to ebb. The ensuing sentences are still packed full of factual information and hence with participial hypo-taxes, but at least they are governed by the progressively more leisurely pace of principal clauses linked by 'and': *mise, et dissegli, e andò. Entrati . . . trovarono che . . . se n'era volato* is still quite dramatic; but then comes the progressive relaxation of the paratactic series *dissero, e ultimamente lasciarono stare, e tornarsi.* Of such artistry there is no trace in earlier narrative literature. . . .

In the case of Frate Alberto . . . we are told his previous history, which explains the very specific character of his malicious and witty shrewdness. Madonna Lisetta's stupidity and the silly pride she takes in her womanly charms are unique in their kind in this particular mixture. And the same holds true of the secondary characters. Lisetta's confidante, or the *buono uomo* in whose house Frate Alberto takes refuge, have a life and a character of their own which, to be sure, is only hastily indicated but which is clearly recognizable. We get an inkling of what sort of people Madonna Lisetta's relatives are, for there is something sharply characteristic in the grim joke, *si possero in cuore di trovare questo agnolo e di sapere se egli sapesse volare.* The last few words approach the form which German criticism has recently come to call *erlebte Rede* (free indirect discourse). Then too the setting is much more clearly specified than in the *fabliau.* The events of the latter may occur anywhere in rural France, and its dialectical peculiarities, even if they could be more accurately identified, would be quite accidental and devoid of importance. Boccaccio's tale is pronouncedly Venetian. It must also be born in mind that the French *fabliau* is quite generally restricted to a specific milieu of peasants and small townspeople, and that the variations in this milieu, insofar as they are observable at all, owe their existence exclusively to the accidental place of origin of the piece in question, whereas in Boccaccio's case we are dealing with an author who in addition to this Venetian setting chose numerous others for his tales: for example Naples in the novella about Andreuccio da Perugia (II, 5), Palermo in the one about Sabaetto (VIII, 10), Florence and its environs in a long series of droll tales. And what is true of the settings is equally true of the social atmosphere. Boccaccio surveys and describes, in the most concrete manner, all the social strata, all the classes and professions, of his time. The gulf between the art of the *fabliau* and the art of Boccaccio by no means reveals itself only in matters of style. The characterisations of the personages, the local and social setting, are at once far more sharply individualised and more extensive. Here is a man whose conscious grasp of the principles of art enables him to stand above his subject matter and to submerge himself in it only so far as he chooses, a man who shapes his stories according to his own creative will.

As for Italian narrative literature before Boccaccio, the specimens known to us from that period have rather the character of moralizing or witty anecdotes. Their stylistic devices as well as the orbit of their views and concepts are much too limited for an individualised representation of characters and settings. They often exhibit a certain brittle refinement of expression but in direct appeal to the senses they are by far inferior to the fabliaux. . . .

Whatever we choose from among the products of the earlier period – be it the crude, boorish, sensory breadth of the fabliaux, or the threadbare, sensorily poor refinement of the Novellino, or Salimbene's lively, vividly graphic wit – none of it is comparable to Boccaccio. It is in him that the world of sensory phenomena is first mastered, is organised in accordance with a conscious artistic plan, caught and held in words. For the first time since antiquity, his Decameron fixes a specific level of style, on which the relation of actual occurrences in a contemporary life can become polite entertainment; narrative no longer serves as a moral exemplum, no longer caters to the common people's desire to laugh; it serves as a pleasant diversion for a circle of well bred young people of the upper classes, of ladies and gentlemen who delight in the sensual play of life and who possess sensitivity, taste, and judgement. It was to announce this purpose of his narrative art that Boccaccio created the frame in which he set it. The stylistic level of the Decameron is strongly reminiscent of the corresponding antique genus, the antique novel of love, the fabula milesiaca. This is not surprising, since the attitude of the author to his subject matter, and the social stratum for which the work is intended, correspond quite closely in the two periods, and since for Boccaccio too the concept of the writer's art was closely associated with that of rhetoric. As in the novels of antiquity, Boccaccio's literary art is based upon a rhetorical treatment of prose; as in them, the style sometimes borders on the poetic; he too sometimes gives conversation the form of well-ordered oratory. And the general impression of an 'intermediate' or mixed style, in which realism and eroticism are linked to elegant verbal formulations, is quite similar in the two cases. Yet while the antique novel is a late form cast in languages which had long since produced their best, Boccaccio's stylistic endeavour finds itself confronted by a newly-born and as yet almost amorphous literary language. The rhetorical tradition – which, rigidified in medieval practice into an almost spectrally senile mechanism, had, as recently as the age of Dante, been still timidly and stiffly tried out on the Italian *volgare* by the first translators of ancient authors – in Boccaccio's hands suddenly becomes a miraculous tool which brings Italian art prose, the first literary prose of postclassical Europe, into existence at a single stroke. It comes into existence in the decade between his first youthful work and the *Decameron*. His particular gift of richly and sweetly moving prose rhythms, although a heritage from antiquity, he possessed almost from the beginning. It is already to be found in his earliest prose work, the *Filocolo*, and seems to have been a latent talent in him, which his first contact with antique authors brought out. What he lacked at first was moderation and judgement in using stylistic devices and in determining the level of style; sound relationship between subject matter and level of style had still to be achieved and become an instinctive possession. A first contact with the concept of an elevated style as practised by the ancients – especially since the concept was still influenced by medieval notions – very easily led to what might be termed a chronic exaggeration of the stylistic level and an inordinate use of erudite embellishment. This resulted in an almost continuously stilted language, which, for that very reason, could not come close to its object and which, in such a form, was fit for almost nothing but decorative and oratorical purposes. To grasp the sensory reality of passing life was completely impossible to a language so excessively elevated.

In Boccaccio's case, to be sure, the situation was different from the beginning. His innate disposition was more spontaneously sensory, inclined towards creating charmingly flowing and elegant forms imbued with sensuality. From the beginning he was made for the intermediate rather than the elevated style, and his natural bent was strongly furthered by the atmosphere of the Angevin court at Naples, where he spent his youth and where the playfully elegant late forms of the chivalric culture of Northern France had taken stronger hold than elsewhere in Italy. His early works are *rifacimenti* of French romances of chivalric love and adventure in the late courtly style; and in their manner, it seems to me, one can sense something characteristically French: the broader realism of his descriptions, the naïve refinement and the delicate nuances of the lovers' play, the late feudal mundaneness of his social pictures, and the malice of his wit. Yet the more mature he grows, the stronger become the competing bourgeois and humanist factors and especially his mastery of what is robust and popular. In any case, in his youthful works the tendency towards rhetorical exaggeration – which represented a danger in Boccaccio's case too – plays a role only in his representation of sensual love, as do the excess of mythological erudition and of conventional allegorising which prevail in some of them. Thus we may assert that despite his occasional attempts (as in the *Teseida*) to reach out for something more, he remains within the limits of the intermediate style – of the style which, combining the idyllic and the realistic, is designated for the representation of sensual love. It is in the intermediate, idyllic style that he wrote the last and by far the most beautiful of his youthful works, the *Ninfale fiesolano*; and the intermediate style serves too for the great book of the hundred *novelle*. In the determination of stylistic level it is unimportant which of his youthful works were written partly or wholly in verse and which in prose. The atmosphere is the same in them all.

Within the realm of the intermediate style, to be sure, the nuances in the *Decameron* are most varied, the realm is no narrow one. Yet even when a story approaches the tragic, tone and atmosphere remain tenderly sensual and avoid the grave and sublime; and in stories which employ far more crudely farcical motifs than our example, both language and manner of presentation remain aristocratic, inasmuch as both narrator and audience unmistakably stand far above the subject matter, and, viewing it from above with a critical eye, derive pleasure from it in a light and elegant fashion. It is precisely in the more popularly realistic and even the crudely farcical subjects that the peculiarity of the intermediate elegant style is most clearly to be recognized; for the artistic treatment of such stories indicates that there is a social class which, though it stands above the humble milieu of everyday life, yet takes delight in its vivid representation, and indeed a delight whose end is the individually human and concrete, not the socially stratified type. All the Calandrinos, Cipollas, and Pietros, the Peronellas, Caterinas, and Belcolores are, like Frate Alberto and Lisetta, individualised and living human beings in a totally different way from the villein or the shepherdess who were occasionally allowed to enter courtly poetry. They are actually much more alive and, in their characteristic form, more precise than the personages of the popular farce, as may be apparent from what we have indicated above, and this although the public they are meant to please belongs to an entirely different class. Quite evidently in Boccaccio's time there was a social class – high in rank, though not feudal but belonging to the urban aristocracy – which derived a well bred pleasure from life's colourful reality wherever it happened to be manifested. It is true, the separation of the two realms is maintained to the extent that realistic pieces are usually set among the lower classes, the more tender and more nearly tragic pieces usually among the upper. But even this is not a rigidly observed rule, for the bourgeois and the sentimentally idyllic are apt to constitute borderline cases; and elsewhere too the same sort of mixture is not infrequent (e.g. the novella of Griselda, X, 10).

The social prerequisites for the establishment of an intermediate style in the antique sense were fulfilled in Italy from the first half of the fourteenth century. In the towns an elevated stratum of patrician burghers had come to the fore; their mores, it is true, were still in many respects linked to the forms and ideas of the courtly structure, but, as a result of the entirely different social structure, as well as under the influence of early humanist trends, they soon received a new stamp, becoming less bound up with class, and more strongly personal and realistic. Inner and outer perception broadened, threw off the fetters of class restriction, even invaded the realm of learning, hitherto the prerogative of clerical specialists, and gradually gave it the pleasant and winning form of personal culture in the service of social intercourse. The language, so recently a clumsy and inelastic tool, became supple, rich, nuanced, flourishing, and showed that it could accommodate itself to the requirements of a discriminating social life of refined sensuality. The literature of society acquired what it had not previously possessed: a world of reality and of the present. Now there is no doubt that this gain is strictly connected with a much more important gain on a higher stylistic level, Dante's conquest of a world, made a generation before. . . .

Its most conspicuous distinguishing characteristics, if we compare [our text] with earlier narratives, are the assurance with which, in both perception and syntactical structure, it handles complex factual data, and the subtle skill with which it adapts the narrative tempo and level of tone to the inner and outer movement of the narrated events. This we have tried to show in detail above. The conversation between the two women, the spreading of the rumour through the town, and the dramatic scene at Lisetta's house are made

a clearly surveyable, coherent whole within which each part has
its own independent, rich, and free motion. . . . In our story, after
the relatives reach home *con gli arnesi del agnolo*, Boccaccio continues as
follows: In *questo mezzo, fattosi il dì chiaro, essendo il buon uomo in sul Rialto,
udì dire come l'agnolo Gabriello era la notte andato a giacere con Madonna Lisetta,
e da cognati trovatovi, s'era per paura gittato nel canale, nè si sapeva che divenuto se
ne fosse.* [Broad day come, the good man with whom Fra Alberto had
taken refuge, being on the Rialto, heard how the angel Gabriel had
gone that night to lie with Madam Lisetta and being surprised by her
kinsmen, had cast himself for fear into the canal, nor was it known
what had become of him.] The tone of seeming seriousness, which
never mentions the fact that the Venetians on the Rialto are bursting
with laughter, insinuates, without a word of moral, aesthetic, or any
other kind of criticism, exactly how the occurrence is to be evaluated and what mood the Venetians are in. If instead Boccaccio had
said that Frate Alberto's behaviour was underhand and Madonna
Lisetta stupid and gullible, that the whole thing was ludicrous and
absurd, and that the Venetians on the Rialto were greatly amused by
it, not only would this procedure have been much clumsier but the
moral atmosphere, which cannot be exhausted by any number of
adjectives, would not have come out with anything like the force it
now has. The stylistic device which Boccaccio employs was highly
esteemed by the ancients, who called it 'irony'. Such a mediate and
indirectly insinuating form of discourse presupposes a complex and
multiple system of possible evaluations, as well as a sense of perspective which, together with the occurrence, suggests its effect. . . .

Nor does Boccaccio scorn the direct method of characterisation.
At the very beginning of our text we find two popular phrases which
serve to set forth Lisetta's stupidity directly and graphically: *che poco
sale avea in zucca* and *che piccola levatura avea*. Reading the beginning of the
novella we find a whole collection of things similar in form and
intent: *una giovane donna bamba e sciocca*; *sentiva dello scemo*; *donna mestola*;
donna zucca al vento, la quale era anzi che no un poco dolce di sale; *madonna
baderla*; *donna poco fila*. This little collection looks like a merry game
Boccaccio is playing with his knowledge of amusing colloquial
phrases and perhaps it also serves to describe the vivacious mood of
the teller of the tale, Pampinea, whose purpose it is to divert the
company, who have just been touched to tears by the preceding
story. In any case, Boccaccio is very fond of this sort of play with a
variety of phrases drawn from the vigorous and imaginative lan-

guage of the common people. Consider for instance the way in which (in novella 10 of the Sixth Day) Frate Cipolla's servant, Guccio, is characterised, partly directly and partly by his master. It is a striking example of Boccaccio's characteristic mixture of popular elements and subtle malice, ending in one of the most beautiful extended periods that he ever wrote (*ma Guccio Imbratta il quale era*, etc.). In it the stylistic level shifts from a most enchanting lyrical moment (*più vago di stare in cucina che sopra i verdi rami l'usignolo*) through the coarsest realism (*grassa e grossa e piccola e mal fatta e con un paio di poppe che parevan due ceston da letame*, etc.) to something approaching horror (*non altramente che si gitta l'avoltoio alla carogna*), yet all the parts form a whole by virtue of the author's malice which glints through everywhere.

Erich Auerbach

The Legendary Style
of the
Decameron

In order to view Boccaccio's *Decameron* in its cultural perspective, it is traditional to refer to the *Novellino*, the French *fabliaux*, and certain passages from Cavalca's *Vite de' SS. Padri* and Passavanti's *Specchio della vera penitenza*.

In the *Novellino* there is a wealth of all kinds of *dicta* and *facta*; however, the didactic and moral content is not encompassed in a central idea. Not a really autonomous work, the book fits rather into the category of encyclopedias and collections. Nor does the clarity of style compensate for the fundamental paucity of invention. The gulf between the *Novellino* and the *Decameron* is indeed deep.

The *fabliaux* are replete with pungent situations, but they make their point in other ways and do not impart the sense of constructive literary adventure that is characteristic of the *Decameron*. The wordiness of the *fabliaux*, as in goliardic songs, is foreign to Boccaccio's purpose. In justification of the 'form', as he terms it, of his short stories, he observed: 'None of them is so shocking that, if put into decent words, they would embarrass anyone.' And even here, taking into account the disparity between the quality of the content and the manner of expression, his statement is valid.

The *Vite* of Cavalca and the *Specchio* of Passavanti at times manifest a sure touch in the characterization of sinful deeds and carnal temptations. With the help of these two *Trecentisti* we are better able to understand why Boccaccio sought protection from criticism by saying that certain equivocal situations were exposed to view even by monks in their sermons. However, the works of Cavalca and

Abridged by Robert S. Dombroski from *Romantic Review* XLIII (1952), pp. 166–84, 186–9. Reprinted by permission of the author and publisher (Columbia University Press).

Passavanti, being late documents, are not the best introduction to
the medieval tradition. Why not revert to the Latin *Legenda aurea* of
Jacopo da Varazze, a charming and for centuries a very popular
work, which Boccaccio knew?

The *Legenda aurea* takes up and brings to maturity a long tradition
that begins at least as far back as Gregory the Great. It is a question
of a real literary genre which, while assuming popular aspects,
expresses theological and philosophical themes of an origin not the
least popular. This genre – which I call simply 'the legendary genre' –
fulfils an exemplaristic and didactic function. Its well-defined
stylistic forms had a longer span than is usually believed. Not only
the fantasy of the Middle Ages, including Dante, but the very fantasy
of the so-called Renaissance and of Boccaccio himself, as will be
argued here, was expressed in legendary forms. In discussing the
Decameron, we must first turn to the strange world of legends. What
may seem a detour is rather the most direct route toward the world
of Boccaccio.

I

To what kind of literary elaboration religious matters in the *Legenda
aurea* were subjected can easily be seen from the following episode,
which here is in part translated and in part summarised, following
a proportionate distribution of the short prologue, the extended
crisis, and the very brief epilogue.[1]

'Andrew, Bishop of Fondi, although a bishop, allowed a nun to
dwell in his home. The old enemy imprinted her image in his mind's
eye so that, while in bed, he was consumed by evil thought.' Now
it happened that a Jew arrived in Rome and finding no lodgings,
sought refuge in the Temple of Apollo. Although he was not
baptised, in awe of that profane place, he made the sign of the cross.
This act helped him escape unharmed from a nocturnal meeting of
demons. At midnight, there assembled a crowd of evil spirits, and
Satan, seated among them, questioned them and listened to the

---

[1] Jacobi a Voragine, *Legenda aurea, vulgo Historia lombardica dicta*: recensuit Dr
Th. Graesse, Vratislaviae 1890; editio tertia. The passages I quoted can
easily be located under the title of each legend; therefore I am omitting
superfluous indications. At times I myself have translated from the original,
and at times I have made use of the rendition of Granger Ryan and Helmut
Ripperger.

impious acts of each one. The first, kneeling in front of Satan, confessed to having devastated an entire province with social upheavals
and wars. '"How much time has this taken thee?" asked Satan.
"Thirty days", he answered. "Why has it taken thee so long to do
this?" asked Satan.' And without heeding the answer, Satan ordered
the lazy devil to be flogged without mercy. The same punishment
was meted out to a second devil, who in twenty days had produced
storms at sea and had shipwrecked boats, and to a third who had
wasted ten full days in bringing about only a bloody matrimonial
battle. But the fourth demon, although he had used up forty long
years, received completely different treatment. Satan, descending
from his throne, embraced him, placed on his head his own crown
and invited him to sit next to him. What had that worthy man con-
trived? Having attached himself to a hermit, he had caused him to
fall into a sin of the flesh, 'in lapsum carnis'. And now approached a
fifth and last demon. He recounted how much carnal desire he had
infused in Andrew, Bishop of Fondi, for that same nun, 'adding that
the day before, at Vespers, he had succeeded in making the Bishop
give her a caressing slap in the rear' ('addens, quod heri hora
vesperarum usque adhuc eius mentem traxerit, ut in tergum eius
blandiens alapam daret'). Satisfied with the good start, Satan ordered
the demon to leave and to return and receive a special prize – 'pal-
mam singularem' – when he had succeeded in making the Bishop
fall into more substantial sin. But the Jew, who had overheard the
whole conspiracy, went to the Bishop and warned him; the latter
repented and baptized his benefactor.

This whole tale, included under the title of De exaltatione Sanctae
crucis, has its exemplaristic moral: the sign of the cross made by the
Jew in the pagan temple leads to his conversion and to the repentance
of the Bishop. But the literary moral differs a bit; we can explain it
by means of information supplied by the author himself. He tells us
that he borrowed the plot of the story from the third book of the
Dialogues of Gregorius Magnus and that he himself constructed the
long episode of the meeting of the demons. But this very scene, with
its wealth of invention and its vivid colours, concludes by turning
even edification into a joke.[2] . . .

---

[2] Da Varrazze has lifted the pungent phrase from Gregory, who omits
the first four devils. Cf. Sanctus Gregorius Magnus, Dialogarum libri quatuor
(III, VII), in Migne, Patrologiae latinae, LXXVII.
    On the comic genre of the Middle Ages cf. E. R. Curtius, Europäische

If we are in search of episodes, we can glean a mighty harvest. We will confine ourselves to the minimum so as to keep at bay the 'six thousand six hundred sixty-six demons' which might possess us. Not only are the erotic hints innumerable, especially with reference to the demonic temptations and the pagan persecution of beautiful and pure Christian women, but there are countless sketches of heroes that can easily be transferred to Boccaccesque situations. Here is Quintinianus 'ignobilis, libidinosus, avarus,' infatuated with Agatha, and desirous of marrying her so as to enjoy her beauty, better his own social position, and appropriate her wealth. But since the holy woman resists him, he sends her to a prostitute named Aphrodisia and to her nine daughters of equal turpitude, so that for thirty days they can influence her and in some way cause her to change her mind. Here is a sorcerer leading Theodora into adultery by this reasoning: 'What happens during the day God knows and sees, but what is committed at sunset or at night, escapes the eye of God.' Here are the evil machinations of Cyprian. He was addicted to sorcery and it was thought he transformed women into mares and indulged in many other acts of magic. Burning for love of the virgin Justina, he had recourse to magic in an attempt to bend Justina to his will or to prevail upon her to succumb to Acladius, who had similarly become infatuated with her. He summons the demon and orders him to induce Justina to yield to him. Many times the demon visits the virgin until he succeeds in implanting unchaste thoughts in her mind and in leading her to the threshold of perdition by means of that sophistic reasoning which is used ironically in Decameron: 'What then is the meaning of God's command: "Increase, and multiply and fill the Earth"? For fear, sweet friend, lest by abiding in virginity we set the world at naught. . . .'

The least that can be said is that a work like the Legenda aurea offered Boccaccio many suggestions and gave him such a lively subject matter that it was virtually impossible for him to resist appropriating it to his own use. It makes one wonder whether Boccaccio's fantasy was stimulated not by the real and therefore limited corruption of his time, but by such literary presentations as we have reported above. Hermits, bishops, nuns, adulterous wives, transformers of women into mares, equivocal reasoning,

---

Literatur und lateinisches Mittelalter (Bern, 1948); 'Exkurse', IV, 'Scherz und Ernst in mittelalterlicher Literatur', and especially (4) 'Hagiographische Komik'. It seems to me, however, that the question is far from solved.

descriptive determinations were all there, eagerly awaiting the new touch.

Making light of religious subjects was in accord with the ecclesiastical practice of reaching the sinner, not frightening him away, inducing him not to consider himself outside the Church, or in conflict with its dogmatic tenets. The *Legenda aurea* is a work of edification rather than of mystic exaltation. It appealed to the great mass of transgressors and contemplated all imaginable weaknesses. If men and women who attained sainthood had the same temptations and committed these very sins, no one need despair because of his own failures. The *Legenda aurea* in its entirety is a caustic compendium against despair. . . .

The *exemplum* finds its form in a spontaneous and simple way. One of the rhetorical devices most frequently employed is gradation, or crescendo. The two versions of the legend of Andrew, Bishop of Fondi, that of Gregory the Great, and that of Jacopo da Varazze, are marked by the high literary skill with which, in the second version, the assembling of the devils is arranged in an effective crescendo. . . .

The legendary style may vary and grow more or less complex. At times, legends which illustrate the same theme and reproduce the same plot are arranged in a series according to the degree of intensity. Even Boccaccio often proceeds thus; in the *giornate*, with obligatory topics, every storyteller intends to outstrip his predecessor.

These gradations fill three different structures which constitute three main forms of legend, mirroring as many different kinds of example.

1. The legend of conversion. This describes the swift passing from one manner of behaviour to another. Conversion is at times both gratuitous and meritorious: at times brought about by irresistible grace. . . . The examples of conversion polarise the black and the white, the colours of wickedness and salvation, into two spheres in sharpest contrast. One sphere is filled with evil and nothing but evil; the other is a repository of all theological virtues. Here, gradations take up both spheres, but with a central breach, which separates them and creates a contrast between them.

2. The legend of the interferences which cause a soul to vacillate. Generally this type of legend has three sections. In the first, a holy soul, distinguished by its faith and its vocation, is introduced. In the

second, the interferences and effects of diabolical temptations or of heathen snares, with the attendant waverings, are described. In the third, the victory of vocation and faith is extolled. . . .

3. The legend of firmness of faith and of intention. Here the body of the legend is a simple crescendo, as the example of Saint Marina shows. A good man who had just been widowed retired into a monastery and exhorted his only child, Marina, to follow his example. Marina, impelled by an irresistible calling, puts on a man's habit, enters with her father into the same monastery, and takes the name of Brother Marinus. There she is delegated the duty of going out to gather wood. Her little journeys for this purpose lead her to make the acquaintance of a nice family, with which she occasionally stays. In this family there is also a young girl who is having a love affair with a knight, by whom she is with child. In order to avoid the disgrace of wilful carnality she accuses Brother Marinus of rape. Marinus, without revealing her sex, without even attempting to defend herself, accepts with infinite patience all the punishing and humiliating consequences of this calumny, as well as the long penances that the brothers impose on her. Only after many years, indeed on the very day of her death, do the brothers ever discover that she is a woman, when they go to wash the body and prepare it for burial. A variation of this theme is the example of Saint Margherita: making use of the same expedient, she also enters a monastery of monks and because of her piety, she is chosen to become the supervisor in a convent of nuns. A nun becomes pregnant and Margherita is accused. . . .

Almost all of the *exempla* start at a very high point of tension. . . . It is a typical feature of exemplaristic prose that the narrative takes its inception from an already critical situation. Every author pursues the theme to the highest pitch of the marvellous that his imagination can conceive.

Nevertheless the legends are studded with realistic traits: true or false bits of evidence, but always precise, indications of time and place, descriptions of milieux, often worked out with taste and exactitude. Dante's and Boccaccio's concretizations, aside from their poetical work, are no longer surprising when account is taken of texts like the *Legenda aurea*. In this literature, including the great *Trecento* writers, realism plays the role of an 'intensifier', which is intended to increase the relative degree of the marvellous and prove that wonders and miracles exist and are constantly operative. *Realitas ancilla miraculi.* . . .

II

One would be inclined to think that, with his open and boastful vindication of the rights of nature, Boccaccio accepts the challenge of Christian exemplarism. But a formulation so binding would be a betrayal of the *Decameron*'s tone. Let us say rather that he plays with an erotic and jocular subject matter identical with or similar to that found in abundance in the *Legenda aurea*. Resorting to a trick common to the comic and satirical genres, he profits from the fantastic exaggerations with which Christian exemplarism supplied him, in order to stamp upon them a shape contrary to that intended by Jacopo da Varazze, with the purpose not of humbling, but of exalting beyond all verisimilitude, 'the rights of nature'. Let us see, then, what these rights of nature in the *Decameron* involve.[3] . . .

Probably the great short story writer would not have discussed his own conception of love in the famous Introduction to the Fourth Day if his detractors had not forced him to defend himself. But his argumentation was very feeble, clearly because a defence of his excesses is not possible in rational form. He brings forth the tenacity of love of 'Guido Cavalcante and Dante Alighieri when already advanced in years', and of 'messer Cino da Pistoia when a very old man'; but they are doubtful excuses which harmonize poorly with the fruit of his imagination. He asks the support of the laws of nature, but how many laws of nature are violated by his characters? He refers to his work as being addressed to an unlettered audience, but this act of modesty is repugnant to his conscience as an artist, and he lets escape a statement to be taken seriously: 'In composing my stories, I stray not so far from Mount Parnassus or from the Muses as many may suppose.' And then renouncing logic and reason, he entrusts his apology to a story, the hundred and first of the *Decameron*.

It is the story of the 'green geese'. A good man, prostrate with grief at his sudden widowhood, decides to lead an ascetic life and retires with his young son to a cavern in the hills surrounding

---

[3] For the *Decameron* too, at times I myself have translated it, at times I have used the translation of Leopold Flameng, with occasional changes.

Florence. The years pass in this solitude, he ages, and the son grows up without ever having seen a woman. Now it comes to pass that the hermit, having to go to town, takes the youth with him, who, seeing women for the first time, with great wonder asks his father what they are. Hearing that they are evil things and are called geese, 'not mindful of palaces, nor oxen, nor horses, nor donkeys, nor money, not even of anything else that he could have seen, suddenly he said: "Father mine, I pray thee get me one of those green geese."' The father energetically opposes the idea and the story abruptly ends.

Telling the story of the green geese, Boccaccio had in mind a legend which illustrates the firm and complete renunciation of sex and of terrestrial love to the point of absolute negation. It is the same legend which we have seen above and which reappears under the name of Marina, Margaret, Pelagia, Eugenia, Euphrosyna, Theodora, Apollinaria. This young girl dresses like a man, and repairs to a monastery. She persists in a heroic as well as absurd way in concealing her sex. In the Da Varrazze version, the legend of Marina begins thus: 'Marina was an only daughter. Her father, being widowed, entered a monastery; and then, dressing his daughter in man's clothing, he asked the abbot and the other monks to receive his only son in the monastery. His request was granted and the maiden lived among the monks, and bore the name of Brother Marinus. When she was twenty-seven years of age, her father, feeling the approach of death, called her to his bedside and told her never to reveal her womanhood to anyone.' We know how firmly Marina kept her promise.

Boccaccio merely appropriated this *antefactum*. The story of the geese is patterned on a father who, being left a widower, 'resolved to be no more of this world, but to give himself to the service of God and to do likewise with his little son.' Just as the widower of the legend shares the cloistered rule with his daughter, so the widower of the story shares with his son a hermitical discipline; and as the former asks his daughter to forget about her sex, similarly the second resorts to remote expedients to keep his son ignorant of his masculinity. And we know how Boccaccio proceeded from this premise. However, if the story of Marina is a legendary *exemplum* of Christian renunciation, Boccaccio's tale is a legendary *exemplum* of the impossibility of renunciation.

The story of the geese constitutes the real prologue and, so to speak, the ideal substratum of the entire *Decameron*, as much for the choice of content as for its formal elaboration. The love for green geese can induce a man to change naked women into mares for his pleasure, to visit a woman at night without destroying her illusion that her lover is the Angel Gabriel, to exchange his own wife for his friend's, for the reciprocal pleasure of the couples, or so much other mischief. All these cases, proceeding from a common root like the story of the geese, are bound to prove its validity and to maintain its exemplaristic nature.

The determination and function of love in Boccaccio are certainly not modern. Modern representation of love starts out with a dramatic turmoil, like the conflict between passion and reason. Either reason triumphs, as in rationalistic morality, or passion is supreme, as in romantic ethics. In either case, the modern rights of the individual existence are affirmed by means of conflicts, interferences, repressions, sentimental and mental complications. . . .

All of this has no relation to Boccaccio's 'naturali affezioni' and 'leggi di natura'. Boccaccio seems a simpleton when placed in this world of modern psychology. At this point let me refer again to the passage of the youth who for the first time sets his gaze on women: 'Not mindful of palaces, or oxen, or horses, or donkeys, or money, not even of anything else that he could have seen, suddenly he said: "Father mine, I pray thee get me one of those green geese."' This is clearly a parable. It means that in Boccaccio's representations, love is isolated and almost extirpated from the thick and inextricable texture of psychic and moral reality and is maintained always in this impossible sphere of abstraction, without conflict or repressions, without complications of a mental or of a sentimental nature. And if many and fantastic complications are present in the *Decameron*, they do not stem from the essence of love or from those psychological and moral interferences from which qualms are generated, but from interferences and incidents that link the *novelle* to the most diffuse genre of adventures. The world itself, *novella*, retains many of the meanings of the adjective *novum*, among them: 'unexpected', 'unheard of', 'marvellous.' Loosened from the bonds of the human lot, indeed unaware of them, love is magnified and proceeds toward an unreal and unlimited goal. Boccaccio's fancies of love are thus brought into competition with fancies of religious legends. . . .

III

The oddities of Boccaccio-like love are no less fantastic then the miracles propagated by a literature in which the Bishop of Genoa excelled. Boccaccio's love forces exist only in fantasy and therefore, like the religious legends, taking in the *antefacta*, the form of a manifest absurdity, they start at a very high point of tension: a young lover suddenly undergoes physiological and intellectual metamorphosis; a little hermit is unable to distinguish between women and geese; more than one wife does not notice that she is in bed with another man than her husband; an abbess wraps the priest's breeches around her head; a young merchant, mystified by empty chatter, thinks he recognizes a prostitute to be his sister and experiences her sisterly love; Griselda is endowed with such docility that critics find the story absurd and meaningless. What more could Boccaccio have done to emphasise the legendary character of his inventions? Indeed we shall find that the *Decameron* reproduces the three structures of the legends: that of conversions, that of adventures generated by unexpected interferences, and that of firmness.

1. Boccaccio's miracles are exemplifications of the sudden passing from one moral state to another because of an irresistible compulsion. Cimone and the little Florentine hermit are physically and morally changed as soon as they are touched by the grace of femininity. 'Love's arrow having then, through Iphigenia's beauty, penetrated into Cimone's heart, whereinto no teaching had ever availed to win an entrance, in a very brief time, proceeding from one idea to another, he made his father marvel and all his kinsfolk and every other that knew him.' It is a question, obviously, of conversion; in fact Boccaccio has adhered to their traditional type, polarising contrasting colours. Prior to his meeting with Beauty, Cimone is presented as an uncivilised being with a 'rough and uncouth voice' and 'manners more befitting a beast than a man'; subsequently, 'he first, to the utmost wonderment of everyone, in a very brief space of time, not only learned the first elements of letters, but became very eminent among the students of philosophy, and afterwards (the love of Iphigenia being the cause of all this) he not only reduced his rude and rustical manner of speech to seemliness and civility, but became a past master of song and sound and exceeding expert and

doughty in riding and martial exercises, both by land and by sea.'
Similarly, previous to his meeting with the geese, the little hermit is
all imbued with the 'glories of eternal life and of God and the
Saints'; subsequently, he initiates certain things which the author of
the Decameron does not need to relate. . . .

We shall now extend definitely the designation exemplum from
religious and moral prose to that of the Decameron: nor could we do
otherwise. Whatever we may say in regard to love in Boccaccio, to its
organisation and concretisation, is to be seen only per exempla. The
exemplaristic form is recognizable at once. In it the theme is wholly
bare and may be cast in numberless figurations, in order to re-
emerge constantly with its fixed, hammering character. In the
Decameron, likewise, the original motif is continually reaffirmed with
an insistent and often brutal constancy. Boccaccio's lovers are
involved, couple by couple, in dissimilar adventures, and because of
this each short story has its own value; but unless they are betrayed
by a cruel injustice (IV, 1) they invariably end in bed, or in an
embrace on a bench (VIII, 8), or even in less comfortable places
(VII, 2). With this primitive and simple act every short story returns to the primitive and simple root from which all these tales
draw their vital sap and pattern. This hammering character is
especially evident in the second exemplaristic structure, that of
interferences and adventures.

2.   Let us take a really extreme case (IX, 2), since it is imagined as
occurring in a convent 'very famous for sanctity and religion'. An
enamoured nun finds a way of bringing to fruition at nighttime her
own desires and those of her suitor. Unfortunately, the other nuns
notice it. Having trapped the sinner, they knock at the door of the
Abbess, without suspecting what she may be doing. The Abbess
dresses in a hurry, rushes out of her room, summons the Chapter,
and sitting in judgement has the young peccant colleague dragged
before her. Terrible reproaches rain down upon the culprit, until the
latter, pointing to the Abbess' coif, causes the whole audience to
realise that her kerchief is the breeches of the priest. The Abbess
'changed her note, and proceeding to speak after a fashion altogether
different from her beginning, came to the conclusion that it is impossible to withstand the pricks of the flesh, wherefore she said that
each should, whenas she might, privily give herself a good time,
even as it had been done until that day. Accordingly, setting the

young lady free, she went back to sleep with her priest and Isabetta returned to her lover, whom many a time thereafter she let come thither, in despite of those who envied her, whilst those of the others who were loverless pushed their fortunes in secret, as best they knew.' From that day on, the demands and rights of nature triumphed in the convent.

The short story of the nun and the Abbess offers an opportunity to bring into better focus the structure of the second exemplaristic pattern. The theme is posited: here the sensual gratification of a nun who does not aspire to sanctity, elsewhere the perfect vocation of a saintly woman. Forces contrary to the thematic thesis are made to intervene: here the opponents of the rights of nature, elsewhere diabolical temptations or heathen snares. The 'upset' arising therefrom is subsequently described with a gradual adventurous crescendo, and driven to its uttermost point. Finally, the denouement occurs with the return of the initial thematic motif, which triumphs over all. . . .

Boccaccio's leading strand is not always love. Sometimes Fortune takes over the main role; thus in the tales of Andreuccio da Perugia (II, 5) and Nicolò da Cignano (VIII, 10), although females play a counterpart in them. Merchants both, Andreuccio and Nicolò, with well lined purses, have arrived in a great city full of allurements and dangers. Through more than the ordinary Boccaccesque accidents they are stripped down to the last penny. But through just as many accidents and crafty tricks they recover all they have lost, even to the last penny. Everyone knows that Andreuccio 'returned to Perugia, having invested his money in a ring, whereas he came to buy horses'. Here, too, the same narrative rhythm is repeated: theme of the tale (money), opposite forces and various accidents (complete loss of financial belongings), integral return to the thematic state (recovery of the initial fortune).

In his stories, Boccaccio employs a stylistic and linguistic scale which descends to the forms of homely dialogue, to dialectic terms, to obscene *double entendre*. The *Legenda aurea* too is rife with scenes that are anything but courtly. Here is another one, to refresh the reader's memory. Publius falls in love with Anastasia, and not being able to obtain his purpose with her, tries to compensate with the kitchen-maids. He tries to have his will with them, but, being providentially struck with insanity, proceeds to embrace bean pots, frying pans, and copper kettles: 'cacabos, patellas caldaria et similia amplectans osculabutur'. He emerges all smeared with black, disfigured, and with garments torn to pieces: 'nigerrimus et deformis et vestimentis conisis'. Such or similar language is to be found in the *Decameron*. From the rarified and dreamy atmosphere of the gardens where, with courtly elegance, seven Florentine gentlewomen and three gentlemen relate alluring tales, sing their songs, exchange lively and at the same time polite compliments, without descending to less than correct actions, we seem to have reached a cynical realism – even though the foolish unreality of the tales remains in full validity.[4] . . .

Slight results are attained if, in order to understand Boccaccio from every angle (linguistic, stylistic and artistic), the critic resorts to classical literature on the one hand, to vernacular literature on the other, paying no attention to the intermediate texts like the *Legenda* (I do not say that this is the only one). Medieval literature supplied him – as we have seen – with exemplaristic forms tested by long tradition, with imaginative motifs easy to utilise, and at the same time [allowed him] to recast the subject matter already present in that tradition, and with extremely precise syntactic structures. We are all agreed that when Boccaccio imitates Ciceronian Latin, he spoils everything. No compliment is paid to him if we view him only as a pre-humanist. From so many insignificant humanists who today enjoy undeserved historical vindication, let us choose the latinising vernacular of a serious man like L. B. Alberti. Humanism also prompts him to indulge in interminable and stagnating verbal amplifications; whereas Boccaccio tends to foreshorten and race on to a set goal. Boccaccio, like Jacopo da Varazze, is extremely skilful in using gradation and crescendo with his interweavings: a style which, we find, is peculiar to legend and *exemplum*.

3. The exemplaristic patterns persist throughout the *Decameron*. The content varies from time to time, and it is not always indecent. Boccaccio's love is characterised by much licentiousness, but it also has its loyalties, its pride, its generosity. Fairly often, amorous adventures recede into the background, and the emphasis is on the fickleness of fortune – an old theme, descanted upon *per exempla* from classical antiquity down to the *Novellino*. The last Day of the *Decameron*

---

[4] For this continuous alternating of the Christian-medieval style between a *sermo sublimis* and a *sermo humilis*, see E. Auerbach, *Mimesis, dargestellte Wirklichkeit in der abendländischen Literatur* (Berne, 1946) and especially the illuminating Chapter VII: 'Adam und Eva'. [For English edition see p. 69, below.]

deals only with serious topics: examples of honesty, gratitude, liberality, abstinence. And these virtues too are in such abundant measure that their resonance is as ample and adventurous as that of Roland's horn. Like every true artist, Boccaccio remains constantly loyal to his form. The *Decameron* closes with the difficult figure of Griselda, a magnificent example of firmness.

A nobleman decides to get married. Much to the surprise of his relatives and friends, his choice falls upon a girl belonging to the lowest and poorest social stratum. From her, he demands nothing. He only asks whether she is willing not to be surprised at anything he may do or say and to comply with his wishes. The girl consents. Then, in the presence of all, the lord commands her to strip naked. Having re-clothed her with splendid garments, he leads her to the wedding. 'The young wife seemed to have, together with her clothes, changed her mind and manners.' She put off her uncouthness, and much to the amazement of everybody, for her happiness and that of her lord, learned how to behave like a gentlewoman of ancient lineage. After a while, she presented her husband with a daughter, over whom the father greatly rejoiced.

But on a certain day, the lord took it into his head to 'seek, by dint of long tribulation and things unendurable, to make trial of her patience.' He begins by telling her that people have not forgotten the low estate from which she came. The woman answers: 'My lord, do with me that which thou deemest will be most for thine honour and solace, for that I shall be content with all.' Shortly after, the lord sends an emissary to take her little girl away from her, with obscure words, as if hinting that the child is to be killed. To her husband's messenger the woman recommends: 'Take her and punctually do that which thy lord hath enjoined thee; but leave her not to be devoured of the beasts and birds, except he command it thee.' The woman grows pregnant again and this time is delivered of a son. This second child is taken away from her in the same obscure manner. The wife repeats to her husband: 'My lord, study to content thyself and to satisfy thy pleasure and have no thought of me, for that nothing is dear to me save in so much as I see it please thee.'

Confronted with such docility, the lord allows thirteen years to elapse, and then, 'deeming it time to make the supreme trial of her endurance, declared, in the presence of his people, that he could no longer endure to have her to wife.' He deprives her of everything and orders her to go away. She obeys, saying: 'My lord, I ever knew my mean estate to be nowise sortable with your nobility, and for that which I have been with you I have still confessed myself indebted to you and to God, nor have I ever made nor held it mine, as given to me, but have still accounted it but as a loan.' And with a single shirt, which she has requested, in order to cover her body which will always belong to her husband, she leaves the house. Meanwhile her lord prepares for a new wedding. He needs a servantmaid who is conversant with housework, and therefore he calls back as a servant his repudiated wife. The ceremony is being prepared. Guests and relatives arrive, also a younger brother of the second wife. She appears, beautiful and extremely young. The repudiated wife goes to meet her and greets her: 'Welcome and fair welcome to my lady.'

The lord manifests his will. Finally he reveals that the young lady and her younger brother are the children born to him by his wife, so loyal and sorely tried. Her 'long patience' has the reward which it deserved. The lord restores her to the splendour to which he had formerly raised her, and reveals to her that everything has taken place according to a 'preordained end'.

It was necessary to elaborate at length on this tale – one of the most misinterpreted of the whole *Decameron* – in order to disclose its wealth of organisation and its recondite meaning. Psychological criticism has made out of the lord a man full of 'manifest oddities', a kind of tyrant worthy not of the *Promessi sposi*, but of the worst among the third-rate Italian tragedies. According to that criticism, the woman is 'a poor idiot', who tolerates 'the most ferocious cruelties and insults'. In conclusion, the tale 'is without meaning'.[5]

On the contrary: we are confronted with the most complex *exemplum* which Boccaccio ever handled. Its content is not only serious but grave; and this is perhaps what has caused more than one critic to lose his bearings. A love, first given in superabundance to a loyal woman, is taken away from her with successive 'wrenchings', in a series of increasingly arduous trials, and is finally restored to her with equal superabundance. This is the scheme, as old as the *Vitae Sanctorum*, of the *exempla* of humility and of sufferance. From this angle, the foolish pliancy of the woman, the odd 'cruelty' of her

---

[5] Such is Momigliano's opinion in his edition: *Il Decamerone, 49 novelle commentate*, 2nd ed. (Milano, 1936).

lord, the meaning of our tale, its very essence, become clear. In fact, the tale is the result of more parables than any writer, before or after Boccaccio, has ever dared to cope with. The counterpart must be sought in the legends depicted by painters.

In Boccaccio's fresco every section – every parable – closes with a recurrent motif: *fiat voluntas tua*. The lord asks faithfulness and obedience from a humble girl, and she promises. The lord bares her flesh in the presence of all, and she consents. The lord gets angry, starts to menace her, and she says, 'Do with me what thou will'st': *fiat voluntas tua*. The lord's messenger comes to deprive her of her little daughter, and she says, 'Do punctually that which thy lord hath enjoined thee', that is, she exorts him to repeat with her: *fiat voluntas tua*. The lord is about to wrest her little son from her, and she says: 'Nothing is dear to me save in so much as I see it please thee.' She complies with the mystic rule: 'E 'n la sua volontade è nostra pace.' The lord strips her of all other possessions, and she, in the act of returning her nuptial ring to him says: 'Whatever I had I have still accounted it but as a loan', that is, she renounces every right and annuls her own will. The lord lowers her to the status of a maid, introduces the new bride to her, and she thus reveals herself as the perfect handmaiden subserving the lord's will. The lord has brought his purpose to the 'preordained end'. From the dark night in which he had withdrawn, he pours on the humble and loyal soul the superabundant reward of his grace.

In order properly to focus this tale, it was necessary to examine it in the light of its own poetic, and to analyse into its single component parables the complex and gradually developed metaphor of which it is made up. The whole composition has a rhythm marked by that recurrent emphasis – *fiat voluntas tua* – which is intensified at set intervals, seconding the increasing mystery of each parable. Only if we take it for what it is – a *mystery* – does the tale disclose its content and its stylistic and artistic merits. The liturgic mode in which it develops is reminiscent of the *sacre rappresentazioni*, the sacred texts, and, above all, the Book of Job.

The inscrutable judgement of God wishes that Job, deprived of all, even of his sons, should remain naked as he was when he issued forth from his mother's womb. But faith does not abandon that suffering man: 'And he said, Naked came I out of my mother's womb, and naked shall I return thither: the Lord gave, and the Lord hath taken away; blessed be the name of the Lord. In all this Job sinned not, nor charged God foolishly' (*Job* I, 21–2). The analogy is evident. It remains to be seen which extension Boccaccio may have attributed to it, which symbol he may have assigned to his last legend.

Enrico de' Negri

Boccaccio

It has been remarked before now that while true men of action are usually embittered if reduced to impotence, inertia and incapacity, placid and dreamy men find these things enrich and enhance the very real pleasure they derive from their imagination. It is surely not an accident that writers of adventure stories are mostly sedentary people.

Moreover these imaginative yet lazy men, these insatiable yet stationary pursuers of action, are by nature and necessity very far removed from any form of moral reflection. It is peculiar to the moralist that he cuts down the number of possible alternatives and acts resolutely and consistently within them. The moralist defends himself from the imagination as from the most dangerous of mirages, above all when the imagination plays an action that is entirely governed by the caprices of chance, action for action's sake. In fact action for action's sake, whether dreamed up or practised, requires a flexibility, a flightiness, an indifference, that do not harmonise with moral conscience.

I have always thought that Boccaccio – that placid and comfort-loving 'Giovanni of tranquillity' as he is usually portrayed to us – was in the depth of his soul, by way of compensation and perhaps of sublimation, a great lover of action. Surely he was the kind of man who cannot enjoy ease and comfort unless he imagines himself in danger and discomfort, who needs to conjure up a fantastically active life so as to be able to pursue his quiet existence in peace. One thinks of a man like Sacchetti, the pleasing domestic and provincial story-teller, as the exact opposite of Boccaccio. Sacchetti finds complete fulfilment in shrewd and effective representation. His imagination does not take him outside the confines of his own narrow world. All he wants as a story-teller is to give pleasure – his work, like his life,

Abridged by Robert S. Dombroski from Alberto Moravia's *Man as an End: A Defence of Humanism*, translated by Bernard Wall (London: Secker and Warburg, 1965), pp. 134–55. Copyright 1965 Secker and Warburg Ltd: reprinted by permission of the publisher.

is calm. But consider the voluptuous delight with which Boccaccio's episodes are elaborated, enriched and decorated; the liveliness with which he presents his characters, as though jealous of them. Consider the enormous variety of his settings: at sea, in cities, woods, rooms, caves, and deserts; and the way his characters comprise all conditions, nationalities, and periods – facts which go to show that the important thing for Boccaccio was less to give pleasure and surprise than greedily to fill himself living within the widest variety of people, situations, places, and periods. His cosmopolitanism is made up of extent and quantity rather than of civilization and education. Florence and its surroundings were too small to satisfy his thirst for action. He needed the East, France, Naples, Venice, Rome and Sicily, the ancient world and the high Middle Ages, and not only places and periods familiar to him, but those he knew of by hearsay. Most writers move within a given space and time. Where this does happen, as with Boccaccio, it means that the process of liberation and consequent widening of vision has reached fruition. Boccaccio's uprootedness and freedom, which seem so extraordinary to anyone who knows how rare such conditions are, are the primary reason for his universality.

There have been various ways of explaining the amorality and callousness that many believe they can detect in Boccaccio's work. He has been called a sensualist, as if sensuality necessarily excluded moral conscience. His lack of severity of spirit has been ascribed to the decadence of customs, the death of medieval chivalry, the transition to the modern middle-class age, and the change from the ancient ideas of transcendentalism to the immanence of the Renaissance.

But I for my part am convinced that morality is not a thing – like fashions or other superficial characteristics – that follows in the wake of historical change. Unquestionably Boccaccio was as moral a man as Dante or Manzoni. We should not let ourselves be misled by the fact that his stories contain so many adulteries and deceptions as well as a kind of superficiality and indifference. A careful reading of the Decameron reveals it as a book of only moderate sensuality, and never, or hardly ever, is sensuality the main subject of a story. And as for superficiality and indifference, they are only a defect when viewed extrinsically; to carry through a work of this kind they are a necessity.

Let us try to compare Flaubert and Boccaccio for a moment.

Flaubert's problem was quite different. He was concerned with providing in each of his books a more or less disguised portrait of
himself and hence with knowing and judging himself. Knowing and
judging himself led logically to knowing and judging the world
around him. In this sense moralism was as necessary for Flaubert as
amoralism was for Boccaccio, as we shall see in due course. The
fact that he described ordinary, normal, common things was simply
a result of this undertaking. Only ordinary, normal, common things
can provide the moralist with material that does not frustrate him
or disperse his cohesion. The moralist needs to believe in the existence of a stable social set-up, of interests and passions that cannot
evade judgement, of a serious and concrete world in which human
beings bear full responsibility for their actions. The play of fortune,
adventure and chance are excluded from his world, or if they find
their way into it they are inexorably drawn into the framework of a
moral judgement. A hare-brained and adventurous fellow in a
Boccaccio story would be turned by the moralist into a swindler
and a criminal; adventure becomes error, sin, a trick or crime. Moreover, variety serves no purpose, for one single fact scrutinised with
attention is quite enough for the moralist's ambition. He does not
wish to live many lives, but only one – his own. Flaubert felt the
tyranny of this situation, and more than once deluded himself into
thinking that he could escape it. Salammbô is the result of one such
attempt at escape. But Flaubert's spirit was not to be set free merely
by being transferred into distant and mythical ages. Salammbô is just
as heavy and narrow as Madame Bovary. The monstrous coherence of
Flaubert's path ends up in the blind alley of Bouvard et Pécuchet.

Boccaccio's task was quite different. He wanted neither to judge
himself nor to know himself, and still less to condemn or reform.
The corruption and decadence of customs left him indifferent not
because he shared in them but because they were factors that were of
no use to him. Moralists are praised too often for pillorying certain
vices. When we reflect that, given their temperaments, they desperately need those vices then we can see that their merit is not all
that great. On the other hand Boccaccio, with his thirst for adventure, needed quite different things. First of all he needed not to be
weighed down and impeded by serious or strict moral concepts, not
to have to continually establish a relationship of moral judgement
between himself and his characters, between himself and the world.
So much for the negative side; as for the positive side, what

Boccaccio needed was action pure and simple. Action of any kind, for the value of action lay in its being action pure and simple. Action of any kind, for the value of action lay in its being action, not in its being good or bad, sad or gay, imaginary or real. And when we think how infinitely beautiful and various and in all things enjoyable and desirable the world appeared to the enchanted Boccaccio, we see what a deprivation it would have seemed to him, amid such variety and wealth, to choose a little corner in which he could grow roots, to sacrifice so many possibilities to a concern for only one.

For these reasons it is vain to blame Boccaccio for not being moral, for being sceptical and superficial. It is contradictory to admire, say, the story of Andreuccio da Perugia and then blame Boccaccio for superficiality. What would have remained of Andreuccio's adventure if Boccaccio had probed into what lay behind his fecklessness and dash? The play, the lightness, the charm of those pages would have evaporated. It is useless to dwell on Boccaccio's flaw which to readers of today is a black separating gulf – the flaw of seeming to give absolution to his crime-prone and dishonest characters. We must realise that this absolution is the price paid for countless poetic events and curious magical details. Boccaccio seems to be saying to the reader: 'Let's agree once and for all that my characters are doing what they're doing for their own good reasons which it would be boring to pinpoint and evaluate. So relax; let them carry on, and let us enjoy ourselves.' A love of action that tends to precipitate action so as to enjoy it as soon as possible is, in my view, the mechanism with which Boccaccio's world operates. Notice how Boccaccio's way of telling a story is exactly the opposite to that of modern novelists. If we look at the first page of Madame Bovary, for instance, we certainly shall not find a statement of the book's main theme, nor the premises from which the development logically stems, set down with conventional clarity. We shall not find Madame Bovary, born in such and such a place, married to such and such a man, had such and such ambitions', and so on. Flaubert, like nearly all modern writers, does not set out to make his characters act, but to create them; and his attention is set on a reality of whose developments he himself is ignorant. This is the reason why books like his almost give us the impression of living through the events that we are reading; and, as happens in life, we do not know today what may happen tomorrow.

On the other hand Boccaccio, whose main concern is to make

his characters act and act wholeheartedly without hesitation, provides us headlong at the beginning of each story with the characters and data essential to the intrigue. Then once he has cleared the ground of these, he can devote himself body and soul to the development of the action. It is this convention, this preliminary liberation of the author from the burden of the characters and their motives, that enables Boccaccio to ornament his action with such magic, sensuality and light-heartedness.

For this reason it is mistaken in my view to see Boccaccio as an erotic writer. The truth is that though most of the stories in the *Decameron* pass for love stories, Boccaccio is not very interested in love. The role of love here, as in reality, is as a mainspring of human action and once the spring has been released Boccaccio turns his attention exclusively to action. In other words, love is a sub-heading for one kind of action and no more desirable as such than many other sub-headings. This becomes plain when we observe Boccaccio's ignorance about normal, emotional, psychological love; for him love has no savour unless it is adventurous, difficult, full of vicissitudes and equivocations. And Boccaccio hurries through love as he does through so many other emotions, giving it a few words at the beginning of his stories.

> Lorenzo ... who was goodly in person and gallant ... when Isabetta bestowed many a glance upon him and began to regard him with extraordinary favour ... Which Lorenzo marking, he began to affect her ... and 'twas not long before ... they did what each most desired ...

This handful of words relates Isabetta's love for Lorenzo in the most exemplary love story Boccaccio has written.[1] Boccaccio hurries through love, its birth, the people, the facts, so as to get, we feel, to what concerns him most, the famous passage about the 'pot' in which Isabetta, after burying the head of her dead lover, plants 'some roots of the goodliest basil of Salerno'. And about this pot, and the beauty of the plant and the way the brothers get to know that the pot contains the lover's head, Boccaccio spreads himself with a kind of tender cruelty. Once he has cleared the ground of the psychological and emotional data, he can, as usual, sit back and lavish all his care on the action and the objects on which it depends.

---

1 [IV, 5 – ed.]

We have already said that Boccaccio's passion for action gave a subtler, keener edge to his enjoyment of his comforts as a peaceful man, a humanist, and an honoured and solid citizen. And we have, in the structure of the *Decameron* itself, a reflection of a peaceful life rendered more delightful through the continual conjuring-up of exciting adventures and outlandish escapades. Indeed, the whole idea of the plague and the happy group of young people retiring to the country villa to tell stories, is significant, for the young people's safe withdrawal to the country, while the plague works havoc in the city, reflects Boccaccio's love of danger and his fascinated contemplation of the harsher, crueller things of life while safely basking in his own immunity. Moreover, we must not let ourselves be deceived by the seemingly 'historical' and 'pitiful' character of Boccaccio's plague. The plague – which he describes almost voluptuously and from a literary and aesthetic point of view, with obvious references to other plagues in books, and especially the vivid and detailed one in Thucydides – might well not have existed except as a foil to the delightful and reassuring description of the happy group in their *buen retiro*. As regards historical accuracy and pity, we should compare Boccaccio's plague with the one in Manzoni, which really is historically accurate and deeply pitiful in spite of its morbid and decadent overtones. Compare, for instance, the famous passage from Manzoni: 'A woman came down from the doorstep of one of those exits and approached the convoy ...' with Boccaccio's cold and externalised exclamations which seem to betray not only the complacency of someone who has escaped death, but even a touch of irony:

> How many grand palaces, how many stately homes, how many splendid residences, once full of retainers, of lords, of ladies, were now left desolate of all, even to the meanest servant! How many families of historic fame, of vast ancestral domains, and wealth proverbial, found now no scion to continue the succession! How many brave men, how many fair ladies, how many gallant youths! ...

With Manzoni, the sadistic taste for death, destruction and chastisement is genuinely outmatched by Christian compassion, whereas in Boccaccio we sense the thrill of someone far away in a pleasant place, removed from all danger, who contemplates a great calamity and speculates in a waking dream as to its details. And, in smug contrast, we have 'the little hill on the summit of which was a palace, with galleries, halls and chambers disposed around a fair and spacious court, each very fair in itself and the goodlier to see for the handsome pictures with which it was adorned'. We have the 'meadow where the grass grew green and luxuriant, nowhere being scorched by the sun'. We have the garden with its paths 'each very wide and straight as an arrow and roofed in with trellis of vines', and walled in with roses 'white and red, and jasmine'. We have the 'basin of whitest marble' rising in the middle of a lawn 'so green that it seemed almost black' and 'tables being already set and fragrant herbs and fair flowers strewn all about'. And there is the 'little lake' where 'the fish darted to and fro in multitudinous shoals', and the 'vale' where there were beds 'equipped within and without with stores of French coverlets and other bed-gear'. There is the 'little church nearby' where the group goes for 'divine service'; and the 'copse' full of 'roebucks and stags and other wild creatures as if witting that in this time of pestilence they had nought to fear from the hunter' and, indeed, all the other pleasing and peaceful things which, in the introductions, serve to offset the plague and the stirring events of the stories. In fact the calm and tranquil passages about peaceful occupations far removed from passion reflect life as Boccaccio lived it; for he was a frequenter of courts and côteries, whereas the plague and the events of the stories are the longings of his imagination which helped him to luxuriate yet more in the quiet serenity of his life. That this is so is proved by the way in which he relegated the pleasures of country life to a marginal role in the book – not where they would be if they were the true source of his inspiration. Whereas Tasso, for instance, two centuries later, set such pleasures at the heart of his *Aminta*; for his life was neither calm nor pleasant, and he had every reason to long for an idyllic life of luxury. If Boccaccio had confined himself to describing the calm, light-hearted life of the villa, he would have been a mere Arcadian; if he had confined himself to adventure he would have been a romantic yarn-spinner. But the combination of the villa and the stories reveals the dualism in the depths of his soul. The plague, with its horror, enhances the pleasures of the villa, just as corpses in a cemetery enrich the earth and nourish the flowers that grow in it. So it was a welcome, delightful plague, as contrasted with Manzoni's plague, Defoe's demoralising plague, Thucydides' historical plague, and Poe's grotesque plague. But inventories of plagues in literature have been made before now, so let us return to Boccaccio.

We have no intention here of analysing all Boccaccio's stories so as to illustrate our point as to the mainpoint of his inspiration. Such an analysis would be tedious and mechanical. Think of Bonaparte's book on Poe where the same procedure is applied to every story, and the same discoveries made, until near-boredom sets in. Nevertheless the first story in the *Decameron*, the one about Ser Ciappelletto, seems to me highly important and typical of a whole vein of Boccaccio's kind of narrative, so I would like to discuss it — the more so as many readers may find that that story, lacking in action and real events as it is, contradicts what has been said so far.

The tale of Ser Ciappelletto is well known and has no need to be retold. Boccaccio establishes at the outset, in his usual conventional and brisk way, the criminal and impious character of Ser Ciappelletto who is given to every form of corruption; and thence, with the help of a complicated and rather improbable sleight of hand, he puts him in a situation where he can play the saint and, from his deathbed, carry out a long and blasphemous joke at the expense of his confessor. At first sight this might seem to be a satire on the rites and credulity of priests, a highly irreverent satire and, in last analysis, an unwarranted one. But on closer inspection Boccaccio's main concern is seen to be not the satire itself but the mechanism by which it is obtained. In other words his interest is not in the things themselves but in their interplay when thrown violently together. His interest is not in priests or in the Christian religion, any more than in Ser Ciappelletto: it is in the development of the joke, and perhaps even more in the interplay of force and action that sets the joke in motion.

The theatre, whether classical or modern, is full of deceits and jokes. Moreover the theatre comes nearer to action than any other literary genre. Where there is deceit, the deceiver finds himself in a peculiar position of freedom and power in relation to the deceived. He knows he is deceiving, whereas his victim does not know he is being deceived. His freedom is unlimited so long as the deception lasts and his action, based as it is on contemplative satisfaction, is entirely gratuitous and an end in itself. Deceiving, moreover, means acting without danger, escaping the immediate consequences of action, acting from the cosy and perfectly safe ground of make-believe. It is precisely that kind of action that the lazy and easy-going Boccaccio must have enjoyed. Deception is a dream of action which has recourse to secrecy because it cannot be developed in an open way. They enjoy deceit who feel that the demands of open and brutal action are beyond their scope. In deceit cleverness has its revenge on force and all other irrational factors. Now Boccaccio's pages are full of deceits of this kind.

But we do not mean to imply that Boccaccio's own nature had leanings towards dissimulation and fraud. Indeed, if we realise that action pure and simple almost always lacks bite, and that deceit is intimately linked with the type of bourgeois and conventional lives that Boccaccio wanted to depict, then we shall see why nothing can be deduced from the frequency of the *Decameron*'s deceits as to similar characteristics in the author. Boccaccio's taste for deceit reveals, if anything, something akin to that constant longing of mankind: the longing for invisibility. Who has not dreamt at least once that he had a wand, or a powder, or some other device for making himself invisible, and, once invisible, that he had gone off to the ends of the earth to play practical jokes on important people, to escape punishment, and generally behave with perfect immunity in the most dangerous circumstance? Now the situation of the deceiver is equivalent to a kind of invisibility. The deceived does not see the deceiver as he really is, so the deceiver can act with all the freedom and consistency that he would have if he were invisible. As can be seen, it is a dream of power and action if ever there was one. . . .

Action free from any ulterior motive, action as an end in itself, action for action's sake, in a word adventure, always lies at the heart of Boccaccio's most secret aspirations. But as we have already said, this kind of action runs the risk of seeming unwarranted and hence unreal. Ariosto, another contemplative writer in love with action, remedies this drawback by means of irony; Boccaccio, less disillusioned than Ariosto, counters it with what we would call (to use an overworked term) a kind of magic realism. That is, a visionary yet concrete precision of detail, combined – within a rarefied and ineffable atmosphere – with an extraordinary sense of the coincidences offered by reality itself at the moment of narration. I have said that this magic realism enables Boccaccio to avoid the pitfall of unreality peculiar to adventure. But perhaps it would be more accurate to say that this magic derives precisely from his indifference to the ethical factor, from the scepticism which people still insist on seeing as one of the defects of Boccaccio's art. For what is a dream, where magic seems at home, if not a reality from which all rational, practical, moral and intellectual elements have been banished, and in which the fantasies of the unconscious are expressed? For moralists reality tends to demand a judgement and thus it harmonises realistically with characters and events. But for adventure-dreamers reality is just as ineffable and mysterious as the places, objects and people that we caress with our deepest instincts when we are asleep. The surrealists, in their researches, have sometimes isolated and blown up details in old pictures and thereby revealed the magical and metaphysical character of many of these details – which have a lucid incoherence unknown to the modern impressionists and realists. This is because, like Boccaccio, the old masters often dreamed, and dreams are fertile ground for analogies and enigmas. When seen through a magnifying glass, some of Boccaccio's backgrounds, places and notations become arcane and suggestive, like the tiny *natures mortes*, corners of landscapes, and background-figures of some of our fourteenth-, fifteenth- and sixteenth-century painters. Action, pure action, without intended meaning or ethics, gains depth, lucidity and mystery from those details that no amount of serious moral intention could give it.

An outstanding example of this blending of magic detail with passion for action is provided by the story of Andreuccio da Perugia. Here, moreover, the thirst for adventure is overt and total. There are none of those erotic elements that at first sight may seem to be inseparable from Boccaccio's art. Andreuccio is a young man, nothing else; we know nothing about him except that he came to Naples to buy horses. In a word, Andreuccio lies entirely within the action, and from the action he derives, if not his character, at least his consistency; apart from the action he has no features, no character, no psychology. The starting-point of the tale is the intrigue initiated by the Neapolitan prostitute for Andreuccio's undoing. Without involving himself too far in the probability of the story of a sister lost and found, Boccaccio immediately enters into a compulsive, dreamy atmosphere which is truly magical. We have the 'curtained bed', with 'dresses in plenty, hanging on pegs' in the prostitute's house; we have the 'narrow blind alley' into which the unfortunate Andreuccio falls; we have the 'fellow with the black and matted beard ... yawning and rubbing his eyes as if he had just been roused from his bed, or at any rate from deep sleep; we have those two thieves who, on hearing Andreuccio's story, exclaim, 'Of a surety, 'twas in the house of Scarabone Buttafuoco'; and, finally, we have the cathedral in which the archbishop has been buried, the cathedral where – though not described – we seem to see the tall shadowy nave, the vast paved floor dimly shining, the massive brown groups of pillars and columns and, at the end, all twinkling with candles, the altar with the prelate's sarcophagus. Andreuccio enters the tomb and there the thieves leave him. Shut up in the tomb with a dead man, he is in an anguishing situation almost worthy of Poe. But the church echoes with footsteps, other thieves come along (and, incidentally, how many thieves there are in Boccaccio! – but in a world of humanists, merchants and courtiers, the criminal world is the only one that *acts*), the lid is raised from the tomb and the anguish evaporates. And now the point is, what does it matter if Andreuccio, the honest merchant, becomes a thief and a desecrator of tombs; what does it matter if later (as Boccaccio tells us, not without ingenuousness) his companions congratulate him and help him make away with the stolen goods – granted that the writer has borne us through the adventure in one breath? . . .

But it was not only in space that Boccaccio sought scope for his passion for action; he sought it also in time. I have always considered historical novels and stories an absurdity unless history, instead of presenting itself to the author as a kind of *place d'armes* in which time (to take the words of the imaginary seventeenth-century writer of the Introduction to *The Betrothed*) passes the years in review and draws them up in battle array, unless history brings the years back to the surface of memory like some ancestral recollection, or poetic longing, or nostalgia. Boccaccio, though he lived in a time that no one could suspect of historicism – between the Middle Ages, which rejected history in the name of theological immobility, and the Renaissance, which was equally foreign to the spirit of history owing to its Plutarchian cult of the personality – Boccaccio must nevertheless have had a mythical and obscure sense of the almost legendary past of the high Middle Ages and the Lombard invaders, if only transmitted by oral tradition and family memories. Apart from other stories where the period is uncertain and wrapped, as it were, in the darkness of a magic long-ago (such as the one about Tancredi, Prince of Salerno; Nastagio degli Onesti, and Alibech in the desert of the Thebaid), we find a sense of a Lombardic and barbarous Middle Ages in King Agilulf and Queen Teodolinda, told out as it is in the stained glass of a cathedral, and there is also some kind of prenatal memory present as if someone were recounting things neither invented nor heard but experienced in another life. The Italian groom belonging to the oppressed race who is in love with the Lombard Queen, risks death to lie with her and, this achieved, spends his life remembering those minutes of royal love, is a very complex figure in whom are blended the passion for action and a sort of nostalgia for a dark barbaric era that lacked the light of art or culture yet fostered strong whole-hearted passions, like the protagonist's for King Agilulf's wife. There are plenty of kings and queens in Boccaccio, but these two are the only ones that achieve social relief and concreteness, contrasted as they are with the low-born groom. Agilulf and Teodolinda,[2] we feel, reign barbarously by right of conquest over an enslaved people. The groom has no hope and is content just to be near the queen, tending the horses. But this timid fetishism does not satisfy his passion indefinitely. When desire gains over prudence, he decides to risk his life and try to possess the queen. As usual, once the decision is taken, and the plot formulated, Boccaccio hurtles into the action – which, as he proceeds, is deepened and enriched by the background details.

The attentive reader is sure to remember the place in which the groom's adventure occurs. This is King Agilulf's palace, probably a rough castle of wood with square palisaded towers like the ones Agilulf's ancestors built in the clearings of the northern forests, a fitting setting for a king who at night goes to seek his wife wrapped in a great mantle and carrying a 'lighted torch' in one hand and a wand in the other. It is also a fitting setting for the groom who disguises himself as the king and, making the 'drowsy' chambermaid open the doors to him, lies down silently beside the queen in the darkness. Basically it is the same kind of deception as in many another licentious story, but the remote period, the place, the palace that seems to have emerged from a Germanic saga and the royal atmosphere, confer a poetic quality on what elsewhere might be a mere diversion or joke. Once the deception is discovered, the king makes straight for the place where he imagines his unknown rival to be.

This is the 'long dormitory' above the horses' stables – words charged with evocations of feudal servitude. Here in different beds 'well-nigh all' the king's household sleeps. 'Well-nigh all', for the

---

[2] [III, 2 – ed.]

Lombard kings had no courts, the king being a feudal man like everyone else. His peers were not in the palace but in other castles scattered across Italy; in the royal palace there dwelt only the members of the royal family, and the family's servants. We imagine the 'long dormitory' as narrow and low with pallets for all (or 'well-nigh all') the servants stretching as far as the eye can see under a beamed ceiling. The king enters the corridor, walks slowly along the row of beds, and feels the heart of each sleeper with his hand. Note how this deep deathlike sleep of all the servants, worn out by the day's toil, is in accord with the image of the long dormitory. The king cuts a tuft of hair from the head of the one whose heart seems to him agitated. But the groom, outwitting the king, cuts a similar tuft from the heads of all his companions. So the next day, when the king sees all the family servants partially shorn, he has to admit defeat from his unknown rival.

I have gone into this story at length because it seems to me one of the best in the *Decameron* and one in which the passion for action seems to attain the highest level of articulation and depth. Moreover, with its homely human tone and gay deceit, it marks the transition of Boccaccio's art from the stories we might call 'lucky' (that is those in which the vicissitudes lead to a happy ending in a clear and light-hearted atmosphere) to stories we might call 'unlucky', where the adventures have a tragic ending. Our traditional image of Boccaccio depends mainly on the first type, and especially on those stories with erotic and comic plots. But it is a partial image and takes less than half Boccaccio into account. In fact Boccaccio felt equally deeply about happiness and unhappiness, and this because they are the two faces of Chance, the only god who survives the disappearance of all others and still shines brightly in the serene sky of the *Decameron*. For Boccaccio chance plays the part of fate in Greek tragedies, but we owe his love of chance not to cynicism but, like everything else, to his taste for action and adventure. For what is chance in Boccaccio's stories but the expression of a devoted passion for the manifold in life? All who put their trust in chance put their trust in life as in a river with multiple currents to which we should abandon ourselves in the knowledge that they will ultimately lead somewhere. Chance, moreover, allows every action to be its own self-justification as it occurs. Hence the freedom, the variety, the beauty of all actions without exception, their grafting not onto a dull and limited moral world but onto the most charming and colourful of aesthetic worlds. Chance and mischance are beautiful alike, to be caressed and wondered at with feelings of lascivious desire. All ends up in beauty. . . .

The fact that it is chance that lies behind the vicissitudes of the stories and not a high moral consciousness or system of thought, in no way proves that Boccaccio was a lazy or frivolous writer. Chance, that deceptive and enigmatic goddess, puts the more lovable and younger faculties to the test first and foremost. Faith in chance is a prerogative of the young, of all those whose vitality has not yet been stultified and put at the service of some idea or interest. Boccaccio, who was young in spirit, trusted in chance out of excess of imagination and vitality rather than scepticism and frivolity. And after all, to oust all the dull ghosts from heaven and put in their place the blindfold goddess at her wheel means removing the grey monochrome richness and variety. Such chance, such interplay of agile and free forces is unknown to us, alas, and what we often mistake for dull and sinister chance is a destiny that is inscrutable but no less logical and pitiless for that.

Alberto Moravia

Forms of
Accommodation in
the *Decameron*

It is difficult to write about the Decameron because it falls, as a work of
art, somewhere between the heterogeneity of a random collection
and the homogeneity of a purely personal expression. It does not,
to be sure, fall half way between these poles. Although Boccaccio's
sources were manifold, he imposed on all these stories something
like a recognisable moral style as well as recognisable narrative habits.
As a result, one can properly discuss the typical situations and
characters and values of his book on the assumption that they reflect
a common sensibility and outlook. But the assumption is not everywhere equally justified. In certain stories, on certain pages even, the
reader knows that he is closer to the essential Boccaccio than elsewhere, even if he is grateful that the essential artist chose to stray so
often from his essence. One may be grateful, that is to say, for the
story of Natan and Mitridanes (X, 3) even if one recognises in it a
mode less characteristic than the story of Ciappelletto (I, 1). In this
occasional and happy eccentricity, challenging and complicating the
book's coherence, lies the trap for the critic. For any pattern he
thinks he discerns will generally be marred by the irreducible
exceptions, stubbornly violating all symmetries and generalisations.
In this state of affairs it behoves one to search out the characteristic,
intuit the tendency and capture the drift (while noticing the in-
consistent) rather than insist on the paradigm. I hope that the proposals which follow will be understood to assume this necessary
modesty.

Recent scholarship has rightly stressed the naturalism of the

Abridged by Robert S. Dombroski from Italica, XLV, 3 (1968), pp. 297–
312. Reprinted by the permission of the author and the publisher
(Italica).

Decameron[1], but has not perhaps stressed adequately those forces which counterbalance it, forces deriving from Boccaccio's very strong and instinctive faith in social order. It is not sufficient to say, for example, that Boccaccio's marriages are good only because they conform to nature and when they are not imposed by society. They are also good because they are sanctioned by society, and because they lead to the family, which for Boccaccio is the most important of social institutions. The comic treatment of adultery in the *Decameron* bears witness, not to his cynicism but to his faith in marriage. There are in fact very few broken marriages in the book; the most conspicuous case – that of Ricciardo da Chinzica (II, 10) – is treated with so much more withering humour because the original union represents a particularly flagrant crime against the institution. The stories of the Fifth Day, concerned with the lovers' happy endings ('ciò che ad alcuno amante dopo alcuni fieri o sventurati accidenti, felicemente avvenisse'), all place that happiness in marriage. Boccaccio's underlying caution towards sexual licence is reflected in the value of *onestà* invoked by the frame plot and in the actual restraint practised by the ten young people. What happens when natural love follows its bent without the social sanction of marriage is recorded in the third story of the Fourth Day, wherein three couples elope in defiance of society to end in recrimination, betrayal, squalor, and death.

Boccaccio's faith in marriage extends implicitly to the family as a whole and ultimately to the community and the state. The most dramatic stories of the Second Day – those of Madonna Beritola and the Count of Antwerp – are so affecting because they constitute miniature epics of a family, a household, and the same values enrich the later stories of Torello and Giletta di Nerbona. The union or reunion of husband and spouse, parent and child, remains for Boccaccio an unadulterated good. The faith in the larger community emerges less explicitly from the pages of the *Decameron*, but it is tacitly ubiquitous. The number of wise and upright rulers is strikingly large in comparison to the much smaller number of corrupt or domineering tyrants. A reflection of this social faith can be found in the narrative habit which opens each story with a careful indication

[1] I refer chiefly to the learned and provocative book by Aldo D. Scaglione, *Nature and Love in the Late Middle Ages* (Berkeley and Los Angeles: University of California Press, 1963).

of the city where it takes place, and within the city, the identity of the head of the household. These characteristic indications are conspicuously missing from such a collection as the Novellino. All the protagonists who leave their homes finally return again necessarily to provide a proper and ritualistic conclusion. The modern post-Romantic plot of the protagonist freed from his inhibiting social roots (Portrait of the Artist as a Young Man, Sons and Lovers, Les Faux-Monnayeurs, Der Zauberberg) is unthinkable in the world of the Decameron. It is unthinkable even, and most significantly, in the framing plot, which represents the young people returning to their community even when the return is physically dangerous and the community is in dissolution. The horror of communal dissolution depicted so vigorously in the Introduction is itself a measure of the value of social stability.

That value is certainly felt by all readers and needs elaboration here because criticism has remembered it only intermittently. Indeed one may extend the value of social stability even further to argue that it is built into the very structure of Boccaccio's novella. Almost all the stories conclude with a projection, explicit or implicit, of an achieved equilibrium into an indefinite future. The equilibrium is not achieved by a whole community, but it depends upon a continuing social order which is exemplified and manifested by the miniature order of the story's conclusion. It is rare that a story ends with a fulfilment of passion, as one might expect if nature were dominant. It ends much more frequently when the social problem posed by the fulfilment has been solved, and solved more or less permanently.

There is no question that sexual passion does pose problems for society, no question that nature and community are opposed – if not inevitably, then very frequently. Passion is by no means the only threat Boccaccio recognises; it is supplemented by cupidity and superstition and cruelty and stupidity and prodigality, by various forms of social ineptness or indecorum or violence, and by the great dark agent of Fortune. All of these constitute threats to society, and yet the most common, the most interesting, the most powerful, remains the amoral yearning of desire, cutting athwart class and marriage and ecclesiastical inhibitions, customs and propriety and commerce and plighted troth. The stories of the Decameron are typically concerned with the way society absorbs these threats, and above all the sexual threat. If the stories are not so wide as to focus on a whole community, they are not so narrow, not so psychologically curious, to focus on the drama of a single consciousness. They are concerned with a knot of individuals, a small circle, a grouping of friends or lovers or members of a family, whose relationships the story alters. The capacity of the minor group, the knot, to absorb the threats to its survival demonstrates the resilience of the whole society.

In a few stories, chiefly those of the Fourth Day, the continuing equilibrium of the conclusion is pathetic; it stems from loss, death, and defeat, and it dramatizes society's occasional failure to absorb. But in the collection as a whole, the pathetic stories serve to heighten the achieved equilibrium of the remaining stories, where the absorption is luckily or cleverly or radiantly successful. We begin with an initial equilibrium which has maintained itself for a considerable period of time before the story begins; a pre-narrative indefinite balances the post-narrative indefinite extension. But the initial equilibrium is none the less vulnerable by definition, since it is threatened by those forces or events which set the narrative in action. We are led from that relatively fragile equilibrium through a series of events which challenge it, and finally to a stronger equilibrium — stronger because it survives (as the ending almost always implies) unchallenged. The story ends with the working out of a tougher, less vulnerable stability.

How is it worked out? How is the absorption managed? Sometimes by Fortune, but in the best stories, more commonly or more suggestively by some human manipulation guided by the intelligence. Bosco and Petronio have called attention to the value the *Decameron* places upon a certain kind of shrewd intelligence or worldly wisdom evoked by the word *saviezza*. I want to argue that the quality of *saviezza*, however important and ubiquitous, is not in itself the central virtue of the book, but rather another virtue for which no single term, Italian or English, quite suffices. *Saviezza*, with its blend of caution, astute prudence, and worldly judgement, is too passive, too conservative a trait to manipulate effectively human relationships. It cannot in itself reverse the dangerous swing away from stability; it cannot contain those which menace the established communal knot. To achieve that goal, the one goal that matters supremely in the *Decameron*, a kind of creativity is needed, a brilliant inventiveness, a resourceful cunning capable of righting the slipping balance in a burst of unexpected improvisation. This creativity ranges from the histrionic genius of Ciappelletto in defence of his Florentine hosts (I, 1) to the scheme of the English princess threatened with a misalliance (II, 3), or the inspired device of Andreuccio threatened with incarceration (II, 5), or the arrangements of Antigono which break the cycle of lust encircling Alatiel (II, 7), or the complex manoeuvrings and disguisings of Tedaldo degli Elisei to ensure his mistress' love, and to prove her husband's innocence (III, 7), or the eloquent extemporising of Il Zima as he bilks the covetous Francesco Vergellesi (III, 5), or the spectacular epiphany staged by Nastagio degli Onesti for the benefit of his beloved (V, 9), or the artful poetic justice visited upon the seductive schemer Jancofiore by Salabaetto (VIII, 10). In all these stories and many others, the accommodation is achieved by a kind of therapeutic invention. The inventiveness, which assumes the judgement of the *savio* and learns to collaborate with Fortune, seems to me the wellspring of the book's human assurance. Its poise depends not so much, or not merely, upon prudence as upon a kind of spontaneous artistry.

The artistry in its most modern forms is visible in the witticisms of the Fifth and Sixth Days. The art in these anecdotes is apparently verbal, and yet it is, even here, more than verbal. It involves an alert calculation of human character, of human relationships and the dynamics of a problematic social situation – all this plus the quicksilver intuition of a saving solution. One example among many is the reply of the Marquise of Monferrato (I, 5) to an equivocal question from the king of France. The Marquise, 'savia et avveduta', is shrewd enough to grasp the threat involved in the king's visit, but her shrewdness needs to be fortified by a kind of inspired strategem. Her inspiration leads her to serve dishes based only on hen's flesh and to find, at the critical moment, the obliquely expressive response to his insinuation:

'Dama, nascono in questo paese solamente galline senza gallo alcuno?'

La marchesana, che ottimamente la domanda intese, parendole che secondo il suo disiderio. Domenedio l'avesse tempo mandato opportuno a poter la sua intenzion dimostrare, al re domandante, baldanzosamente verso lui rivolta, rispose:

'Monsignor no, ma le femine, quantunque in vestimenti et in onori alquanto dall'altre variino, tutte per ciò son fatte qui come altrove.'

['Madam, is it only hens that flourish in these parts, and not a single cock?'

The Marchioness, who understood his question perfectly, saw this as exactly the kind of Heaven-sent opportunity she had hoped for in order to make clear her intentions. On hearing the King's inquiry, she turned boldly towards him and replied:

'No, my lord, but our women, whilst they may differ slightly from each other in their rank and in the style of their dress, are made no differently here than they are elsewhere.']

The dinner becomes a kind of metaphor which the marquise manipulates; she has found a way to speak without speaking. And since the king understands, and gives up his pursuit, her art achieves his object: it has contained and defeated his desire without violence. Passion and decorum have been accommodated – elegantly, economically, without the ugliness of anger or the vulgarity of the explicit. But although the stress falls properly upon her artful grace, the story recognizes that this grace must be seconded by the king's own alert understanding and self-mastery, and it concludes with praise for these secondary but necessary virtues:

Il re, udite queste parole, raccolse bene la cagione del convito delle galline e la vertù nascosta nelle parole, ed accorsesi che invano con così fatta donna parole si getterebbono, e che forza non v'avea luogo; per che così come disavvedutamente acceso s'era di lei, saviamente s'era da spegnere per onor di lui il male concetto fuoco. E senza più mottegiarla, temendo delle sue risposte, fuori d'ogni speranza desinò, e finito il desinare . . . ringraziatala dell'onor ricevuto da lei, raccomandolo ella a Dio, a Genova se n'andò.

[On hearing this, the King saw clearly the reason for the banquet of chickens, and the virtue that lay concealed beneath her little homily. He realized that honeyed words would be wasted on a lady of this sort, and that force was out of the question. And thus, in the same way that he had foolishly become inflamed, so now he wisely decided that he was honour-bound to extinguish the ill-conceived fires of his passion. Fearing her replies, he teased her no further, but applied himself to his meal, by now convinced that all hope was lost. And as soon as he had finished eating, in order to compensate for his dishonourable coming by his swift departure, he thanked her for her generous hospitality and departed for Genoa, with the lady wishing him God-speed.]

So it frequently happens in the *Decameron* that the success of an invention depends not only on its own brilliance but the capacity of those affected to accede, to fall into line, to compromise. Thus the Saladin magnanimously gives up his acquisitive design on Melchisedech (I, 3) and Currado Gianfigliazzi forgives Chichibio (VI, 4) out of appreciation for his resourcefulness under duress. In all these cases the essence of the saving inspiration is its unconventionality, which calls attention by its novel felicity away from a potentially disagreeable situation. The wit, the art, constitute a kind of social therapy, although the story seldom insists on an unrealistic moral transformation. The King of France will not permanently renounce the flesh, nor the Saladin his pursuit of money. The accommodation is modest, pragmatic, calculated to the frail measures of man. But it suffices to the situation, and in the process it tends to communicate an oblique moral criticism: a rebuke of Cane della Scala and Erminio de' Grimaldi for their avarice (I, 7 and I, 8) or of the inquisitor for his hypocrisy (I, 6) or the King of Cyprus for his cowardice (I, 9) or the bishop of Florence for his indecency (VI, 3) or a certain gentleman for his garrulity (VI, 1). Almost all the *motti* of the First and Sixth Days function in this fashion, delicate and probing, painful and salutary. And all of the butts so recognize them, with rueful appreciation.

In the fuller narratives of the remaining days, the art of human manipulation may bypass language (as does Masetto Lamporecchio for a time in II, 1) but generally employs it more amply as an instrument of the strategic intelligence. The commonest goal of the intelligence is of course sexual security. The formula that sexual pleasure in the *Decameron* becomes a reward for intelligence is generally true. What is striking is the rarity of those cases in which the intelligence manipulates the person desired. (Most of these cases, such as they are, fall on the eighth day, to which I shall return.) The much commoner case involves the deception of some representative of the social order – a husband, a father (II, 1, V, 4), or, in the *tour de force* of III, 5, an innocent priest. The artistic triumph lies not so much in sexual possession as in deception, a deception which is in its way an accommodation like those we have already seen. The natural impulse is absorbed and its potential venom removed by some happy fiction like the confession of the lady in VII, 5, or the pear tree of Lidia (VII, 9). The *inganno* is socially unconventional but it passes the pragmatic test: it succeeds. It constitutes a cheerfully amoral therapy which the story concedes to be important. If social sanctions did not matter, there would be no need for deception and the story would have no existence.

The dramatic life of Boccaccio's sexual *inganni* lies in the marvellous style of the deceivers. The device itself is not enough: it has to be *carried off*, and the zest of the story lies in the brio of the performance. Boccaccio is not content to assert its effect; he gives us the scene verbatim, with all its shadings and nuances. He renders carefully the distinctive colouring of each performer: the demure placidity of Monna Sismonda (VII, 8), the outraged respectability of the wool-merchant's wife (III, 3), the shrewish scolding of Peronella (VII, 2), the magisterial dignity of Don Felice (III, 4), the smiling and imperturbable assurance of the lady in VII, 5. The pleasure for us in these stories and so many others lies in our admiration for the artistic finish, for the style of the execution enhancing the felicity of the invention. This delight in the rendering of style, one may say in passing, is precisely the attribute which binds Boccaccio most tightly to the culture of the Renaissance. Medieval literature of course is full of trickery, from the *chansons de geste* to the *Roman de Renard* and the *fabliaux*. But the medieval imagination is mainly concerned with the device itself. Boccaccio shows himself closest to the Renaissance in just those stories where he draws most heavily on medieval material. No story in the volume is closer to the *fabliau* than the story of Tofano (VII, 4); what is new and most Boccaccioesque is the outrageous and extended series of speeches given to the wife at the climax. Boccaccio, unlike the authors of his source, took the trouble to write out the whole splendid passionate prevarication, so that we participate not only in the idea but the theatrical experience. This fidelity to the adverb, this ear for rhetoric, clearly places the *Decameron* (*pace* Branca and Whitfield) among the classics of the Renaissance.

The adulterers' flair for style shades over into the delight of other tricksters whose motives are financial rather than sexual, or of still others who persecute their natural victims, the stupid and superstitious, with a kind of inventive malice without motive which approaches art for art's sake. In the latter category fall preeminently those two tireless and pitiless jokers Bruno and Buffalmacco, whose humour appeals a little more ambivalently to our century than to theirs. The five stories devoted to their shenanigans might be said to fall outside the schema of absorption or accommodation which I have been trying to sketch. It could be argued that these stories constitute artistically 'pure' examples of human manipulation without any therapeutic function, since the butts – Calandrino and Master Simone – represent no real threat to society. But perhaps these stories (VIII, 3; VIII, 6; IX, 3; IX, 5) do contain none the less a certain primitive therapy. The kind of foolishness incarnated by the butts might be said to constitute at least a social irritant, at the most a social danger, which a healthy society will strive to expose and correct. 'Non mi pare che agramente sia da riprendere' says Lauretta, '. . . chi fa beffa alcuna a colui che la va cercando o che la si guadagna.' [. . . 'One should not judge a person too harshly for playing a trick on another, if the victim is being hoist with his own petard, or if he is simply asking to be made a fool of.'] Calandrino's folly is never permanently corrected, but it is exposed through the play of his tormentors; the small, recurrent disequilibrium between folly and punishment is persistently righted. Master Simone, whose pretensions to dignity are stressed at the opening, may learn a minimal degree of humility from the outcome of his adventure, and we need not read the concluding sentence as wholly ironic:

> Così adunque, como udito avete, senno s'insegna a chi tanto non n'apparò a Bologna.
> [So now you have heard how wisdom is imparted to anyone who has not acquired much of it at Bologna.]

Bruno and Buffalmacco may play their roles, albeit unwittingly, as the exuberant agents of a society reacting to the irritant of dullness. Something of this same role is discernible in the operations of those confidence agents working ostensibly for money, and especially in such master performers as Fiodaliso (II, 5) and Cipolla (VI, 10), immortal histrions of cupidity, rooking the *sancta simplicitas* of the innocent with a genius transcending the meagre requisite skill. Our appreciation of these actors may imply a tacit judgement that simplicity threatens the social order more seriously than greed.

Boccaccio's interest in 'performance' and his use of theatrical epiphanies have not altogether received the attention they deserve. Almost all his heroes and heroines reveal a flair for theatrics;

almost all are good at improvising, although the scale of improvisation runs from the briefest *motti* through the master productions of Ciappelletto and Cipolla. The therapeutic art of manipulating human relations finds its fullest expression in putting on a literal art. An impressive number of stories conclude with some climactic scene which is arranged or stage-managed or extemporised by the creative intelligence. The staged deceptions of the Seventh Day have already been noted; on other days the dramatic epiphany may take the form of an *éclaircissement*, a revelation of the actual truth. The common elements in both groups are on the one hand the impresario-improvisor and on the other the audience of one or many to be enlightened or gulled. Examples of the *éclaircissement* scene are frequent on the Second Day (the princess of England before the Pope, II, 3; Madonna Beritola and her family, II, 6; the Count of Antwerp before the King of France, II, 8; Zinevra before the Sultan, II, 9) but above all on the Tenth Day (1, 2, 4, 7, 9, 10) where the impulse to generosity seems typically to require a public recognition of its virtue. The public *éclaircissement* tends to appear in the 'soft' stories which involve reconciliation and reunion, whereas the staging of deception belongs of course to the 'harder' accommodations of adultery and cunning. But it helps if we can see the one production as the mirror image of the other. Such climaxes as those arranged by Ghino da Tacco (X, 2), Gentile (X, 4) and the Saladin (X, 9) can teach us that the revelation of generosity needs at least as much contrivance as the concealment of intrigue. In the story of Tedaldo (III, 7) the concluding *éclaircissement* combines, through a kind of prestidigitation uncommon even in Boccaccio, the hard accommodation of adultery with a soft reunion of spouses and brothers. Here by means of the hero's legerdemain, his rhetoric, his disguises, his alert perception, his sense of timing, his sex appeal, and his luck, all the characters are made happy and the accommodation is ratified publicly by the presence of the thronged guests. The use of the feast as the scene of the revelation (repeated in II, 6; V, 8; X, 4; X, 10), with its associations of festivity, magnanimity, sensual pleasure, and communal warmth, is characteristic and resonant with dramatic suggestiveness.

In the second half of the book the art of human manipulation loses a tinge of its warmth and gaiety as it becomes progressively engaged in enterprises that are morally ambiguous. The 'hard' accommodations of deception tend to cluster among the thirty-one stories running from Cipolla (VI, 10) through Donno Gianni

(IX, 10), a group containing many of the most entertaining but also the cruellest and most brutal of the collection. There is indeed a kind of downward drift in this group which can be symbolised by the robust fun of the first story in contrast to the literal bestiality of the last. The accommodation of VIII, 8 (Zeppa and Spenelloccio) which concludes with the fourfold acceptance of double adultery, reaches a degree of seamy audacity unique in the *Decameron*. Within the stories of the Seventh Day alone, a kind of moral deterioration leads to the unpleasant story of Lidia (VII, 9), and in the two succeeding days the commercialisation of sex (VIII, 1; VIII, 2; VIII, 10) and physical cruelty (VIII, 3; VIII, 7; IX, 7; IX, 9) intrude themselves uncomfortably. The group consists of a kind of anatomy of the *inganno*, seen from all possible perspectives but increasingly from an angle of equivocal morality. We may well ask if the text betrays any awareness of these ambiguities, and I think the answer emerges as a cautious affirmative. The awareness appears in at least four various and subtle but unmistakable forms, of which the first is the descending arrangement we have just noted. A second form lies in a kind of plot which appears increasingly in the stories of the Eighth and Ninth Days, a plot which one might borrow from Shakespeare to call 'measure for measure', and which Boccaccio himself calls 'l'arte ... dall'arte schernita'. That phrase appears in Pampinea's introduction to the most painful of all the stories, the revenge of the scholar upon the widow (VIII, 7):

> Carissime donne, spesse volte avviene che l'arte è dall'arte schernita, e per ciò è poco senno il dilettarsi di schernire altrui.
> [Dearest ladies, one cunning deed is often capped by another, and hence it is unwise to take a delight in deceiving others.]

Pampinea's warning that wanton trickery implies 'poco senno' remains to raise questions about many of the ensuing stories and is echoed by Dioneo's remarks opening the story of Salabaetto:

> Io intendo di raccontarne una tanto più che alcuna altra dèttane da dovervi aggradire, quanto colei che beffata fur era maggior maestra di beffare altrui che alcuno altro che beffato fosse di quegli o di quelle che avete contate.
> [... The one I propose to relate should afford you greater pleasure than any of the others, inasmuch as it concerns the duping of a lady who knew far more about the art of deception

than any of the men or women who were beguiled in the tales we have heard so far.]

This motif of turning the tables, of using art to correct the misuse of art, organises both of these stories, as in various ways it organises the stories of Gulfardo (VIII, 1), of Zeppa and Spinelloccio (VIII, 8), and of Ciacco (IX, 8). All of these retributions reflect an understanding that the *inganno* is a double-edged instrument, useful to reverse another's cunning misconduct, but all the more dangerous if abused.

This growing discomfort is reflected in the third evidence of moral awareness – the uneasy receptions accorded by the ladies to the most questionable tricks, such as the scholar's of VIII, 7, and that of Bruno and Buffalmacco in VIII, 6. But the most striking evidence appears in the transfer of the crown from Emilia to Panfilo at the close of the Ninth Day's entertainment. In its context, the queen's allusion to 'amendment' seems to me something more than a formula of courtesy.

> Signor mio, gran carico ti resta, sì come è l'avere il mio difetto e degli altri che il luogo hanno tenuto che tu tieni, essendo tu l'ultimo ad emendare; di che Iddio ti presti grazia, come a me l'ha prestata di farti Re.
> [My lord, you are left with an arduous task, for since you are the last, you must make up for the failings of myself and my predecessors in the office to which you have now acceded. God grant you grace in this undertaking, as He has granted it to me in crowning you our king.]

This half-veiled expression of hope for an altered climate is sustained in the new king's first speech:

> Innamorate donne, la discrezion d'Emilia, nostra Reina stata questo giorno, per dare alcun riposo alle vostre forze, arbitrio vi diè di ragionare ciò che più vi piacesse; perchè, già riposati essendo giudico che sia bene il ritornare alla legge usata, e per ciò voglio che domane ciascuna di voi pensi di ragionare sopra questo, cioè di chi liberamente o vero magnificamente alcuna cosa operasse intorno a' fatti d'amore o d'altra cosa. Queste cose, e diciendo a faccendo, senza alcun dubbio gli animi vostri ben disposti a valorosamente adoperare accenderà, chè la vita nostra, che altro che brieve esser non può nel mortal corpo, sì

perpetuerà nella laudevole fama; il che ciascuno che al ventre solamente, a guisa che le bestie fanno, non serve, dèe non solamente disiderare, ma con ogni studio cercare et operare.

[Enamoured ladies, . . . our queen of today, Emilia, prudently left you at liberty to speak on whatever subject you chose, so that you might rest your faculties. But now that you are refreshed, I consider that we should revert to our customary rule, and I therefore want you all to think of something to say, tomorrow, on the subject of those who have performed liberal or magnificent deeds, whether in the cause of love or otherwise. The telling and the hearing of such things will assuredly fill you with a burning desire, well disposed as you already are in spirit, to comport yourselves valorously. And thus our lives, which cannot be other than brief in these our mortal bodies, will be preserved by the fame of our achievements – a goal which every man who does not simply attend to his belly, like an animal, should not only desire but most zealously pursue and strive to attain.]

The return from licence to law asserted here has reference ostensibly to the imposition of a theme on the last day's stories, but we are free to assume an ulterior stress which Panfilo does not formulate. And we are free to connect the telling phrases – 'a guisa che le bestie fanno' – with the theme of the preceding story and its concluding speech:

Deh! bestia che tu se', perchè hai tu guasti le tuoi fatti et i miei? [Pah! what an idiot you are! Why did you have to ruin everything for the pair of us?]

Panfilo's speech points towards the nobler accommodations of the Tenth Day, which replace egotistic with magnanimous manipulation. In some of the last day's stories (notably that of Natan – X, 3, and Tito and Gisippo – X, 8) a certain remoteness in the atmosphere and rigidity in the characterisation betray the imaginative strain involved in this replacement. Several stories are pushed back to a greater aesthetic distance, as though our scepticism towards unusual generosity needs to be dissipated by a more conventional and less 'realistic' world. Thus the art of necromancy, which has heretofore served as an instrument to beguile the gullible (VIII, 7; VIII, 9) is now presented as a legitimate art (X, 4; X, 9) which helps to effect the happy conclusion. Some readers may gather that they can believe in magnanimity when they believe in necromancy. Such readers are likely to find further support in the very last story, told by the subversive voice of Dioneo, where Griselda's incredible selflessness might be construed to parody all the preceding generosity, and where Dioneo's introductory summary – 'una matta bestialita' – seems to echo deliberately Panfilo's high-minded speech of the preceding day.

All of these bases for misgivings do not, however, seem to me sufficient reason to reject the genuine idealism of the Tenth Day, given the authentic life and dramatic vivacity which inform so many of its stories. Here the virtue of self-disciplined restraint, the capacity to accede, which emerged as a secondary quality earlier, tends almost to become the central virtue Thus the old king Carlo comes, in Robert Frost's phrase, to 'yield with a grace to reason' and so in varying ways come the abbot of Cligni, Mitridanes, Ansaldo and Giberto, Lisa, and the lovestruck Tito. But there remains in this last group of stories the element of creative invention operating to rearrange human relationships, and operating (in such figures as Ghino di Tacco, Natan, Gentile de' Carisendi, King Pietro, and the Saladin) if anything more felicitously than ever. Indeed these nine stories of magnanimity, in their juncture of a finer creativity and a higher self-denial, reach out to extend the formula of accommodation to a profounder principle of success. This firmer equilibrium, this wiser and more tender healing, deserves rather the term 'reconciliation'. In all these stories some kind of final union or reunion is reached within the context of a family, but I would want the term to suggest an ulterior reconciling as well, a deeper pacification between the subversive or the irresponsible, or the dangerous, and the harmony of the community. This surely is what we find in the most representative stories of the Tenth Day, concerned as they are with reconciling to society the lawlessness of Ghino, the lust of King Carlo, the futile infatuation of Lisa, the military exile of Torello, the inconvenient passions of an Ansaldo and a Tito.

In a sense, the action of the framing plot itself represents a coming to terms with the dangerous and anti-social force of pestilence. Here doubtless it would be inaccurate to speak of reconciliation with so blind and arbitrary an antagonist. But we may well note the parallels between the self-reliant resourcefulness of the ten young people and the artful improvisations of the characters they create. The temporary withdrawal from the plague-ridden city constitutes in its way an accommodation with horror. For the withdrawal is not a flight from the social order nor a permanent abdication, nor – what is first proposed – the impractical retreat of seven defenceless girls. The withdrawal amounts rather to the kind of pragmatic stratagem which the stories teach us to admire, and in the central role it assigns to the arts of music, dance, and taletelling, it emulates the creative artistry of the stories' solutions. The miniature community includes, moreover, its own subversive presence in the figure of Dioneo, and one of the most suggestive aspects of this frame plot lies in the way Dioneo's engaging improprieties are themselves absorbed. In the recurrent give-and-take over Dioneo's freedoms, both sides agree to compromise; he is allowed the licence to choose his stories freely and he is allowed to impose the equivocal topic of the Seventh Day, but he is not allowed to sing an indecorous song, and his ribaldry is permitted to influence, but not determine, the quality of the group's social intercourse. Dioneo is contained as the plague is averted, by the virtues of youthful good sense, moderate pragmatism, and a creative independence limited by 'leggiadra onestà'.

It is no wonder that Erich Auerbach misses in the pages of the *Decameron* that tragic realism which moves him and all readers in Dante's *Commedia*. The closing pages of the Boccaccio chapter in *Mimesis* are indeed magisterially severe; they make the strongest possible case against the immature range of the book's seriousness, with all the formidable weight of Auerbach's erudite and Olympian justice.

> It is precisely when Boccaccio tries to enter the realm of problem or tragedy that the vagueness and uncertainty of his early humanism becomes apparent. His realism – which is free, rich, and assured in its mastery of phenomenon, which is completely natural within the limits of the immediate style – becomes weak and superficial as soon as the problematic or the tragic is touched upon.[2]

That assessment is penetrating and damaging, but ultimately it may be a little misplaced. It is not surprising that the comic spirit of

---

[2] Erich Auerbach, *Mimesis: The Representation of Reality in Western Literature*, trans. Willard R. Trask (Princeton 1953), p. 231. [Reprinted above, pp. 69–81].

accommodation with its general patchwork resists by definition the
terrible confrontations of tragedy. The problematic in one form or
another is everywhere in the *Decameron*, as it must be somehow in
any narrative which has a plot. But it exists in most of the stories as
a peril in embryo to be gotten round. The implications of the peril
are not spelled out because their elaboration would destroy the
comic poise. It must be admired that when in certain stories (like the
romances of Ghismonda – IV, 1) the implications are made explicit,
then a certain theatrics of melodrama diffuses the hard clarity of the
potential tragic feeling. But in most of the book the shadow of pain
and loss remains metaphoric, synecdochic, until it is dispelled in
the triumphant brilliance of human wit. The basis for this triumph
lies in the wit's fundamental freedom, a freedom that Dante did not
recognise.

The *Decameron* is so exhilarating because it introduces us to a
certain pristine delight, a delight in the creative possibilities of
human experience. It teaches us the joy of contriving human situations and shaping human relationships when these things are done
with intelligence and artistry and style. It teaches this, as all art
teaches best, by example. It communicates the vital enthusiasm
which stems from making things happen. It asserts with *allegresse* the
liberty to play with the world as with a theatre, and to use its radical
theatricality to arrange and to heal. It demonstrates the artifices of
reconciliation as it makes shifts to mediate between licence and
restraint, passion and order, the self and the living community. It
fixes on the problem of Machiavelli, the struggle of craft to contain
the unruly, the struggle of bank and torrent, but it accepts that
struggle with a grace which is its own. It recognises like Pirandello's
plays the inescapable fraudulence of mortal affairs without aban-
doning its poise. Playful and worldly, unencumbered with mythology, it creates its own unmatchable myth: a faith in the esemplastic
pleasure of being human.

Thomas M. Greene

The *Decameron:*
The Marginality of
Literature

There has been no sustained examination of Boccaccio's reflections on the meaning of literature in the *Decameron*.[1] Probably because Boccaccio himself in his Introduction places his fiction in a garden, a critic of the stature of Charles Singleton[2] has spoken of the *Decameron* as escapist literature. The plague that necessitates the escape is seen to provide the literal alibi which makes any profound preoccupation with the world irrelevant.

If this were all, the *Decameron* would still be in itself a substantial cultural achievement. To quit the arena of history and voluntarily lapse into intransitive aesthetic fruition is perhaps a fundamental revision of St Augustine's Christian doctrine that the aesthetic experience be instrumental to man's spiritual ends; that literature, like the prophetic writings, be the nexus between man and God. But Boccaccio, paradoxically known as *Joannes tranquillitatum*, is radically unable to rest content with a formulation of an absolute and stable antithesis between the aesthetic order and historical existence, just as he is equally unable to accept the Christian view of a creative unity between literature and life. Far from being an evasion into frivolity, the retreat to the garden is a dramatic strategy which enables Boccaccio to reflect on history and to find, in this condition of marginality, of provisional separation from the historical structures, a place for secular literature.

Abridged by Robert S. Dombroski, from *University of Toronto Quarterly* XLII, 2 (Fall 1972), pp. 64–81; reprinted by permission of the author and the publisher, University of Toronto Press.

[1] All quotations are from *Il Decameron*, Nuova Edizione a cura di Charles S. Singleton, 2 vols. (Bari: Laterza, 1955).

[2] Charles S. Singleton, 'On Meaning in the *Decameron*', *Italica* XXI (1944), pp. 117–24.

Literature, in a real sense, is always written on the margin, where there is an emptiness, and in the desert, outside the city of life: the patristic writings are *marginalia* to the *Logos*, commentaries of literature across the desert to the City of God. Writing glosses is also the most conventional activity of the humanists. When Boccaccio, for instance, finished writing his *Decameron*, he compiled a mythological dictionary and footnotes to Dante.[3] But the *Decameron* itself is not an exegesis of the *Logos*, the way Dante's *Comedy* in many ways is. Yet its mode of being is one of marginality in relationship to existing literary traditions, cultural myths and social structures, to that which, in one word, we call history.

The dramatic relation between literary marginality and history does not have a clear-cut configuration in the *Decameron*, both because the world of history is seen as an absolute negativity, corroded by the plague, and because Boccaccio intentionally writes secular literature. In the absence of the *Logos* what meaning can literature possibly have? What is its function in this world of death? What does it accomplish in the neutral area Victor Turner calls 'betwixt and between'?[4]

Within this context, we must reject Auerbach's remarks that the *Decameron* never transcends the purely phenomenal aspects of historical experience and that it 'becomes weak and superficial as soon as the problematic or the tragic is touched upon'.[5] Boccaccio's primary concern is rather to reflect on the continuities and the discontinuities between literature and history. He clearly understood that literature always has a historical dimension, yet its historicity is deliberately impoverished, shrunk to the unserious and the banal. When literature fails in its impulse to capture and interpret the mass of empirical fragments in a significant historical structure, it brings itself into being as a degraded object of erotic mediation. The *Decameron* is, in many ways, a reflection of the essential discontinuity between

---

[3] *Il Commento alla Divina Comedia*, ed. Domenico Gueri (Bari: Laterza, 1918). The mythological dictionary, on which Boccaccio had been working for many years is, of course, *The Genealogy of the Gods*.

[4] Victor Turner, *The Forest of Symbols* (Ithaca: Cornell University Press, 1970), pp. 93 ff. See also Turner's *The Ritual Process* (Chicago: Aldine Publishing Company, 1969).

[5] Erich Auerbach, *Mimesis: The Representation of Reality in Western Literature*, trans. Willard R. Trask (New York: Anchor Books, 1957), p. 202. [Reproduced above, pp. 69–81.]

literature and historical reality and on the deliberate self-reduction
of literature to the ontological status of a 'thing'. . . .

Undoubtedly, the pastoral mode constitutes the primary strategy
of Boccaccio's fiction. He attempts to weave and subsume into the
continuity of the pastoral structure the various levels of the book.
The retreat of the *brigata* to the *locus amoenus* to tell stories, away from
the terror of the plague-stricken city, finds its counterpart in
the author's own distance from an inordinate love of the past. The
fluctus concupiscentiae which threatened his life was also averted by the
'piacevoli ragionamenti d'alcun amico' (Proemio, 3). Accordingly,
the *Decameron* is consistently traversed by a double pastoral; the
pastoral of the garden corresponds to historical chaos and the
pastoral of the author to erotic chaos. Since literary entertainment is
common to both of them, we shall speak of a pastoral of literature.
The pastoral of literature goes beyond the author's aesthetic recollection of the radical disorders of the flesh: it absorbs the readers
who must be distracted from the despair of love into its own rhetoric
of evasion. In all these cases, the absolute presupposition of the
literary garden is death; literature is seen as the positive vehicle by
which to transcend the experiment of death, by forgetting it.

The retreat into the garden is thus obviously an effort to cope
with loss and a conversion to life. Aptly enough, the *Decameron*
begins with a dramatic emblem of life, with reference to the anni-
versary of the Incarnation, the symbolic date of the beginning of the
world:

> Dico adunque che già erano gli anni della fruttifera Incarnazione
> del Figliuolo di Dio al numero pervenuti di milletrecento-
> quarantotto, quando nell'egregia città di Firenze, oltre ad ogni
> altra italica nobilissima, pervenne la mortifera pestilenza, la
> quale o per operazione de' corpi superiori o per le nostre inique
> opere da giusta ira di Dio a nostra correzione mandata sopra i
> mortali, alquanti anni davanti nelle parti orientali incominciata
> ... verso l'Occidente miserabilmente s'era ampliata. [Intro-
> duzione, 3 ff.]
> [I say, then, that the sum of thirteen hundred and forty-eight
> years had elapsed since the fruitful Incarnation of the Son of God,
> when the noble city of Florence, which for its great beauty excels
> all others in Italy, was visited by the deadly pestilence. Some say
> that it descended upon the human race through the influence of

the heavenly bodies, others that it was a punishment signifying
God's righteous anger at our iniquitous way of life. But whatever its cause, it had originated some years earlier in the East . . .
[and] unhappily spread westward, growing in strength as it
swept relentlessly on from one place to the next.]

While Boccaccio attempts to situate the plague in historical space
and time, he uses what in medieval rhetoric is a conventional *topos*
of exordium. The vernal equinox, occurring on the Feast of
the Annunciation, 25 March, is the emblem of the beginning of the
world, the fall of man and his redemption. The date stands at the
exact centre of the historic process and is a typological recapitulation
of the great events of salvation history. Conventionally, medieval
works of fiction begin with this typological *ab initio*. Most promi-
nently, the *Divine Comedy* and the *Canterbury Tales*, with significant
differences, employ this rhetorical device as a deliberate sign that
the book is a synopsis of the pilgrimage of human history and a way
of creatively participating in the *renovatio mundi*.

The use of this *topos* in the *Decameron* also transcends mere rhetorical interest. Its conceptual function is clear in the description of
the plague. The plague, rooted in the historical particularity of 1348,
is expanded by Boccaccio into a metaphor for the totality of history.
By describing it as a continuous east–west movement, Boccaccio is
applying to the plague the Christian interpretation of the historic
process. The doctrine of history as a spatial-temporal *translatio* from
east to west, patterned on the movement of the sun, with the Incarnation at its centre, is inverted in order to dramatise the totality of
history *sub specie mortis*. No redemption, therefore, is intended by the
reference to 25 March. The intensification of the fecundity engen-
dered by the Incarnation through the epithet 'fruttifera' only underscores the ironic disparity between the typological abstraction and
the reality of death. Typology, which is the prophetic interpretation
of the structure of history, is annihilated in the world of death.

It is this general vision of history as absolute death that compels
Boccaccio to search for a pastoral heterocosm and to claim for the
Decameron what might be called a metahistorical autonomy. The very
word *Decameron* has in itself a symbolic resonance that can hardly
escape students of the Middle Ages. The title is patterned, as has been
commonly acknowledged, on the medieval *Hexamera*, schematised
accounts of the succession of events in the history of the world which

were modelled on the six days of creation. Boccaccio secularises the title by significantly altering the six days into ten days. In medieval numerical symbolism, moreover, ten is the number of temporal perfection, of self-enclosed totality. With its claim to be a sufficient and coherent enclosure the *Decameron* is projected as an anti-world, an atemporal aesthetic garden juxtaposed to the history of mutability and death.

The secularisation of this seemingly privileged literary cosmos is stressed by two other correlated motifs. The first is the transition from the corrupt city of the world to the garden of literature which takes place through the Church. The Church is an enclosed garden, commonly described as the *hortus conclusus*, a Christian variant of the pastoral mode because it is interpreted as the prefiguration of the Garden of Eden. It is in the Church, in itself a liminal place, because it is the space where disjunctive experiences converge (time–eternity), that the *brigata* convenes and decides to escape to a pagan refuge, a *locus amoenus*. The garden of literature begins as a parody of institutional liminality.

Although this first detail reinforces our general interpretation that the *Decameron* is a provisional conversion to a secular order, I would not emphasize its importance if it were not part of a consistent pattern of changes of locale. At the end of the Sixth Day, the *brigata* moves into the 'valle delle donne', an idyllic landscape where on the Seventh Day, ironically, they discuss the deceits within the structure of marriage; the ordered idyllic background is a mockery of marriage, because marriage, ever since St Paul and the patristic allegorisations of the *Song of Songs*, is the sacramental figure of an immanent experience of edenic unity.

This second detail which emphasises the process of secularisation of the literary garden is more important because it brings into question the aim of this literary venture. While still in the Church, the *brigata* decides to structure itself as a hierarchical *communitas*, turning the experience in the *locus amoenus* into an ironic reversal of the city: 'Disse allora Ellissa: "*Veramente gli uomini sono delle femmine capo, e senza l'ordine loro rade volte riesce alcuna nostra opera a laudevole fine.* . . ."' [Introduzione, 21] ['Then Elissa said: "It is certainly true that man is the head of woman, and that without a man to guide us it rarely happens that any enterprise of ours is brought to a worthy conclusion."'] The biblical allusion in this passage, like its irony, is transparent. St Paul in the *Letter to the Ephesians* wrote of the mystical body of the Church as follows: 'Wives, be subject to your husbands, as to the Lord; for the *husband is the head of* the wife, even as Christ is the head of the Church.'[6] The Pauline doctrine of the mystical body, expressed through the marriage analogy, is uniformly used as the rationale of the body politic in the political theology of the Middle Ages. The irony, of course, consists in the fact that Boccaccio secularises St Paul's vision of order precisely in the Church, and thus goes into a double mockery of the city and the Church, which theoretically incarnate that order. The whole of the *Decameron* is, in a sense, a quest for order and unity achieved, somewhat ambiguously, through marriage. In the story of Griselda, marriage itself is the metaphor for the reinstatement of opposites to a prelapsarian and sacramental unity.

The Pauline allusion to the edenic myth of order and hierarchy makes manifest the utopian impulse of the escape and connects the escape dialectically with history: the literary experience is an anti-world, disengaged from history only in order to reflect from this marginal state both on itself and on the chaos of the world, and ultimately to return to the world with a vitally renewed apprehension of its structures. In this context, the irony we have stressed is not the simple irony of reversed meaning, but a systematic and all-encompassing mockery of the structures of society. The very chastity of the *brigata* in the *locus amoenus* is a brilliant parodic counterpoint to the frank sexuality of some of the tales, possibly a self-mockery of the storyteller, in the same way that the vision of order formulated in the Church is, as we have seen, a parody of the lawlessness and anarchy of the city.

The view of literature as a middle ground between two absences, between utopia and social structures, as a provisional retreat from the city in an atemporal space, is intensified by the *brigata's* ritual of return, at the end of the story-telling, to the Church where they had originally met. The *brigata* dissolves at the end because no finality is possible for the pastoral interlude.

There is, however, a radical disproportion between, on the one hand, this view of literature mediating between order and chaos and aspiring to be an alternate world and, on the other hand, the systematic degradation of the text to the role of a 'Galeotto'. The very subtitle of the *Decameron* reads 'prencipe Galeotto'. Boccaccio's own

---

[6] Ephesians 5, 22–3.

gloss on 'Galeotto fu il libro e chi lo scrisse' of *Inferno* V establishes a clear perspective on the inner form of the *Decameron*. Dante's Gallehault is the book in its function as intermediary of love between Paolo and Francesca, the dramatic equivalent of Pandarus in Chaucer's *Troilus and Cryseyde*. Aware of literature as an erotic snare – a commonplace of medieval romances – Boccaccio seems intent on assigning to this text the role of erotic mediator, and thus unmasking the threats and seductions of his own artifact.

The audience itself that Boccaccio chooses, the 'oziose donne', exposes the trap of the literary act: writing for the ladies, however coy a claim it can be, is concomitantly an admission of aestheticism and futility. Even St Augustine's aesthetic doctrine of the 'uti et frui' to which we have alluded in our preliminary remarks, is depreciated: women who will read the tales '*diletto* delle sollazzevoli cose in quelle mostrate et *utile consiglio* potranno pigliare. . . .' [Proemio, 5] ['will be able to derive, not only pleasure from the entertaining matters therein set forth, but also some useful advice. . . .'] The world of pornography is revealed as the essential structure which supersedes the impossible effort to write serious literature.

Boccaccio, therefore, clearly establishes in his Introduction a state of tension between two types of literary mediation, the erotic mediation and the prophetic mediation. What is the link between them? Is Boccaccio inviting us to read the text simultaneously on two levels? Or does the reduction of the text to the role of the procurer serve to question literature itself and its vital role in the reordering of the world? These questions are explored in some of the *novelle* to which we now turn.

The very first *novella* of the *Decameron* throws into focus several aspects of the relationship between typology and literature to which we have alluded. Critics have chosen to read it in ways that cripple and sterilise it. They have emphasised the credulity of the friar confessor, the shrewd bourgeois cynicism of the merchants, or more subtly, the 'arte di vivere' of the protagonist. The *novella*, to be sure, is so rich that it can sustain a great many commentaries. For our part, we shall try to read it as a deliberate metaliterary act, or more precisely, as a tale about the deception of language. Boccaccio, in other words, at the strategic and crucial moment of venturing into a universe of tales, stops to unveil the possible mystifications of literary creation and its link with history.

The preamble to the tale uncovers its thematic basis. There is, on the one hand, a statement on the flux and corruption of the temporal order; on the other hand, a formulation of the efficacy of prayer to mediate between the confusion of the world and the stability and unity of God. These two problems are pivotal to the inner structure of the tale because its thematic core, by contrast, is the attempt of the language of man to order and formalise the chaos of experience.

The tale is articulated in two ironic halves: in the first half, we are given an impersonal and objective account of the life of Ser Cepperello: through the rhetorical figure of *adynaton*, the reader is emphatically asked to discern in this figure an inversion of the human order. His total alienation is dramatised through the transparent emblems of his being, a foreigner, a usurer, a sodomite and sinner. The second half is a rewriting of the first, a palinode, so to speak, in the sense of a symmetrical ironic reversal of the first half. On the point of death, Ser Cepperello makes his confession, during which he goes into a consciously falsified retrospective account of his life.

The pretext for the confessional falsification is to simulate a Christian life in order to avoid exposing his hosts, two Florentine usurers, to public contempt. In a sense, the confession becomes a distorted self-creation, the last act of an existence of uninterrupted forgery and deception which, therefore, gives a paradoxical coherence to Ser Cepperello's whole life of blasphemy. The confession is an act of usury because it is an unreal production; Ser Cepperello reproduces a mere appearance, an unreal image of himself, and usury, in its primary symbolic value, is always the parody of *poiesis* because it is an emblem of imaginary unreal productivity. Ser Cepperello's verbal self-fabrication becomes an unquestionable reality to the friar who hears his confession. The friar, in turn, after the death of Ser Cepperello, builds a sermon on the false confession and proclaims him a saint. The self-loving man who was alien to the world and who lived in profanation of the world, is sanctified, and becomes, through his verbal disguise, the centre of cohesion and stability of men.

Clearly, Boccaccio is not interested in the problem of the triumph of perversion or in bourgeois cynicism except in a peripheral way. He is raising, at the heart of the tale, the problem of the truth of language, its proliferation and contagiousness, its uses and role within history. He underscores the ambiguity of the confession by using a double perspective on what Ser Cepperello says: from the

friar who is listening to the confession the description rapidly shifts
to the adjacent room where the two Florentine brothers are over-
hearing their verbal exchange and laughing at the lies of their friend.
More directly, during the sacramental confession, the problem of
truth is more explicitly raised:

> 'Padre mio, di questa parte mi vergogno di dirvene il vero,
> temendo di non peccare in vanagloria.' Al quale il santo frate
> disse: 'Dì sicuramente, ché il vero dicendo né in confessione né
> in altro atto si peccò già mai. . . .' [I, 1, p. 32]
> ['Father, I am loath to tell you the truth on this matter, in case
> I should sin by way of vainglory.' To which the holy friar
> replied: 'Speak out freely, for no man ever sinned by telling the
> truth, either in confession or otherwise.']

This allusion is picked up at the end of the confession, where the
verbal performance is linked to the problem of faith in language:

> Veggendo il frate non esser altro restato a dire a Ser Ciappelletto,
> gli fece l'assoluzione e diedegli la sua benedizione avendolo per
> santissimo uomo, sì come colui che pienamente credeva esser
> vero ciò che Ser Ciappelletto avea detto: e chi sarebbe colui che
> nol credesse, veggendo uno uomo in caso di morte confessan-
> dosi dir così? [I, 1, p. 36]
> [Perceiving that Ser Ciappelletto had nothing more to say, the friar
> absolved him and gave him his blessing. He took him for a very
> saintly man indeed, being fully convinced that what Ser Ciap-
> pelletto had said was true; but then, who is there who would not
> have been convinced on hearing a dying man talk in this
> fashion?]

The friar believes in the confession, and the people believe in the
holiness of Ser Ciappelletto, because there is a shared faith in the
Word that gives sense to words and sustains them. But to understand more fully the relationship between secular and prophetic
literature, we have to analyse the literary traditions which constitute
the fundamental structure of the tale. The tale is simultaneously a
parody of the hagiographic mode, of the confessional mode, and of
the religious sermon. It is because of the parody of these rhetorical
genres that we can consider the tale of a metaliterary act. Boccaccio
connects the two genres of hagiography and confession and exploits
them in order to raise the problem of the relationship between a

literary making of the self and history. The confessional element, probably because it appears as a sacrament, has been neglected as a literary form. Like most literary confessions, the tale gives, albeit in a grotesque inversion, an autobiographical review of the significant events of the life of Ser Ciappelletto from the vantage point of death; it shows the conversion of the hero and his reconciliation with history; finally it attests to the hero's explicit purpose of 'saving' his friends. The confession is a lie, and Boccaccio's distinctive aim is to degrade and parody the structural substance of the classical confessional form. The conversion, which is the crucial turning point in the novel of confession, is reduced in the tale to a mere change of name. Ser Cepperello is changed to Ser Ciappelletto, which means 'cappello, cioè ghirlanda'; the new name, in other words, does not dramatise an inner change; rather, it becomes an ironic allusion to the halo of the protagonist's future sainthood through Boccaccio's own etymologising. The hagiographic mode is the basis for the parody of the process of reconciliation of the self with history.

As has been shown, hagiography provides the blueprint for the dramatic process of the tale insofar as the story of Ser Ciappelletto is essentially structured on a saint's life. But hagiography also provides the historical dimension for various reasons. It makes possible the transition from the private confession to the world of history because it makes Ser Ciappelletto the centre of the community. More fundamentally, it constitutes in itself a typological structure. The *Legenda aurea*, on which the tale is patterned, is essentially the history of the chain of saints from Abel to the Last Judgement.[7] It is a typological mode because it defines the process of extrapolating from the multifariousness of historical reality the significant inner events of history. In its general structure, therefore, it provides the true history of the city of God on earth; its particular function in the tale is to provide the nexus between the self and the prophetic history of the world.

The sermon is the last rhetorical target of the tale. Language is again the chief performer. Because of the sermon, the focus is on language in its direct prophetic function: after the aesthetic self-dramatisation, patterned on typological and sacramental modes, language is used as a prophetic proclamation. The derivation of the

---

[7] Enrico de' Negri, 'The Legendary Style of the *Decameron*, *The Romantic Review*, XLII (1952), pp. 166–89. [Reproduced above, pp. 82–98.]

sermon from the confession shows how one rhetorical form is generated from another: in the tale, in effect, we move from confession to the sermon and finally to the popular legend in a continuous process of fictional excrescence. This rhetorical proliferation, and its effects on listeners, forcefully dramatise the inherent ambiguity of language. Like the plague, literary language is contagious; it has an autonomous and treacherous existence, organically multiplying itself and drawing into its inauthenticity the whole audience. There is the implication, furthermore, that a link between the self, history and God, through literary typology, may exist only if there is a faith in the *Logos*. But the whole tale subverts the literary forms in which a typological structure of reality is envisioned. It demystifies and empties of its faith-content the myth of the unity of literature and life.

In the preamble to the tale, as we pointed out, the emphasis falls on the general chaos of the world, followed by a statement on the efficacy of prayer to bridge the gap between God and man. At the basis of typological literature there is an impulse to counter this chaos. The function of secular literature, by contrast, seems to be one of consumption of literary artifacts, a way of placing these rhetorical modes within the general confusion and duplicity of life. Secular writing involves itself, furthermore, in this pervasive corrosion and, significantly, contracts itself into the unseriousness of a 'joke'. What remains intact and vital in the general dissolution of forms in the tale of Ser Ciappelletto is the trick played by him on the friar in order to save his Florentine hosts.

There is an obvious incongruity between the brilliance of the literary forms concocted and parodied and the pretext from which the fictional mechanism originates and which alone is preserved. Boccaccio subtly discloses how the domain of parodic literature is narrowed down to the 'trick'. The analogy with the problems set forth in the introduction is striking. Set in the context of death, literature is in the impossible situation of providing truth and permanence. It can only actively confront the mythic literary forms and dissolve itself into cheap and trivial uses.

It might be objected that this tale is, after all, not so serious, that its tone is unmistakably comical and, therefore, that it might even be difficult and artificial to superimpose similar responsibilities on a fundamentally funny story. To answer these imaginary objections, let us turn briefly to a consideration of these problems in the Sixth

Day of the *Decameron* and particularly to another *novella*, which is equally funny, that of Frate Cipolla (VI, 10).

The Sixth Day, in general, is very important in terms of our discussion because its declared focus is the uses of language; the tales gravitate around the concept of literary taste and literature as part of human leisure. In the tale of Cisti (VI, 2) language is endowed with efficacy to redeem Cisti in the social hierarchy in the sense that the language he uses with Geri levels the social differences between them. But Boccaccio prefaces this redemptive view of language with an apt description of Fortune not as the random, blind chance of the pagans, but an Intelligence of God. The world is given a metaphysical coherence, in other words, and within this context, language has its efficacy. The story of Frate Cipolla, on the contrary, amplifies the problems of the inherent duplicity of language treated in the tale of Ser Ciappelletto. In a sense, it supplements the first tale because the verbal illusionism, this time, comes from a friar. . . .

Boccaccio involves the whole world of rhetoric in his tale and discloses the absurdity of metaphoric language in his parody. The friar, in fact, 'sì ottimo parlatore e pronto era, che chi conosciuto non l'avesse, non solamente un gran rettorico l'avrebbe estimato, ma avrebbe detto esser Tullio medesimo o forse Quintiliano.' [VI, 10, p. 25] ['he was such a lively and excellent speaker, that anyone hearing him for the first time would have concluded, not only that he was some great master of rhetoric, but that he was Cicero in person, or perhaps Quintilian.'] The world of rhetoric is carefully thematised in the tale: the sermon turns into a brilliant exposure of the possibilities for deception in fictive language. When Frate Cipolla manipulates his listeners by the sermon, the focus falls upon the parody of the metaphoric language in which religious mysteries are represented:

Egli primieramente mi mostrò il dito dello Spirito santo così intero e saldo come fu mai, ed il ciuffetto del serafino che apparve a san Francesco, ed una dell'unghie de' gherubini, ed una delle coste del Verbum-carofàtti-allefinestre. . . . [VI, 10, p. 31]
[First of all he showed me the finger of the Holy Ghost, as straight and firm as it ever was; then the forelock of the Seraph that appeared to Saint Francis; and a cherub's fingernail; and one of the side-bits of the Word-made-flash-in-the-pan.]

If metaphor attempts to unite the separate elements of the world and discover the fundamental identity of things, in this context it is an absurdity, because its literalness annihilates the symbolic language of religious experience. As in the case of the tale of Ser Ciappelletto, social cohesion is not affirmed by verbal acrobatics of a mystifier, because the community, by virtue of its shared faith in God, antecedes the experience of language. On account of this fundamental futility, the sermon readily dissolves into cant.

Boccaccio, furthermore, exposes the mechanism of deception in language by the ingenious interaction of a subplot in which the friar's servant, Guccio Imbratta, attempts to seduce a maid of the inn where they live. The dramatic function of this subplot is clear: by the confrontation Boccaccio creates a doubling of plots, each mirroring and dissolving the other; by crude eroticism, it exposes the master's own seduction of the people in the Church. We might even point out how this master–slave relationship, which is part of a more complex dialectic in the *Decameron*, is anticipated in the very introduction to the Sixth Day in which the *brigata* and their servants mirror each other in the act of storytelling. The self-reflection implies a suspension of social hierarchy at the moment in which they are involved in the marginal world of books.

The tale of Frate Cipolla, like that of Ser Ciappelletto, comes into being from an extraliterary impulse. At the heart of the tale there is the trick that two friends play on the friar by substituting charcoal for a feather. Throughout the sermon they remain dissociated from the people, outside the seduction of language but fascinated by the friar's cunning. The trick of the two friends and their admiration for the sermon dramatise the whole process of literary creation, from the cheap reality of its intent to the mystification of representation. At the same time, their detached perspective on the fiction and Frate Cipolla's theatricality mark the degradation of language as prophecy to language as sheer performance.

In the light of this *novella*, it is time to return to the imaginary objections which we formulated after the discussion of Ser Ciappelletto. This story is also a flagrant joke, as funny as the story of Ser Ciappelletto: we cannot minimise it. How do we account, then, for the comical tone of the two tales? In a sense, Boccaccio has internalised the possible response of the reader in the two tales, first through the two Florentine brothers, secondly through the two tricksters. But the fun is also the storytellers'. Their fun is the index of the ambiguous fascination of the storytellers, because they are midway between detachment and involvement with the artifices of reality that they create. The verbal performances are temptations because they are possible ways of being for the *Decameron* itself, in the same sense that Francesca, for instance, is a temptation to Dante because she is Dante's possible self. Furthermore, Boccaccio intentionally degrades the status of the tales to the frivolous and idle because by being jokes they can question all reality around them without themselves claiming a privileged mode of being. What is involved in all of this is the whole nature of the playful and comical in the *Decameron*. Boccaccio devotes the entire Seventh Day to the motif of the joke or 'beffa'. These jokes are ludic moments, literally illusions, experiences in which not only is reality doubted, but in which illusion and reality inextricably overlap, an absolute space where the real and the imagined, the inner and the outer, are systematically confused. . . .

Most of the tales we have examined revolve around the opposition between prophecy and literature. Literature was the negation of prophecy, its mockery. In a sense, literature seems to be possible precisely when prophecy fails or to indicate the failure of prophecy. In the process of subversion of mythic forms, literature involves itself in the general failure; its self-annihilation is the index of its privilege and its specificity. Yet, when Boccaccio compares in the conclusion sacred and secular forms of scriptures, the opposition can no longer be sustained because there is a universal levelling by death. Along with the assertion of his own instability, Boccaccio's final words are a statement on the ontological instability of the world: 'confesso nondimeno, le cose di questo mondo non avere stabilità alcuna, ma sempre essere in mutamento, e così potrebbe della mia lingua essere intervenuto. . . .' [Conclusione, 327]. ['I will grant you, however, that the things of this world have no stability, but are subject to constant change, and this may well have happened to my tongue. . . .']

The *Decameron* began with the plague and ends with this vision of death. Literature, because of this, is explicitly self-consolatory, an elegy for the precariousness of the literary experience itself: 'nobilissime giovani', Boccaccio writes, 'a consolazione delle quali io a così lunga fatica messo mi sono. . . .' [Conclusione, 323]. ['Noble young ladies, for whose solace I undertook this protracted labour. . . .']

Written with the assumption that the social foundations were shaking and that there is no firm ground in the moral cosmos, the *Decameron* fails to be a lasting sacrosanctum and is equally insufficient to order life. Unable to be either, in the fact of metaphysical annihilation, it contracts under Boccaccio's reductive impulse to the necessary role of the devalued and the useless: a perennial marginality. In this tension, the *Decameron* stands halfway between the universe of plenitude and sense of the Divine Comedy and the programmatic non-sense of the *Orlando Furioso*. . . .

Giuseppe Mazzotta

Selected Bibliography

Reference

Zambrini, F. – Bacchi Della Lega, A., *Bibliografia boccaccesca. Serie delle edizioni delle opere di Giovanni Boccaccio*, Bologna: Romagnoli, 1875.
Traversari, G., *Bibliografia boccaccesca*, I: *Scritti intorno al Boccaccio e alla fortuna delle sue opere*, Città di Castello: Lapi, 1907.
Branca, V., *Linea di una storia della critica al 'Decameron'*, Roma: Dante Alighieri, 1939.
——— *Boccaccio: The Man and his Works*, New York: New York University Press, 1973.
Caretti, L., 'Guida al Boccaccio', in *Studi Urbinati*, XXVI, 2 (1952).
The most complete and critically accurate account of Boccaccio's life to date is V. Branca's biographical introduction to *Tutte le opere di Giovanni Boccaccio*, I, Milano: Mondadori, 1967.

Criticism

Baratto, M., *Realtà e stile nel 'Decameron'*, Vicenza: Neri Pozza, 1970.
Battaglia, S., *Giovanni Boccaccio e la riforma della narrativa*, Napoli: Liguori, 1969.
Billanovich, G., *Restauri boccacceschi*, Roma: Ist. Graf. Tiburino, 1947.
Booth, W., 'Two Stories from the *Decameron*', in *The Rhetoric of Fiction*, Chicago: The University of Chicago Press, 1961.
Cottino-Jones, M., *An Anatomy of Boccaccio's Style*, Napoli: Cymba, 1967.
Croce, B., 'Il Boccaccio e Franco Sachetti', in *Poesia popolare e poesia d'arte*, Bari: Laterza, 1933.
Fido, F., 'Il sorriso di Messer Torello (*Decameron* X, 9)', *Romance Philology*, 23 (1969), pp. 154–71.
Fontes, A., 'Le theme de la *beffa* dans le *Decameron*', in Rochon, A., et al., *Formes et significations de la 'Beffa' dans la litterature italienne de la Renaissance*, Paris: Universite de la Sorbonne Nouvelle, 1972.
Getto, G., *Vita di forme e forme di vita del 'Decameron'*, Torino: Petrini, 1958.

Hauvette, H., *Boccace: Etude biografique et littéraire*, Paris: Colin, 1914.

Lee, A. C., *The Decameron: Its Sources and Analogues*, New York: Haskell, 1967 [first published, London, 1909].

Neri, F., 'Il disegno ideale del *Decameron*', in *Storia e poesia*, Torino: Chiantore, 1936.

Neuschäfer, H.-J., *Boccaccio und der Beginn der Novelle*, München: Wilhelm Fink, 1969.

Quaglio, A. E., *Scienza e mito nel Boccaccio*, Padova: Liviana, 1967.

Russo, L., *Letture critiche del 'Decameron'*, Bari: Laterza, 1970.

Sapegno, N., 'Giovanni Boccaccio', in *Storia letteraria del Trecento*, Milano–Napoli: Ricciardi, 1963.

Scaglione, A. D., *Nature and Love in the Late Middle Ages*: An Essay on the Cultural Context of the Decameron, Berkeley and Los Angeles: University of California Press, 1963.

Schiaffini, A., 'Il *Decameron*', in *Tradizione e poesia nella prosa d'arte italiana dalla latinità medievale a Giovanni Boccaccio*, Roma: Edizioni di 'Storia e Letteratura', 1943.

Sinicropi, G., 'La struttura del segno linguistico nel *Decameron*', in *Studi sul Boccaccio* 9 (1976).

Tripet, A., 'Boccace et son clerc amoureux', in *Bibliothèque d'Humanisme et Renaissance*, XXIX, 1 (1967), pp. 7–20.

Todorov, T., *Grammaire du Décaméron*, The Hague: Mouton, 1969.

Notes
on the Contributors

ROBERT S. DOMBROSKI, formerly with the University of Chicago, is now Associate Professor of Italian at the University of Connecticut. He is the author of *Introduzione allo studio di Carlo Emilio Gadda* (1974) and various essays on modern and contemporary Italian Literature.

UGO FOSCOLO (1778–1827), prominent poet, essayist and literary critic, is famous for his autobiographical novel *Le Ultime Lettere di Jacopo Ortis* (1798) and the long–short poem *I Sepolcri*. His many writings are available in a number of editions and translations.

FRANCESCO DE SANCTIS (1817–83), the most distinguished Italian literary critic of the nineteenth century, taught at the University of Naples from 1871 and was three times Minister of Public Education. His chief work, *Storia della Letteratura Italiana*, was begun in 1870.

VITTORE BRANCA, Professor of Italian at the University of Padua and Director of the Fondazione Cini, is one of the most distinguished interpreters of the Italian Trecento. He has written and edited numerous books and articles.

GIUSEPPE PETRONIO, Professor of Italian and Dean of the Faculty of Letters at the University of Trieste, has written, among many books, an excellent volume on Enlightenment culture, *Parini e l'illuminismo lombardo* (1961) and another on Italian Romanticism, *Il Romanticismo* (1960).

VICTOR ŠKLOVSKIJ, a prominent exponent of Russian formalism, has published numerous works as a critic and novelist. His recent criticism includes a collection of essays on Tolstoy (1963) and a book on the modes and structures of fiction (1959).

ERICH AUERBACH (1892–1960) was Professor of Romance Philology at the University of Istanbul, taught at Princeton and was Sterling Professor of Romance Languages at Yale University. He wrote several important studies of Dante and Vico. His major work, *Mimesis: the Representation of Reality in Western Literature* was published in 1946 (English translation in 1953).

ENRICO DE' NEGRI, widely known for his interpretations of Hegel and Luther, was Professor of Italian at Columbia and at the University of California, Berkeley. His latest book is *La Teologia di Lutero* (1967). He is currently Professor of Philosophy at the University of Rome.

ALBERTO MORAVIA is one of the most popular of contemporary Italian novelists. His many essays on literature appear in *Man as an End: A Defence of Humanism* (1965).

THOMAS M. GREENE, Professor of Comparative Literature at Yale University and Chairman of that department, has written a book on the epic, *The Descent from Heaven: A Study in Epic Continuity* (1963), another on Rabelais, *Rabelais: A Study in Comic Courage* (1970), and essays on Dante, Shakespeare, and Spenser, among others.

GIUSEPPE MAZZOTTA, formerly with the University of Toronto, is now Associate Professor of Italian Literature and Curator of the Fiske Collection at Cornell University. He has written a Monograph on Dante and is currently writing a book-length essay on the *Decameron*.

EVERY KID CAN WIN

EVERY KID CAN WIN

Terry Orlick & Cal Botterill

nh Nelson-Hall • Chicago

Library of Congress Cataloging in Publication Data

Orlick, Terry.
  Every kid can win.

  Bibliography: p.
  1. Sports for children. I. Botterill, Cal, joint
author. II. Title.
GV709.2.O74 1975   796'.D19'22   74-19385
ISBN O-88229-194-7

Manufactured in the United States of America

For children in sport,
and especially for children
out of sport.

Contents

Foreword   ix
Preface   xii
Acknowledgments   xv

1   What You Can Do for Kids   1
2   The Right Start   6
3   Why Eliminate Kids?   15
4   What About Winning?   27
5   What's Best for Kids?   38
6   What do You Feel?   57
7   What Can We Expect
    from Kids?   93
8   It's Gotta Be Fun   105
9   What about Girls?   119
10 Making Sport a Better Place
    for Kids   134
11 Every Kid Can Win   156

Appendix A   The Child in Sport—
             Recommendations   161
Appendix B   Minor Hockey—
             Recommendations   164
Appendix C   Desirable Athletic
             Competitions—
             Recommendations   166
Appendix D   What about Sportsmanship?   168
Appendix E   Girls in Sport,
             Children's Attitudes—
             Recommendations   173
Appendix F   Girls in Sport,
             Elementary Curriculum—
             Recommendations   176

             Bibliography   178
             Index   185

Foreword

Thank heaven for men who have grown up without forgetting what it's like to be a kid. Not only do Terry Orlick and Cal Botterill remember but they have combined insight and judgment to produce suggestions to alleviate a problem faced by boys and girls all over this continent.

The problem relates to how we view sport and its value to growing children. It will be to the point to identify several persisting beliefs that this book should help to change. These beliefs are seldom voiced but our actions bear evidence of their existence.

The first is the idea that children play sports to entertain adults. Listen to adults talking at kids' games in any sport. You will hear comments like, "Why don't more parents come out?" or, "These kids deserve support, I never miss a game!" Surely sports and games are worthy of playing in their own right. Adults would laugh at the idea that they "deserve support" in the form of the family watching them curl, golf, bowl, or ski. Why should it be different for kids?

The second persisting idea is that games and sports for kids must be organized and controlled by adults if they are to be of real value. Adults are certainly needed, but what is also needed is direct input from the kids themselves to determine what is really appropriate for them. There are also large bodies of knowledge now available in child growth and development, psychology, and sociology, from which ideas must be drawn if more appropriate forms of sports organization for kids are to be developed. Again, this book makes a substantial contribution toward that end.

A third persisting and dangerous idea is that kids are miniature adults. If this view is accepted then it is not surprising that men insist on dressing kids up in replicas of big league uniforms and require them to play in facilities, with equipment, and under rules which are, to a large measure, inappropriate.

Finally, there is the myth that the real value in sport lies in learning to be a winner, that people can be divided into winners and losers, and that sport is a way to make sure you (or your kids) end up in the right group. This book should help us to see the error of this myth. Victory and defeat, as mere outcomes or products, are indeed a pair of impostors as Kipling pointed out long ago. Victory at any cost or against an ill-prepared opponent must be an imposter! Defeat despite one's best efforts cannot be cause for shame. The person one should compete with in life is one's self.

If victory and defeat are imposters the important values of sport are in the processes that kids and adults undergo while they take part. Terry and Cal make a powerful case for shifting the focus of kids' sports away from the narrow concerns of the products, victory or defeat, to the larger concerns of the processes involved. They have indeed remembered the boy in themselves and listened to the kids of today as well as to concerned adults who recognize the need for change.

Children learn most by coming to grips with the world around them, by developing their minds, bodies and emotional equipment through real-life encounters with other people, and with the many environments in which they must live. In a mass, urban, highly technological society children find it almost impossible to get the kinds of experiences they need if they are to become competent, confident adults. Sports and games emerge as one medium, among others, through which such growth can take place. The needs are real. They are present in all kids. If we can find ways to improve sporting environments so that Every Kid Can Win, we will have done something of importance.

Murray F. Smith
University of Alberta

Preface

Over the past several years there has been a tremendous upsurge in the amount of criticism levied at little and minor league sport. While people are quick to criticize, they seldom offer positive suggestions concerning alternative ways of doing things. You rarely hear about the good things that coaches are doing with children. Although we would be the first to admit that we don't have all the answers, we feel that we have some promising positive directions for redesigning children's sport for success.

Our focus in this book is not so much on performance as on the performer. More precisely our concern is with what is in the best interest of each individual child. There have been numerous books and clinics devoted to improving performance (e.g., learning skills, drills, training techniques, strategies, etc.) but none to our knowledge which have focused on the social and psychological well-being of the performers, in this case, the children. This is our focus.

People generally recognize that positive sports experiences can make a significant contribution to the quality of life, and they feel that every boy and girl should have the opportunity to participate in and to enjoy sports. However, it is becoming increasingly evident that sports are not automatically good for children as was once supposed. Rather, sports can influence a child in either a positive or a negative direction depending upon the quality of the exposure. Many people are concerned about giving the child the best possible exposure in sport. It is because we share this concern and feel that we have something worthwhile to offer that we have written this book. It is our hope that this book will cause you to think, to draw upon your own experiences, and to somehow guide your behavior as a result. In this way the children will really be the winners.

In May 1973, a Canadian national conference and workshop was held which focused specifically on the child in sport and physical activity. A few years prior to this, the American Association of Health, Physical Education, and Recreation published a special joint-committee report on the desirability of athletic competition for children of elementary school age. Although some valuable information has come out of these conferences, to date they haven't proven to be of much practical value. Things continue to go on in much the same manner as they have gone on for years. A major problem seems to be that information and positive suggestions never get to the people who need them. The people to whom the child is directly exposed—the thousands of little league and minor league coaches, the parents, the teachers, the officials, the people who run the community leagues—these are the most influential change agents in children's sport. Yet, they seldom, if ever, receive the information concerning the children. This book is a direct attempt to bridge that gap.

Acknowledgments

We would like to thank the many people who, over the years, have created learning environments for us, and who in many ways contributed to our thoughts and lives—

——the numerous people who played a vital role at the University of Alberta;

——our many colleagues as students, athletes, teachers, researchers, and coaches;

——all the priceless kids and young people in our lives whom we came to know through teaching, coaching, interviewing and just living;

——Len Wankel and John Partington for their excellent reviews and comments on the original manuscript;

ACKNOWLEDGMENTS

——the Orlick and Botterill families where it all began; and
——especially Cathy and Doreen who enrich our lives and mean so much.

We appreciate you all and hope that we can somehow make all your contributions worthwhile.

1

What You Can Do for Kids

When it comes to kids, we are all on the same team—that is, trying to do what is best for kids and trying to somehow contribute to the quality of their lives. Most of us devote countless numbers of hours and sometimes our lives to (our) kids. Unfortunately, despite our good intentions we sometimes fail to act in the child's best interest.

Whether we are parents, coaches, officials, or administrators involved in children's sport, we can and do have a direct impact on how kids view sport and how sports affect kids. Collectively, we determine whether youngsters come out, whether they have a good experience, and even whether they drop out. In essence, we determine the quality of the exposure in kids' sports. Parents and coaches in particular play a

1

critical role in influencing kids' sport-related expectancies and behavior. Together, we are largely responsible for what the child expects from sports and what is expected from the child in sport.

Parents are often responsible for whether a young child goes out for a sport, and coaches are usually responsible for whether kids enjoy sports and whether they benefit from them. Both have a tremendous impact on the kinds of behavior kids display both in and out of sports. Rules which are set up by administrators and organizing committees, along with how these rules are carried out by officials (or supervisors), also have a direct effect on kids' behavior.

Children learn by the example you set and by the way you respond to what they do. A child's values, attitudes, and ways of behaving are most often learned from those people who are most important to him/her. A child is continually taking the attitudes and emulating the behavior of people he admires or depends on and people who in some sense control him. Parents are the most significant models of behavior during the child's early years. Children frequently reproduce not only the behavior patterns of their parents but also such things as mannerisms, gestures, and voice inflections which the parents have never attempted to teach directly.

Children seem to learn more from what you are (your behavior) than from what you say. Attitudes and values seem to be more communicable through indirect, rather than direct, means. In other words, deeds are more important than words in that your actions speak louder than your words. For example, if you say sportsmanship and abiding by the rules are important and you behave by screaming and swearing at the referee, it is your behavior which will have the greatest impact on the kids in terms of their learning about values in sport.

These same principles hold true for the coach and older athletes who, outside the family, probably have the most important influence on kids in terms of their attitudes, expectancies, and actions related to sport. The first contact most kids have with organized sport and a "coach" is through some sort of community league team. The minor league coach is often the first male authority figure, other than the father, to whom the child is exposed for an extended period of time. Many kids will look up to the coach and may try to emulate his behavior. By his words and deeds the kids will learn what is important—whether it is sportsmanship, cooperation, or winning at all costs. As a coach, what you are, what you do, and what you say can have extremely important effects on the child's behavior for years to come—both in and out of sport.

A child's behavior is primarily under the control of consequences or reinforcements. Reinforcements can be thought of as rewards or any kind of pay-off that the child considers to be worthwhile. There are countless numbers of reinforcements which have an effect on, or shape, a child's behavior. Because we are social beings and require the support of others, various forms of social approval are extremely effective reinforcers and incentives—especially for children. Some common examples of social approval include: (1) praise or verbal comments indicating approval, encouragement, commendation, or achievement such as, that's good, you are doing fine, you are playing well, you

3

make me happy; (2) affection or positive physical contact such as embracing, patting, holding an arm or hand, nearness, sitting on lap; (3) facial attention such as smiling, eye contact, winking, and so forth. Other influential rewards include such things as fun, improved performance, sense of accomplishment, success, material rewards (e.g., candy, money, tokens), and so on.

The tendency for a child to behave in a certain way is a function of past reinforcement along with the expectation of future reinforcement for behaving in a similar manner. A child may also exhibit a particular behavior as a result of seeing someone else being rewarded for engaging in that behavior. If you are a significant person in the child's life, which is probably the case, then not only are you a model for the child, but you also have control over the reinforcements which are important to the child. It is because of these factors that you have considerable control over (your) children's behavior. Through your day-to-day contact with kids you have the capacity to establish, maintain, or modify their behavior.

You can have the greatest impact on children's behavior by providing both a model and reinforcement for a given behavior. Once children learn that rewards are dependent upon certain kinds of behavior (e.g., good clean fair play as opposed to fighting and foul play), they will tend to behave in this way because they know it is in their own best self-interest to do so. Peers can also serve effectively as models to establish and maintain behavior patterns. For example, a coach can pick out a child who does exhibit positive behavior (e.g., honesty, cooperation, concern for others, etc.) and praise him in front of the others for his admirable behavior. In this way children quickly learn what is desirable behavior by seeing that it has been reinforced. If parents and coaches cooperate in their efforts by rewarding the same kinds of positive behavior, it will rapidly become a part of the child's lifestyle. It should now be evident that you can play a significant role in shaping (your) kids' behavior and direction, as well as their sporting future. It is essential that you recognize your power and do everything possible to best serve the kids. Your first major responsibility is to insure that kids get "the right start," which is the focus of the next chapter.

2

The Right Start

The school day was almost over when the gym teacher walked into the children's classroom and said, "Anyone who wants to play soccer, baseball, or floor hockey can meet me in the gym right after school." There were some elated sounding "yippees" along with the silent shuffling of paper. The bell rang. Billy, still excited, jumped up and said to Johnny, "Hurry up, let's go to the gym!" Johnny replied, "Nah, I hate sports. Anyway I'm going home to watch TV." Each boy left the classroom and went his separate way.

Why do some children react like Billy and some like Johnny? Our contention is that it is largely a function of a child's initial exposure to sports. Billy was lucky enough to be introduced with the right start, while Johnny never had that opportunity.

Basic orientation toward experience is established early in life. If children adopt rewarding activity patterns as a part of their lifestyle during the early school years, they will tend to retain this orientation through adolescence and adulthood. However, the failure to establish positive patterns of active interest in childhood and youth may result in significant gaps which persist throughout life.

Consequently, children's first sports experiences are vitally important. If their initial exposures are positive and enjoyable they may become "hooked" for life. On the other hand, if these experiences are negative and unenjoyable, they can be "turned off" for a long time. Whether the child does have an early positive exposure to sports and physical activities is largely dependent upon minor league coaches, who collectively come into contact with millions of children, along with the parents and teachers of these same children.

The most important thing you can do to insure that the child gets the right start is to see that the child's participation is fun and enjoyable above everything else. The simple fact is that if children are not receiving some sort of positive rewards from their participation, they will not continue. Having fun, playing, and being a part of the action can be extremely rewarding for kids. In fact, interviews with young kids who played organized sports revealed that "fun" and "action" were the things they liked best about sports. A typical response from an eight-year-old when asked why he wants to play sports is "I like it. It's fun!"

As we begin to move away from this fun orientation, kids indicate that they have progressively more negative and unhappy experiences. For example, kids indicate that what they dislike most about sports include such things as "getting yelled at for doing something wrong, getting hit or kicked, dirty play, sitting on the bench, feeling like a failure." Community leagues and school teams often make reinforcement (e.g., social approval, praise, encouragement) dependent upon successful performance before children have had adequate preparation.

In the beginning, if children are evaluated at all, it should be on an individual basis. If a child has made advancements, he should be rewarded and praised rather than being made to feel like a failure by judging him against some predetermined standard, particularly when the standard is unattainable.

If children feel they are failing, they quickly become discouraged. Failure certainly is not rewarding for anyone, while success is a great reinforcer. However, success and failure are dependent upon the standards which are set for the children. Consequently, the standards or goals should be structured, or restructured, for success.

The most important factor determining whether the child feels he has succeeded or failed is not how high or low the standard is set, but the difference between his actual performance and the standard. In other words, the goals set must be achievable. By setting unrealistically high goals you almost guarantee that the child will feel a sense of failure. If standards approximate the top performances, which they usually do, most children are bound to experience repeated failure because of the continuous gap which exists between where they are now and where they think they are supposed to be; for example, the best. Regardless of

8

how hard they try, most children will never close the gap (see C. Sherif and Rattray, 1973).

One way to establish realistic and attainable goals for children is to have them compete against their own past performance. In this way, the goals can be set near enough to their actual performance level to insure that any amount of individual improvement will be experienced as success. This will assure frequent success experiences. As the child progresses, goals can be readjusted to meet specific individual needs and still be kept within reach.

Coaches have often minimized or ignored the critical role which failure, or expectancy of failure, plays in shaping a child's behavior in a sports setting. The child operates on his expectations of success or failure. Activities are dropped or accepted with enthusiasm depending upon the degree to which the child expects he can attain the goals.

Children are not going to (and should not) waste their time *failing* when they have the option to become involved in more positive, life-oriented enterprises. For example, both self-improvement and fun are important goals within every child's reach. It is particularly important in the beginning when you are establishing sports attitudes and behavior that these goals be paramount.

If we remove the sense of accomplishment or the fun element we will also remove the majority of the children.

To insure that sports participation will become an important part of the child's total life experience, it is best to give the child continuous reinforcement and encouragement during the initial exposures to sport. In other words, the parent, coach, or supervisor should go out of the way to make the experiences rewarding for the "beginner." This can be done by making sure the activity itself is always enjoyable, by setting attainable goals and by giving the child continuous social approval. For example, when teaching a child to catch a ball, you might (a) use a big softball which is easy to catch, (b) gently throw or lob the ball to the child, (c) stand close enough to guide the ball for a successful catch, (d) be free with your encouragement and approval (e.g., good catch, good try, that's coming along well), (e) be quick to point out individual improvement, (f) introduce laughter, variety, and fun into the experience (e.g., throwing the ball under the legs, chasing and being chased, rolling, tumbling, laughing, and thoroughly enjoying the activity).

Once the behavior has been established, the activity itself should be rewarding enough to keep the child coming back as long as every now and then he or she achieves a goal, has fun, or gets a pat on the back. You can now be more selective, giving praise and encouragement from time to time. If you continue to reward every attempt after a skill is well-learned or a behavior well-established, the value of the reward will tend to become less meaningful. It is helpful to introduce variety in rewards and essential to observe and become aware of those rewards which are most meaningful to particular children.

The type of reward, as well as the frequency of reward, will depend on its value to the child and the importance of the person giving the reward. However, the general rule to follow is to reward a great deal in the beginning when establishing a new skill or behavior and to gradually reward less as the behavior or skill becomes better developed. The ultimate goal should be to have the child value the activity for itself and the rewards inherent within the activity.

We have the opportunity to influence every child either positively or negatively toward physical activity in the home, school, and community. Each child can experience the value or drudgery of physical activity. The groundwork which leads to the love and pursuit of physical activities, as well as the basis for many physical skills, is established during the childhood years. This does not mean that children cannot or do not begin to appreciate different forms of physical activity after childhood, but it does imply that what happens to the child during the early years can have a significant impact for years to come.

Many young children begin sports because their parents, or other significant people, provide either the example or the encouragement. Often the parents are, or have been, active themselves or just feel that sports are good for their children. When people around the child are interested in and enjoy activities, the child falls readily into the pattern. Without really being aware of it, the parents set up an environment which is conducive to participation. By talking about sport, by watching it, by enjoying it themselves, the stage is set. The kid is exposed, encouraged, and subsequently reinforced. The child is not, or should not be told that he or she must participate—the child should make that decision. If the family sports environment and outside sports environment (e.g., school) have operated positively on the child, he will want to participate and will not in any way have to be forced to go out.

11

EVERY KID CAN WIN

Once a child decides to participate in a sport, he is generally exposed to a coach or activity-instructor of some kind. Many of these people think that their only function is to teach baseball, or hockey, or soccer, or gymnastics, or skiing, or swimming—but if they are involved with the child in sport, their function is far more important. It is to expose each individual child to an exciting, fun-filled world of sports. Their function is to be concerned with the total welfare of each child and to act accordingly. In this regard, to give kids a positive initial exposure to sports is infinitely more important than to win every game or every meet. To win the game and lose the child is a totally unworthy sacrifice. This is not the big league and these are not miniature professionals. You must always keep the child's interest above the winning interest. This is the foundation of the child's sporting life and physical activities will be accepted with enthusiasm or dropped like a hot potato, depending on these initial experiences. Consequently, you must use every means possible to insure that the child's first exposures are positive ones.

In attempting to make sure that these initial exposures are positive, you should note that when a child is just beginning to learn skills, competition can prove to be detrimental to performance. Consequently, if you place children in competitive situations too early, before skills are proficient, they will generally perform more poorly. An audience is also apt to be distracting to little children during the initial stages of learning. Research has established that when a child is still struggling to learn skills, the additional burden of being placed in front of an audience and being pitted against a rival is bound to have a negative effect on the child's performance and perhaps the child himself. This negative effect may be magnified if the child is highly anxious as a result of being placed in a competitive situation that "really counts" when he is as yet incapable of meeting the demands of the situation. However, once the child is capable of meeting the demands of the situation, which is in part due to mastering the necessary skills, competition is likely to enhance performance (see Wankel, 1969, 1971).

Think of the situation when you go into a supermarket and there is a new girl on the cash register. When she practices on her own, or when there is only one patient customer, she tends to do all right. If a large line forms and people begin to make negative comments (can't you go any faster, etc.), the pressure mounts, she becomes flustered, gets very anxious, and makes more mistakes than before. However, in the same kind of a situation (rush hour), an experienced cashier will improve her performance by adjusting to the demands of the situation. Children in sport are much like the new cashier—you cannot overload or overstress them and expect positive results.

Many people (parents, coaches, and others) are concerned about the age a child should begin playing sports. We maintain that as long as sports are fun-filled adventures existing totally to serve the kids, the age a child begins to play need not be of major concern. However, if the experience is a negative one, it is unwise to enroll a child of any age. This means that fun must be a paramount part of the experience, that goals must be within grasp, and that kids must not be mistreated, used, or abused.

If you have concerns about the quality of your child's exposure, many other people probably have similar kinds of concerns. Upon interviewing the mothers of thirty-two boys, eight and nine years old, we found that over 80 percent of the mothers expressed a strong dislike for the winning emphasis, the pressure, and the overcompetitiveness in children's sports. They indicated that they would like to see these things de-emphasized and the emphasis put on fun and enjoyment, along with giving each child an equal opportunity to play. One mother aptly expressed the general feeling of the group when she said, "Couldn't they have a system where everybody could participate and have fun? Why should some little eight-year-old have to win?" It is interesting that many parents felt that they were alone in their concerns. As it turned out, nearly all of them expressed the same kinds of feelings and concerns about kids' sports.

In the final analysis, adults are responsible for the kinds of opportunities, experiences, and reward systems which exist in kids' sports. These systems can be organized to benefit the health and well-being of large numbers of children or they can be organized for the elimination of kids. If we are to function in the children's best interest with regard to the right start, it is imperative that all young boys and girls receive positive enjoyable exposures to physical activity. People who are involved with young children in activity settings should be focusing their attention on giving each child rewarding, fun-filled experiences, with the pursuit of winning kept in its proper perspective.

3

Why Eliminate Kids?

Elimination is a critical problem, perhaps the most critical problem which exists in children's sport.

According to Canadian Amateur Hockey Association statistics, of the 600,000 players registered or affiliated with the C.A.H.A. in 1973, 53 percent were under the age of twelve, 35 percent were from twelve to fifteen, and 11 percent were over fifteen years of age. Hockey statistics over the past five years indicate that only about 10 percent of the players register to continue participating in organized hockey beyond their fifteenth birthday, and similar trends reportedly exist in other organized sports like little league baseball and minor league soccer (Orlick, 1974). This provides clear cut evidence that either kids are being eliminated or they are voluntarily dropping out. Perhaps even more staggering than these statistics is the fact that kids are beginning to drop out of organized sports as early as seven and eight years of age.

In some cases, the elimination of children is calculated and intentional, while in other cases it is completely unintentional. Whether elimination is intentional or unintentional, it has similar effects. Kids come to feel unworthy, unwanted, and unacceptable.

It is absurd that on the one hand we feel that sports are good for kids and on the other hand we set up a system which eliminates poorer performers, girls, late-maturing boys, kids who are not aggressive enough, and so on.

Although the elimination of kids is often unintentional, "cutting" is one form of intentional elimination which can have drastically negative effects on kids. They are "cut" not only physically but also psychologically. Setting limits on the kind and number of kids allowed to be involved is essentially what cutting is all about. This is an all too common occurrence in communities and schools across the nation. An example which comes to mind occurred when two little girls recently went to "try out" for the softball team. Shortly after they left for the field, one of the girls returned home without her girlfriend. Her father asked her what had happened. The little girl replied, "They already had enough people." So it goes. Similarly, we may have 100 boys try out for a basketball team, or 100 girls try out for a gymnastic team—but in each case, only about ten or fifteen *make the team.* Instead of cutting children, we should be personally encouraging them to come out for sport and making it a meaningful place for them.

We should field as many teams as there are interested kids to fill them. It is ridiculous to promote participation on the one hand, and then to cut interested individuals from the team, or to in any way limit their participation. This type of action provides the rejected child with massive negative reinforcement and counters our basic reason for existing (that is, to serve the children). To cut a child because he is not good enough negates our purpose and our responsibility to our children and to society. It is comparable to a doctor refusing to treat his sickest patients to insure that his win-loss record looks good. Those people seeking athletic participation who are cut-off may be the ones who could benefit most from this experience. Just as the least lovable child is the one who needs loving the most, the least athletic child may need athletics the most. The process of cutting is a vicious circle for the one who doesn't make it. He is cut because he is not good enough to make it and is consequently given no opportunity to practice on a regular basis so that he can become good enough to make it—so he is rejected again the following year. We not only are doing an injustice to the individual but also are cutting our own sporting throats. Twenty years later, these cut individuals do not support our programs, and they refuse to pay for new facilities. Through our negative conditioning program we have firmly entrenched in them a negative feeling about sport. The least that this negative feeling will do is to relegate these people to the role of spectators, which is bad enough in itself.

Elimination is a long term process. Although it may occur at an early age, it can last a lifetime. By eight or nine years of age, many children have already turned off sports. In one study, many young children who had opted out of sports indicated that they never wanted to go out again (see Orlick, 1973a). A seventeen-year-old female cross-country skier of national caliber revealed some possible reasons why many children may not want to go out again as well as why she dropped out herself:

Q. Why do you think you stopped skiing?

A. I liked it when I started but later it wasn't fun anymore.

Q. What didn't you like?

A. There was too much criticism ... he [the coach] didn't act like he wanted me on the team ... he never gave any positive suggestions ... just criticism.

Q. Is there anything else that bothered you?

A. Yes, the coaches ignored the younger skiers ... in order to get attention you have to be good ... lots of kids gave it up because nobody took any interest in them.

Q. Is there anything you would like to see changed in the cross-country ski program?

A. Yes, there's no promotion for recreational skiing ... it's only for the ones who want to compete. The program shouldn't be concerned only with producing racers. Kids may want to compete once they learn how to ski ... or just ski later on. Now they never hear anything about it.

Her perceptive insights were borne out time and time again in interviews conducted with athletic dropouts (young and old) in skiing as well as in many other sports.

The reward structure which now exists in organized sports does not appear to be consistent with what is in the best interest of the majority of children. There appears to be an over-emphasis on winning at the expense of fun involvement. This gives rise to an elitist atmosphere wherein many youngsters eliminate themselves before they start, while others begin to withdraw at seven and eight years of age.

In many cases, organized sport (team or individual) appears to operate as an extremely efficient screening process for the elimination of children.

The findings of a study by Orlick (1972*a*) indicate that a major change in emphasis is needed in children's sport in order to operate in the child's best interest with regard to motivation, program, and personnel. Extensive interviews conducted with eight- and nine-year-old organized sports participants, nonparticipants, and drop-outs showed that the children strongly felt that they had to be good either to make the team or to play regularly. Seventy-five percent of the nonparticipant children, *all of whom thought they were not good enough to make the team,* indicated that they would go out for a team if they thought they would surely make it. *Fear of failure,* or the psychological *stress of disapproval, appeared to influence certain children to the extent that they were afraid to participate.* It has become evident that there are many nonparticipants who would like to participate in a variety of sports, and they would participate if they knew they would be acceptable in the sports setting and if they were assured of having a rewarding experience. However, they generally do not feel that this is the case. Rather, they feel that they do not have much to contribute or gain from a sporting system where acceptance is seen as being conditional upon performance (see Orlick, 1973 b).

Children who drop out of sport at an early age appear to be merely reacting to negative situations which are largely due to the structure of the game or the emphasis of the coaches. The majority of the children drop out because they are not given an adequate opportunity to play, or they are not having a positive experience (e.g., it's not any fun). Sitting on the bench, being ignored, or being yelled at for making a mistake, certainly isn't much fun. Generally these kids are not getting positive reinforcement from the coach or from the competitive situation itself. If they are getting any positive feedback, it is outweighed by negative feedback which leads to their decision to drop out. Most negative experiences are related to an overconcern with perfection, particularly at an early age.

One seven-year-old child and two eight-year-old children, who dropped out of sport, bring out this point quite clearly in their responses to the following question: "How good would you like to be at sport?" Their responses were: "Really good ... because if you're not the coach won't think very much about you." "Perfect ... so when I wanted to play, I could play." "Good enough so I could play sports and I wouldn't get fired on anything I went on" (Orlick, 1973a).

The mother of an eight-year-old hockey player summed up the situation well when she said: "How can kids become enthused when they're not allowed to become involved?"

The following interview excerpts are presented in order to help you get a view from the perspective of two seven-year-old drop-outs and two eight-year-old drop-outs.

Case 1: eight-year-old soccer drop-out. (Started at eight, dropped out at eight, about three-fourths of the way through the season.)

Q. Are you going to go out [for soccer] again?
A. I was planning on it, but I don't think I will.
Q. Why not?
A. It's not that much fun anymore.
Q. Did you play for the whole season?
A. For the last three games I didn't play, but the other games I did.
Q. Why did you decide to stop?
A. 'Cause whenever we had a game I was usually an extra so I didn't get to play very much.
Q. So what did you do during the game?
A. Just stand around and let the mosquitoes eat me.
Q. Were there a lot of kids who didn't play?
A. Yes, there were a lot of extras . . . didn't get to play.
Q. Why didn't they get to play?
A. 'Cause there was already enough guys.
Q. What do you like least about sports?
A. Baseball.
Q. Why?
A. Well, most of the time you're in outfield anyway, and you hardly ever catch one . . . they hardly ever come out that far. I get too bored.
Q. Is there anything you'd like to see changed in sports to make them better?
A. Baseball maybe . . . make the field smaller and the bases a little shorter.

21

Q. Would you like to be an athlete or a member of a little league team?

A. No.

Q. Why not?

A. Well, you just waste time . . . like you could do some other good stuff . . . like build something or something like that.

Q. Would you like to be good at sports?

A. Yes.

Q. How good?

A. Perfect.

Q. Why would you want to be perfect?

A. So when I wanted to play I could play.

Q. What do you think it would be like for you this year if you went out for the team?

A. I wouldn't make it . . . I don't think I would.

Q. If you thought you would surely make the team, would you go out for it?

A. Yes.

Case 2: seven-year-old soccer drop-out. (Started soccer at seven, dropped out at seven [within a few weeks after starting.]

Q. How did you like it last year when you went out for soccer?

A. I didn't like it very much 'cause they never let me play. They just let the good guys play . . . the little guys just have to stand around . . . and watch.

Q. Are you going to go out again?

A. If they let me play I would.

Q. Were there a lot of kids who didn't play?

A. Yup, most of the team didn't get to play . . . just some guys did . . . just the big guys. Everybody else just stands around.

Q. Did you stay for the whole season?

A. I stayed a couple of weeks ... then I quit because I never got to be what I wanted to.

Case 3: seven-year-old hockey drop-out. (Started hockey at five, dropped out at seven; started baseball at six, dropped out at seven.)

Q. Why did you stop playing hockey?

A. I started not to like it.

Q. What didn't you like?

A. Well, in hockey I quit because I didn't get the puck passed to me too many times.

Q. You didn't get the puck?

A. Oh ... only once.

Q. Only once in all the time you played?

A. I think so but I'm not pretty sure ... I might have got it a couple of more times than that.

Q. Is that the main reason you don't want to play?

A. Yeah ... you know 'cause I got bored with it.

Q. You got bored? How come?

A. 'Cause every night you could be fooling around at your house instead of wasting your time playing hockey. All's I did was sit around. . . .

Q. What do you mean?

A. Well, like baseball ... it's like hockey 'cause you. . . . I hardly even get a chance ... 'cause I'm always at the end of the line in baseball.

Q. So you don't get a chance?

A. Well, I get up to bat but I wait such a long time, I forget what I'm doing and I struck out ... that's what I did I struck out ... every time I went up. Oh, I hit the ball and

then I got out and then I struck out ... and
then I struck out again.

Q. Is that why you didn't go out for baseball
again?

A. Yeah.

Q. How good would you like to be in sport?

A. Real good.

Q. Why do you think you'd want to be real
good?

A. Because if you're not the coach won't think
very much about you.

Q. Do you think you will ever want to go out
for a sports team?

A. No.

Q. What do you think is the real reason that
you don't want to go out for a team any
more?

A. It just kind of bothers me ... it bores me. ...

Q. If you were better do you think you'd want
to go out?

A. Yeah. ... Right now I don't have very much
fun. In hockey, I didn't get very much
chance to get the puck and in baseball I
didn't hit the ball very much. Now I don't
want to go out any more.

Case 4: eight-year-old baseball drop-out. (Started at
seven, dropped out at eight after one season.)

Q. Have you ever played on any regular league
teams?

A. Yes. I played baseball last year but I don't
think I want to play baseball anymore.

Q. What didn't you like about it?

A. Well, I didn't get to go up to bat any
time. ... I usually just stay on bases and

everything and play shortstop. I got to go up to bat once every time we played. I didn't get to bat that much. They let me play outfielder . . . and shortstop. I wasn't that good an out-fielder anyway.

Q. Is there anything else that bothers you about playing sports?

A. Yeah, if you play and you have a bad match and guys come up to you and say you're no good at playing baseball or anything like that . . . and you haven't had a chance to do anything.

Q. Would you like to be good at sports?

A. Yes.

Q. How good would you want to be?

A. Good enough so I could play sports and I wouldn't get fired on anything I went on.

Q. What do you think it would be like for you if you went out for a team this year?

A. I don't know . . . it might be sort of hard. . . . I don't know if I'd be any good or anything.

In conclusion, it can be said that many boys and girls are being robbed of an early positive sports experience. Little girls are forced to ask the question: "Why can't I play?" And we ask you, why is there nothing, or so little for the girls? Girls have the same need for activity, companionship, and fun-filled play experiences as do boys. However, what little girls do not need is to be faced with the same kinds of piercing questions that little boys constantly have hanging over their heads: "Am I good enough to play?" "If I go out how will others respond to my performance?" "Am I good enough to be acceptable?" And again we ask you, why does a little boy or girl have to be so tremendously

25

overconcerned with his or her performance in order to play? Why are the rewards reserved only for the small percentage that excel? If sports have the potential to be beneficial to all, why eliminate kids?

Until there are some positive changes in regard to the limited opportunities which exist for girls and the reward structures which exist for boys, we will be robbing many kids of an important part of their childhood. Let's give them all a good fun-filled experience!

4

What About Winning?

Obviously we are living in an extremely achievement-oriented society in which the value of winning has skyrocketed.

The statement attributed to the late Vince Lombardi, "Winning isn't everything, it's the only thing," has become an overriding theme in the lives of many North Americans.

It is not uncommon to hear individuals labelled as either winners or losers by other members of society. Our contention is that these particular labels are often based on a rather narrow interpretation of winning. Those who perceive winning as being only scoreboard victories or achievement at the expense of defeating others are losing out on a great deal themselves.

Besides racking up points, people, youngsters in

particular, can win or achieve many immeasurables such as friends, respect, trust, satisfaction, confidence, knowledge, skills, health, fitness, personal well-being, and above all else, happiness. Sport participation has tremendous potential for positive personality development, self-actualization, and socialization, that is, reinforcement of society's desirable norms and values. To jeopardize attaining personal happiness or any of these invaluables would seem questionable, yet victory-*despite*-cost orientations appear more and more prevalent in both games and life.

Despite laws and rules, people in many instances are free to take advantage of others or to infringe on other people's rights. At times the values of fairness and integrity (perhaps the most important values ever recognized by man) are being eroded and overlooked as a result of an overemphasis on the fruits of victory. When the games people play become more important than the people themselves, competition can begin to have a destructive impact on society.

Perhaps a look at many sport programs for youngsters would reveal that *what is being won* is very questionable while *what is being lost* could be crucial. It has been shown that as the child grows older the importance of playing a game fairly declines as the importance of playing well increases (Webb, 1969). Dishonesty, cheating, and fighting at minor games, deliberate attempts to injure others, dehumanization, overt aggression, dropping out, and so forth, would seem to provide evidence that despite the fact that somebody may be winning in kids' sports, there are many youngsters losing.

It is important to realize that childhood is not only

preparation for life, *it is life!* A child is not just a miniature or potential adult who can handle the pressures of
win-despite-cost orientations to sport. Instead, a child
is a developing individual with a need for an identity,
a tremendous capacity for emotions and feelings, and
often a quite limited physical capacity. In most cases,
the processes of self-discovery, enjoyment, self-reali-
zation, and improvement need far more attention with
youngsters than the process of winning which seems to
be inherent.

Whether it is occurring intentionally or not, this
overemphasis on winning is creeping into activities for
youngsters and resulting in a host of problems and
negative experiences. These problems can be described
in terms of three areas of concern.

Restricted and Inappropriate Participation

In the backyards, alleys, sandlots, and streets of
parts of the world, children gather spontaneously for
interaction, games of all kinds spring up, and these
games almost always involve everyone interested in
some capacity or another. The kids involved seem to
care more for one another than for the game itself, and
as a result the participants are usually open to ideas or
suggestions which are in the best interest of all. That
is, the games themselves are flexible to accommodate
the participants and their capacities.

Adults sincerely interested in kids often organize
these games, giving them a structure in which to operate. This need not be detrimental to youngsters, unless
adults impose their fairly inflexible conceptions of the
game and a more professional approach to sport. This

is sometimes the case because it is what they have come to know.

Professional sport and its structure eliminate those who are presently not good enough, and they insure that those who are best get better treatment and more extensive participation. This is entertainment in a competitive world based on economics, and one can expect little else. Is it necessary that these things be a part of the games kids play?

In a pro-style approach to games, the late-maturing child (in terms of growth and development) may be completely eliminated or given little opportunity to take part and learn the game or to acquire any incentive or confidence to pursue it further.

Surely the greatest advocates of pursuing excellence, performance, victory, and so forth would admit that those very goals may be defeated by elimination and/or negative exposures for youngsters in early childhood. When can we be sure that someone will *not* be good? The past is full of examples of extremely late-maturers or people who just began to really concentrate on a particular sport later in life. It has been said that one of the all-time greats of ice hockey, Eddie Shore, had never really skated until he was well into his teens. How many individuals of this caliber are eliminated or discouraged today? Equal opportunities for at least the kids should be one ideal to which our society should cling.

Youngsters of five and six years of age are being informed that they are not good enough and are being cut from teams. Some are being dropped for a better player who can be picked up when the big games come up. Others are sitting on players' benches freezing or being bitten by mosquitoes with the distant hope that they might get a chance to play and that it might be fun. Many are being discouraged by what can be interpreted as pro-style handling of players (e.g., abrasiveness, tremendous demands, lack of sensitivity, dehumanization, etc.). Still others are being discouraged by the hostility, cheating, aggression, and violence that become part of games when defeating the opponent becomes too important.

Above all, there are youngsters who are *disappointed*, perhaps for one of the many reasons stated, but most often because *it isn't any fun*. Level of ability should not be a prerequisite for participation or for having fun in childhood. The star usually has all the confidence necessary, and it is the others who may benefit most from attention during the critical period of childhood. For a lot of kids, winning isn't everything—*being able to take part and have fun means much more*.

Unrealistic and Unreasonable Expectations

When a pro-style, adult approach to sport (which strongly stresses achievement and winning) is presented to kids, it often brings with it unrealistic and unreasonable expectations for children, both in terms of performance and behavior. Whether these expectations are being presented intentionally or not, they are resulting in many pressured and unhappy youngsters. A child is not an adult and often does not have the capability to handle many of the adult situations created in sport.

For example, consider the following questions:

—Should a five- or six-year-old child be expected to handle being "cut" or "dropped" from his "dream" team?

—Should the same child be expected to "hit" others and be more aggressive toward opponents every time he goes out?

—Should a ten-year-old, pitching in the city championship before a huge noisy crowd, be able to deal with the pressure of a small lead with bases loaded and nobody out in the ninth inning? (What if he fails?)

—Should a youngster be expected to handle the abrasive treatment often utilized in professional sports?

—Should a nine-year-old be expected to have much success with "adult-size" basketball hoops, goals, fields, balls, and so forth?

—Should the child have to deal with the disapproval of crowds of people when he happens to fail to meet adult standards?

—Should an eight-year-old be required to wear an adult-style uniform and correspondingly always perform or behave like an adult or entertainer?

—Should kids be expected to be patient while sitting in discomfort on the sidelines waiting to play?

—Should a child be groomed especially for a certain sport, position, or skill without ever knowing his capability at others?

—Should young children be expected to consider winning a game more important than the kids on the other team?

—Should kids ever have to consider sport as work?

—Should the child learn that beating the rules can be an acceptable way to win?

These are the kinds of questions people who are trying to help kids through sports must begin to ask themselves. Is the deck being stacked against them?

It is important to administer programs for kids with a child's-eye view to insure that the situations, expectations, challenges, and encounters presented are realistic and reasonable for them. When youngsters create their own games and challenges, they tend to be self-limiting in terms of their capabilities. When a game gets too hot or uninteresting, it breaks up. Games are also readily adjusted so that most participants have a near fifty-fifty chance of succeeding. The child can achieve a great deal if learning is allowed to occur naturally. In natural learning an important and careful series of progressions takes place whereby the child gains confidence and seldom attempts things unless there is at least a fifty-fifty chance of succeeding. When pressured along to achievement through unrealistic expectations, the child becomes increasingly uncertain, his confidence often suffers, and the personal worth of the experience becomes questionable. Maturity is developed rather than achieved.

Development of empathy (being able to project yourself into the place of the child) as an interested coach, parent, fan, or whatever is perhaps the best way to insure reasonable expectations for children and to improve the quality of experiences presented to youngsters. With some genuine empathy as guidance, fewer things are taken for granted and the people interested in helping youngsters will come closer to achieving their objectives.

One of the finest writers of stories for children, Maurice Sendak, was asked what made it possible for him to communicate so sensitively with the needs and feelings of children (Le Shan, 1968:347). He responded that the most important thing was "to reach and keep hold of the child in me!" Youngsters identify with those who can identify with them and who know their capacities and feelings. Similar to the way children project themselves from time to time into the roles of adults, we must also sense their feelings and situations if we are to present reasonable expectations for them. Wouldn't we all like to maintain the vitality and sensitivity of childhood?

Undesirable, Violent, Immoral, and Unsocial Behavior

Participation in sport has tremendous potential for personality development and socialization. Sport and games present countless opportunities to reinforce society's *desirable* norms and values. However, when winning becomes more important than any other factor, we tend to lose sight of desirable norms and values, and we reinforce behavior which is less than desirable.

When winning becomes too important, the child learns that he has a better chance of emerging victorious if a talented opponent is hurt or frightened of injury. Likewise, kids may learn to trip or interfere with an opponent rather than try to catch him or allow him an opportunity to score. (Is there really such a thing as a good penalty?) A child may learn that bending the rules is more effective than trying one's best. Youngsters may learn to lose respect for others (officials, opponents, fans, or whatever) en route to victory. The behavior that results from these kinds of lessons would certainly have to be termed questionable.

In watching professional sport, the youngster may have initially observed these types of behavior and noticed that they were not always reprimanded but often rewarded because of entertainment value and/or eventual victory. In kids' sports if one's enthusiasm to win or put on a show becomes too emphatic, the same kinds of pro-style behavior tend to be rewarded or at least accepted. Acceptance is what kids seek, and behavior that is accepted by significant people in their lives tends to become part of their lifestyle.

It is hard to believe that kids are learning desirable values from sport when one observes some of the behavior in little and minor leagues and notes some of the disgraceful incidents occurring in kids' games. Fights and brawls at organized kids' games are no longer uncommon! There are confirmed reports of officials being assaulted by youngsters and fans; teams are refusing to shake hands with opponents; attempts to hurt or injure opponents physically are becoming all too prevalent; penalty-studded games are becoming typical; lack of respect for opponents or officials is commonplace; and acceptance of overt aggression seems to be spreading. All that is necessary to verify these statements is to go to some games, to talk to people who regularly attend games, or to follow minor and little league sport in the newspaper.

This past season alone in the Province of Ontario we have had several cases of both players and spectators needing to be hospitalized after fights, and riots have broken out at minor league games. Players have not only lost teeth, but also eyes and even life itself as a result of swinging fists and sticks. In a recent hockey game two teenage boys got into a scrap which, after the game, developed into a fatal fight in the parking lot, wherein one of the boys literally lost his life (*Globe and Mail,* 1974). In another game a boy lost his eye as a result of another player illegally hooking him with his stick (*Globe and Mail,* 1973).

On April 18, 1974, the *Ottawa Citizen* reported that bomb threats, resignations and fear of bodily harm forced the withdrawal of the Bramalea Blues from the Ontario Hockey Association Junior B final series against the Hamilton Red Wings. A spokesman for the Blues said, "for the safety of my players and the value of their lives, I don't think it is worth continuing the series any further." The game that led to this decision, to withdraw from the series, was "a violence filled game" which resulted in 190 minutes of penalties, a brawl in one period which took twenty-five minutes to bring under control, and police having to be called in to break up fighting in the stands and corridors. Several players were injured, two suffered eye injuries, another was attacked by a fan, and still another was beaten by two persons from the opposing team. The trainer, who was also injured while trying to protect one of the players, had to be hospitalized (*Ottawa Citizen,* 1974).

It is rather frightening to think that tomorrow's world might be guided by people with values of the type we have just described. The transfer from sport to life is logical and one really begins to wonder if winning a game can be that important! Social-psychologist

Carolyn Sherif revealed the development of a rather destructive approach to winning which may have serious consequences for youngsters and future generations. After thoroughly reviewing the research concerned with children's competitive and cooperative behavior she concluded that research is "showing a development in the United States of a highly individualistic form of rivalry in which 'If I can't win, no one can.' The object of competition is to beat the rival, regardless of whether one's own performance reaches a level of excellence" (C. Sherif and Rattray, 1973:23). It is not too difficult to imagine the type of behavior which results.

The three major areas of concern in kids' sport which we have described can all be linked fairly closely to an overemphasis on the value of winning. Consequently it is crucial to keep the goal of victory in its proper perspective. The child who loses a game to a more highly skilled opponent, yet is cooperative, respected, satisfied, healthy, self-assured, and happy surely must be a winner! The quality of his life must compare pretty favorably with that of anyone who has learned to win at any or all cost. The total welfare of all exposed to games should be top priority—especially for youngsters!

Just recognizing the tremendous importance of sport being *fun* for children could be the most significant single factor in making you a more effective and positive influence on kids. What about winning? How important is it? It is certainly something to think about.

5

What's Best for Kids?

What is best for kids? This is an extremely crucial question, but one which you will ultimately have to answer for yourself. In attempting to do so, you should consult the kids themselves. This chapter attempts to provide you with some food for thought, as well as some basis on which you can begin to formulate your answers.

Perhaps we can begin by looking at the construction of the game itself. Children generally express some concern over the quality of their sports if they are given the opportunity to do so. In one community, when eight- and nine-year-old children were asked what they liked least about sports, over 80 percent mentioned some negative experience, some boring experience, or some failure experience (Orlick, 1972a).

Many children indicate that they would like sports to be scaled down to their level. Some suggestions the children make toward this end include: make the games easier; cut down the length of the games; increase the actual playing time as opposed to sitting or standing around; cut down on boring repetition such as drills; make the playing areas smaller in fields and rinks; adjust goals to enable more success, like lowering basketball nets; have less practice and more playing; cut down on the roughness; and promote honesty and truthfulness in obeying rules. In general, children express a desire to have more fun and experience more success, as opposed to failure. For example, many children feel that baseball should be changed so that they can be at bat and hit the ball more often and get the ball more often in the field. Some of their specific suggestions for accomplishing this include: making the field smaller, making the bases shorter and the bats bigger, allowing more swings at the ball and more outs to retire a side. In hockey, children indicate that they do not like being pushed around, checked, boarded, and "freezing." They would like to learn some skills better, like (skating), to feel they are more part of the game, to get the puck more often, and to do more playing and less sitting around.

By implementing some of the children's suggestions, we could make many positive adjustments in children's sports. Interestingly enough, some countries are already beginning to make adaptations in equipment and playing areas for children. Some examples of this include miniature-sized ping-pong tables, badminton nets and courts, volleyball nets and courts, reduced-sized volleyballs, basketballs, soccer balls, soccer playing areas, soccer goals, basketball standards (e.g., 5 foot, 6 inches), miniature courts, and so on. Some of these adjustments make it possible for nursery school children to have fun and to experience "success" in something like basketball with a few modifications in the rules. Many additional adaptations could be made in an attempt to redesign sport for success, such as developing miniature-sized curling rocks and ice sheets for children.

It is important to make sure that when an adjustment is made in equipment, rules, and the like, it actually results in more success and more fun for the children. In some cases it may be more advantageous to increase the size of an object (e.g., baseball, puck, bat) while keeping its weight constant, or to keep the size constant and reduce the weight in order to enable more success for the young child. At any rate, by scaling down the games and making the necessary adaptations, we will provide children with a greater chance to attain some success and conceivably to have a more rewarding and enjoyable experience in the sport.

In attempting to provide for all types of children, we should remember that some children are not interested in activities of a highly competitive or team nature (i.e., child versus child or team versus team). More individual and/or noncompetitive activities should be provided to meet the needs of these children, and facilities should also be made available for children to "just play" without any adult intervention. It should not be a case of "superorganized or unavailable," as one parent expressed it. For kids to have the opportunity to play on their own without a lot of structure is essential. This provides important learning situations in which children have to be completely self-reliant for organization, rules, officiating, teaching, learning, practicing, creating, and so on. Many children indicate that they would like to take part in more individual and noncompetitive outdoor activities such as camping, hiking, climbing, exploring, cross-country skiing, sledding, swimming, archery and horseback riding (Orlick, 1972a; Glassford et al., 1973).

To give the kids increased responsibility within the organized sport setting is also important. This can be done by such things as asking them for their advice and getting their opinions on different things related to practices, games, or the sport itself; by encouraging them to make up new kinds of practice games or new ways of practicing skills; by encouraging them to call their own fouls and do their own officiating in practice and games; by encouraging them to organize on their own; and by gradually increasing the decisions and responsibilities which are given to them to carry out.

It is important that the coach sets up an atmosphere in which a child can feel or develop a sense of self-worth. A child's estimate of his own worth or ability is inferred from the words and gestures of other people. Children tend to anticipate and adjust their behavior to the expectations of others. You behave in terms of what you think you are, and what a child thinks he is depends upon what other people think he is.

In order for a child to feel he is a person of worth, other people must treat him like he is a person of worth. This is why approval, praise, and encouragement are so important to a child—to let him know he is an acceptable and worthy individual. As a social

41

being, every child needs this kind of approval. This is also one reason why approval results not only in better learning, but also in better overall adjustment of the child.

Probably the easiest way to develop a feeling of self-worth in sport is to prove to the child by his actions that he is accomplishing something. Physical activity is one place where a child can see and feel improvement quickly. For example, "Two minutes ago you could not do a seat-drop on the trampoline—now you can!" This is indisputable evidence of accomplishment which can make a child feel proud and worthy. Each accomplishment, however small it may seem, should be recognized and rewarded, particularly in the beginning. This will serve to legitimatize the child's feelings, which may be needed at the start. The child will experience countless evidences of self-worth as long as he compares himself (and you compare him) to his own past performance. How you treat the child can have a significant effect on how he sees himself.

Coaches and parents have too often resorted to aversive or negative control when working with children (e.g., criticizing, ridiculing, blaming, humiliating, scolding, yelling, threatening, punishing, withdrawing approval, and so forth). This takes its toll on children as can be attested to by drop-out children and young participants alike. To accept imperfection while a child is learning is important. An overconcern with perfection can make a child feel like a failure, causing him to subsequently lower his feelings of self-worth. You can make a child feel successful by rewarding any improvement or anything good, and by making positive suggestions, or you can make the child feel like a failure by always criticizing and yelling that he did this or that wrong, or that he wasn't as good as so-and-so was. For example, a girl may come in last at a swim-meet and feel happy and successful if you compare her to her own past performance, but sad and unsuccessful if you compare her to the winner of the meet. In terms of overall adjustment, as well as learning, to use the positive approach based on individual improvement is much more beneficial for the child.

If you consistently treat a child like a failure, or if he consistently feels as if he has failed, he will soon see himself as a failure. This will in turn have obvious effects on his feelings of self-worth as well as his performance. It can get to a distressing point, as one mother expressed about her eight-year-old son: "Now he's afraid to try anything because he's afraid to fail."

In his book, *How Children Fail,* John Holt comments: "They [children] are afraid, above all else, of failing, of disappointing or displeasing the many anxious adults around them, whose limitless hopes and expectations for them hang over their heads like a cloud" (1970:16).

Remember to let a child know that he is acceptable even if he doesn't excel. He has to know that it is perfectly acceptable to participate just for fun. The child should not be made to feel acceptable *only* when he performs well. Unfortunately adults sometimes reinforce performance at the expense of the child. An example of a parent resorting to negative tactics in the pursuit of excellence came out in an interview with the father of a ten-year-old hockey player. The father told the child that he would buy him the best new skates available if he made the all-star team. The boy made the team and consequently was given his brand new pair of expensive skates. Shortly after this, his father took the skates back from him because "he didn't play well enough." The father said that the boy "put out from then on."

This boy had a lot more than a pair of skates at stake. His father had essentially told him that unless he made the all-star team, and unless he played well once he made the team, he was unacceptable to his dad. No wonder he put out! (How long can the boy take this kind of adverse control and remain psychologically healthy? And more important—what happens when he can't make it?)

Other forms of negative control include such things as always harping at a child about his mistakes, telling him he didn't play well or he didn't skate well, telling him he missed good chances, and so on. In a recent study, many fathers of young players were found to respond negatively to their sons after they had lost a game (Higgs, 1974). This kind of behavior does not appear to serve any useful purpose. It just produces needless anxiety in the child and makes him feel miserable. Similarly, when a coach singles out a child and chastises him in front of everybody for doing something "wrong" like missing a shot, it is extremely distressing for the child and puts him in a situation in which he is scared to death of making a mistake. The child already knows he's made a mistake or that he's lost—there's no reason for the coach or parent to rub it in. If anything, they should help the child to reduce his anxiety or to adjust to the loss by playing it down. Put yourself in the kid's shoes. What if you made an unintentional mistake or were the cause of something going wrong? Would you want someone making you feel even worse? Wouldn't it be better to help the child look forward with some enthusiasm to the next challenge?

Children tend to operate on their expectancies of reinforcement. For example, if they expect fun, approval, or success from sports, they will be motivated to participate. On the other hand, if they expect disapproval, humiliation, or failure, they will not be motivated to participate. Whether a child actually does participate will be dependent upon the relative strength of these conflicting expectations.

Once in the sports environment, children will tend to behave in the manner expected of them or in the manner which will maximize their rewards. This will be true regardless of whether the behavior is positive or negative; for example, passing to a teammate or fighting. There is evidently an increasing amount of violence not only in society and in professional sports but also in children's sport. For example, when eight- and nine-year-old hockey players were interviewed in eastern Canada, it was found that about 50 percent of them had already been in a fight in hockey, half of them having been in a fight three times or more (Bentley and Hunter, 1973). In one province it became necessary to put cages around the penalty boxes and to eliminate shaking hands after the game to prevent young children from fighting. After kids' games the officials stand guard and/or escort the opposing teams to their locker rooms to prevent fights from breaking out.

You ask yourself, "Why does this occur?" There are probably a variety of reasons, but a major one is that violence is being reinforced, as is clearly pointed out in the following two examples. This first excerpt is taken from an interview with a ten-year-old hockey player.

> Q. What do you like best about playing hockey?
> A. Hitting . . . knocking the guy down . . . I just like hitting.
> Q. What does your coach do when you make a good hit?
> A. The coach gets really excited . . . like in practice when you get a good check . . . he yells "yeah" and slaps his stick on the ice.

The next excerpt is taken from an interview with the proud father of another ten-year-old hockey player.

> Jason's aggressive. . . . He's not afraid to get in there and hit. The other day he hip-checked a kid and knocked him right out of the play. . . . He's not afraid to go into the boards after them. My other son Rod just sticks his stick in there but he won't hit. . . . I try to tell him . . . what can you do with someone like that?

Obviously aggressive behavior is being rewarded in sports such as hockey and football. It is beginning to take its toll both on and off the playing field. One study indicated that ten-year-old all-star hockey players were more likely to respond aggressively with pushing, hitting, and so forth in normal social situations than their peers who were not involved in sports (Leith and Orlick, 1973).

A particular behavior will become commonplace or disappear depending on the rewards which are given for engaging in the behavior. A behavior is terminated through the removal of positive rewards or through the introduction of negative consequences for engaging in the behavior.

If you feel that violence is not an admirable kind of behavior for kids to engage in and you wish to extinguish it, under no circumstances should kids be rewarded for engaging in it. It is up to you to see that only positive modes of behavior, and not negative ones, are rewarded.

People (parents, coaches, teachers, and others) are inclined to take good behavior for granted and pay attention only when a child misbehaves.

Most of us pay attention to violations. For example, when a player gets a penalty in hockey, it is announced over the public address system, "Number 8—Johnny Jones—two minutes for roughing." Attention to inappropriate behavior serves to strengthen the very behavior that the attention is intended to diminish (see Madsen, 1971). By paying attention, we may actually unintentionally reward what we do not want to occur. Some kids behave in certain undesirable ways, like unfair play, infringing on the rights of others, and doing what they are not supposed to be doing, just to get attention. If we cease to give them attention for behaving in this way, they in turn will stop doing it.

We tend to dwell on what is wrong rather than looking for what is right even when teaching skills. Pay attention to the good behavior! Play a little game— try to *catch the child being good* and then reward the child by giving attention, praise, or smiling. Watch carefully and when the child begins to behave desirably make a

47

comment such as, "You're doing fine, Cathy, very good." Persistence in catching children being good and giving praise and attention will eventually pay off in better behavior, better performance, and more fun for all.

Certain kinds of behavior seem to be obviously desirable, like sharing, cooperation, honesty, concern for others, respect for others' rights and feelings, self-discipline, self-reliance, and so forth. Other kinds of behavior appear to be obviously undesirable, like violence, fighting, disregarding rules, cheating, unfair play, lack of concern for others, selfishness, and so on. It would be extremely beneficial for children if you (parents, coaches, officials, members of the community league, etc.) were to get together to outline the kinds of behavior you feel are desirable and undesirable for (your) children in sports. If the behavior can be listed in concrete, observable terms, you can then all work together to actively encourage desired kinds of behavior and actively discourage undesired kinds of behavior.

A specific example of desirable behavior relating to cooperation and concern for others may be something like helping another child with a skill during practice or after a competition. In wrestling, after a match, a boy could show his "opponent" how he pinned him and how he could have escaped. In gymnastics, competitors could help one another with skills after a meet. This type of beneficial socializing may help the children realize that the other team is not really "the enemy."

In trying to promote honesty and fair play, encourage a child in any sport to call his own infractions.

In volleyball he could be encouraged to raise his hand if he touches the net or if the ball is out-of-bounds. Another example may be if a boy or girl unintentionally knocks someone down, he or she could help the person up and apologize for the infraction.

Some specific examples of undesirable behaviors may be such things as punching, elbowing, tripping, yelling profanities at the referee, and so on. It should be made known to the child that this type of behavior is totally unacceptable.

If you were actually to take up this challenge and act upon it, the potential benefit to the kids could be immense. This could lead not only to the formation of desirable rules and behavior for children in sport in your community, but also to desirable behavior for coaches, parents, and officials involved with kids in sport.

Several innovative children's hockey programs which have recently sprung up independently in different parts of Canada have been direct attempts at doing what's best for kids. After speaking with the innovators of four of these programs (George Kingston, University of Calgary hockey coach; Harvey Scott, University of Alberta sport sociologist and former pro-football player; Hal Hansen, University of Ottawa hockey coach; Al Way, innovative minor league hockey coach, Ottawa, Ontario), we saw clearly that they were doing some pretty impressive things with young kids. What follows is a brief description of some of the unique aspects found to exist in any one or all of these programs.

The emphasis in each of these programs is on learning basic skills and having fun doing it. Any boy (or girl, in two of the programs) who wishes to play hockey has a chance to do so and is given an equal amount of time on the ice. The approach is extremely positive with a lot of praise and encouragement given to the kids. For example, if a child falls down and gets back up, rather than yelling at the kid for falling, the response is something like: "That's it Jimmy, that's the way to get back into the action." In two of the programs no official score is kept. They are trying to insure that the fun aspect remains high and to implement the idea that "success" is not dependent upon the number of goals scored or on the number of assists made.

In all of these programs the emphasis is on self-improvement. For example, the kids may be told to "glide on one skate as far as possible" and then to "try to go a little further than you did last time." The coach watches for individual improvement and when he sees the slightest evidence of it will say something like, "Very good John . . . you turned to your left that time . . . that's the best you've done it." Little fun games are used to learn skills, and shinny (spontaneous pickup games) is played cross-ice. Games are generally played cross-ice (three games going at once on a regular hockey rink), which allows all kids to be active at the same time with no one sitting. One coach has the games go for fifteen minutes straight with everybody playing; then there is a five minute break and then he has another fifteen minutes straight. Each child is also given the opportunity to play each position and all coaches actively discourage roughness and foul play.

They are reportedly having tremendous success with the youngest kids, judging by the way the kids are improving, by the fun they are having, and by some of the comments from the parents. Some of the older kids who have been firmly conditioned in the old way of playing for the score, with undue roughness, are not as receptive. "Deconditioning" will not occur overnight, but in time these older kids will again learn to play for enjoyment and to play fairly.

Hal Hansen, president of the Canadian Hockey Coaches Association and member of the Canadian Amateur Hockey Association (C.A.H.A.) Technical Advisory Committee, is a forward thinking individual who has had a wide range of involvement in Canadian minor hockey. For the child in sport he strongly recommends:

> A total de-emphasis on winning games, of becoming league champions, of winning trophies with the emphasis being placed upon individual improvement in the particular skill and the learning of new ways and means to enjoy hockey. . . . An alternative lies in the refocusing of hockey as a sport, an endeavor that provides enjoyment, fitness, and skill improvement. It means a de-emphasis on organization and competition under ten or eleven years of age. It means an emphasis on innovation in practice content, and ice utilization so that sound progressions and learning experiences become evident . . . . We must consider the majority and give them the opportunity to participate fully, to enjoy hockey as a sport, to feel the thrill of learning a new skill, or shooting the puck in a net, or just plain maximum activity in learning situations. (1972)

Hansen is now implementing and conducting research on his innovative "alternative" which should ultimately be to the benefit of thousands of youngsters. Jim Duthie of the University of Windsor Sports Research Institute is also involved in the implementation and assessment of an alternative hockey approach which is a direct attempt to "return the game to the children." Twenty-eight teams in the city of Windsor are participating in a no standings minor hockey league. For their eighteen game season no goals are counted, no points are awarded for games won or lost, and no records are kept of leading scorers. The kids just play the game and seem to have a lot of fun in the process. Initial research observations indicate that kids in this league show "less frustration, anxiety and aggression" than those in more traditional leagues ("No-Win Hockey," 1974).

A progressive young women's high school physical education teacher who switched from a negative to a positive approach has shown that new directions can work even with older kids.

She revealed that she used to always look for what was wrong with what people did, but that over the years she found that the girls responded much better when she looked for what was right. "You can always find something good, no matter how bad a girl's ability is. I try to pick out what's good." Her present approach is one which emphasizes fun for all and a concern for others. When she first started teaching she "followed the book" by doing a lot of drills and then allowing about five minutes to "play" at the end of the period. She soon found out that the kids wanted to "play" and not "work" at drills. She now lets them play for nearly the whole period. If they are having problems they will ask for help. For example, one time the girls asked, "How come we never score any baskets?" At that time she asked if they wanted to do some shooting practice, which the girls were now ready and willing to do.

The effect of this teacher's encouragement of a concern for others became evident in a volleyball game. After about two months of encouraging the girls to make the teams even and to help one another, the following incident occurred. One of the poorer girls came up to serve. The girls on the "opposing team" told her to move in closer to the net to serve, because they knew she wasn't very good. She walked halfway up the court and managed to barely lob the ball over for a "successful" serve. "It was a marvelous thing to see and a marvelous feeling for me." Instead of being glad that the girl couldn't serve (an easy point for us!) as they were in the beginning, they now considered this girl's feelings and helped her. Other things also began to happen, like girls switching sides to even things up if too many "good" girls seemed to be on one team. The girls really began to enjoy their gym classes.

A community league director and the father of a boy whose team won the league championship in baseball had the following observations on the positive approach:

> My son just happened to be on the team that won the league championship last year. I'm positive that it was because of the coach. He never yelled at the kids and everytime a kid came off the field he'd have something encouraging to say . . . a little pat on the back and some little positive suggestion . . . no matter how bad the kid was (e.g., that's okay Kelly,

you gave it a good effort . . . next time maybe try keeping your bat a little more level on the swing). This same little league coach also had the winning team the following year.

Former pro quarterback and head football coach at the University of Western Ontario, Frank Cosentino, is also a strong advocate and model of the positive approach to coaching. He looks for what is good, he is constructive in his criticism, he provides his players with a lot of encouragement, he is empathetic with his players, and he never screams or chews them out. In short, he is a positive-thinking man who has great rapport with his athletes and is sincerely interested in them as individuals as well as football players. Since he began his coaching career, only four years ago, his teams have consistently either won or have been strong contenders for their league title and have also won the Canadian Intercollegiate Championship.

There are other examples of this type of positive approach in different sports which is beginning to take hold. People like those mentioned, as well as others who have attempted to start positive and innovative programs, should be given a lot of credit for going out on a limb in an attempt to do what's best for kids. They may not have all the answers as of yet, but they are well on their way, and it is only by trying new positive approaches that we will eventually come up with what is really in the best interest of kids.

Evidently there are some people presently doing an excellent job with kids in sport, but there are countless more who could be making a similar contribution. Those who seem to be most effective are the ones who have a genuine "relationship" with the kids. They are nonthreatening, straightforward, and enthusiastic. They set a positive atmosphere which permeates the gym, the field, the rink, or the pool. Games and skills are presented in a fun-filled positive way, instructions are simple and easy to follow, and the difficulty of skills is gradually increased. Praise and encouragement are given often, even for partially correct performance or behavior (e.g., I'm pleased with the way you're moving along; you guys did a great job today, etc.). A child is not subjected to offensive, negative criticism for doing something "wrong." Criticism is constructive and is stated in the form of positive suggestions (e.g., try keeping your head up a little more). The children are included in the decision-making process and really feel that the program is their own. It is truly a program *for the kids!*

As long as we keep in mind that the outcome of the child is infinitely more important than the outcome of the game, we will be well on our way toward doing what's best for kids. When an overemphasis is placed on winning, competition breeds the kind of conflict which is not in the children's best interest. People who encourage winning at all costs, cutting and eliminating poorer athletes, violence and fighting, pressure tactics, the complete disregard of rules, and the like, are having a negative effect on children in sport. These individuals, who are organized *only* to win, do more to promote undesirable behavior and to turn kids off sport than any other known factor. The concepts of having to "be first or forget it" or of having to either "do it well or don't do it at all" do not belong in children's sport.

Our contention is that the proponents of these

55

philosophies should be informed of the errors in their ways, presented with positive suggestions for alteration, and encouraged to try some of these alternative methods. If this is done in a positive, constructive manner (which includes explaining why it is best for the kids), people will generally be receptive. There are cases on record of persons who have changed from a completely negative approach to a positive approach based on this kind of feedback. This resulted in children having a good experience, rather than a poor one, which was previously the case. However, if after your sincere attempts, no positive changes are made, it seems that there is no other option left except to remove these people (negative influences) from all contact with children in sport. This appears to be the only way to protect the children.

Since the child has relatively little control over the situation which exists in children's sport, it is up to you to implement changes. He can't do much to change things, but you can. If you see undesirable behavior being reinforced, kids having bad experiences, or children being mistreated in sport, it is important that you try to do something about it.

If you are interested in reviewing some recommendations made by special groups interested in the child in sport, refer to Appendices A, B, C, E, and F.

6

What Do You Feel?

We have expressed some of our feelings about what's best for kids. Now it is your turn to express what you feel and to find out what your family feels! This could be the most valuable chapter in this book, that is, if you take it seriously.

After conducting countless interviews (as a counselor, as a coach, and as a researcher), we have concluded that many parents are not aware of the kinds of experiences their kids are having or what their kids are feeling because they seldom, if ever, sit down and talk to them. Similarly, one parent often does not really know how the other parent feels or how the rest of the family feels about a particular issue. Coaches are often unaware of how their players really feel.

You must try to learn from the children as we have

learned, by listening to what they say and by closely observing how they respond to what you do or what other people do. Our greatest inspirations have come from children. They have been our greatest teachers.

As many of you know, children are perceptive and have a tremendous amount to offer if they are given an opportunity to express their views. Apparently adults must make a more conscious effort to become better listeners. It is extremely important for them to communicate with the children and with each other in order to better understand the other's perspective. This chapter will provide you with some specific interview questions (which we have used and other parents have used) that will enable you to get to know your family better in regard to their feelings and desires related to sports and recreation.

One father who utilized these interview questions with his three children and his wife said that their responses had such an impact on him that he changed his behavior as a result. He never realized the things he was doing or how it was affecting his wife and kids until he sat down with a set of questions and interviewed each family member. He learned a great deal about his family and himself as a result, and he highly recommended that other parents use the interview.

A few excerpts from his interview with his family are presented below:

> Q. Did it seem that I [dad] wasn't very happy after some of the games?
> A. Not all the time, maybe when we lost. . . .
> Q. What did I say to you?

A. You weren't playing well. . . .

Q. Do you expect me [dad] to say something when you don't do well?

A. Yeah. You say that in the car.

Q. Would you like it better if dad doesn't say anything?

A. Yeah! [Note: Interviews with other children have shown that many children already feel "sad," "awful," "disappointed," after making a bad mistake, after playing poorly, or after a loss.]

Up until this time, this father was not aware that he was responding negatively to his son after a loss, or that his son would have preferred him not to say anything. As a result he changed his behavior.

In an interview with his wife, he discovered the following:

Q. Would you like to participate in sports now?

A. I would very much like to get involved in golf and be good at it.

Q. Have you made any plans?

A. Not with you. I can't stand going golfing with you.

Q. Why not?

A. Because I always feel like an albatross around your neck. You're always telling me to keep my head down and look at the ball. We end up fighting before we get off the first tee. So it is something I have to learn on my own then go out and whip your ass. I'll fix you. (Note: The point is clearly made that people must be given freedom to learn on their own, and that in our attempt to help, we must not dominate.)

59

When you conduct your own interviews, you must be sure to merely ask the questions without offering any opinions or suggestions. Remember you are trying to find out only what the other person feels. You will have ample opportunity to express what your feelings are when you are being interviewed. As an interviewer, you simply pose the question and encourage responses by listening attentively, and by asking further questions to clarify what you don't understand. During the interview you should not indicate by your comments or actions whether you agree or disagree with what is being said. Just be attentive and listen. Once all the interviews have been conducted you can discuss the differing perspectives and compare your responses with the case studies outlined later in this chapter under "What Some Kids Feel" and "What Some Parents Feel." (Note: If possible, conduct the interviews when only the two people directly involved in the interview are in the room.)

Children's Interview Questions

These questions will serve as a basic guideline for your interview. You may think of some additional questions which are more pertinent to your particular situation either before or during the interview. The interview questions should be adapted to your specific needs. For example, if your child has dropped out of a sport, you can ask more specifically about the events surrounding that decision. Use those questions that apply to your situation and drop the others. If you do not have time to do the entire interview, do only the short form, the ten starred (*) questions.

What about you—the child

1. Do you like to play sports?
*2. What do you like best about sports?
*3. What do you like least about sports (or what don't you like about sports)?
4. Is there anything else that bothers you about sports?
*5. How could you change sports to make them more fun or to make them better?
6. When you played last year was there anything you would like to have changed?
7. What kinds of sports or activities would you like to do after school or on the weekends, if you could do anything you wanted?
8. Would you like to be an athlete (or a member of a little league team)? Why or why not?
*9. Would you like to be good at sports? (If yes, how good?) Why?
10. Do you like going to practice? Why or why not?
11. When you played last year did you get enough playing time (e.g., ice time or time on the field)? Do all the kids play the same amount of time?
12. How do you feel when you lose or when you make a bad mistake? What makes you feel like that?
13. How good do you think you could be in sports?
14. Would you like to be the star on the team? Why or why not?
15. What do you think it will be like for you when you go out for the team this year?

61

16. Do you think you will always want to go out for a sports team?

Nonparticipants only

1. What do you think it would be like for you if you went out for a team this year?
2. Do you think you will ever want to go out for a sports team?
3. If you thought you would surely make the team, would you go out for it?

What about your mom, dad, and the coach

1. Do you think that mom or dad would like you to play sports? If yes, what makes you think that?
*2. Do you think it would make mom or dad happy if you were really good at sports? What makes you think that?
3. What is your coach like this year?
4. What do you like about your coach?
*5. What don't you like about your coach?
6. What makes the coach most happy (then most mad) in practices? How do you know?
*7. What makes the coach most happy (then most mad) in games? How do you know?
8. What does mom (then dad; then coach) say before you play a game?
9. What is the first thing mom or dad says to you when you come home after a game?
*10. What does mom (then dad; then coach) say after a winning game?
What does mom (then dad; then coach) say after a losing game?
11. Did it seem that dad (or coach; or mom)

wasn't very happy after some of the games? (If the answer is yes—why do you think he/she wasn't happy?)

*12. Does dad say anything when you don't play well?

*13. How do you feel when he says something?

14. What would you like him to say? Would you like it better if he didn't say anything?

15. Do you think dad (mom) would feel bad if you didn't want to play sports anymore?

Adults' Interview Questions

This interview was designed as a guideline to enable you to share your ideas about sport with your family. Husbands can interview wives or vice versa, or perhaps what would be most fruitful is for your children to interview you. It would give the child a chance to be directly involved and would also expose him/her to your feelings. If you do not have time to do the entire interview, do the short form, the seven starred (*) questions.

1. Were you ever active in sports?

2. Do you take part in any sports or physical activities now? If not, would you like to? Do you have any plans of doing so?

*3. Would you like your children to participate in sports?

*4. Why would you like them to participate (or why wouldn't you like them to participate)?

5. What level would you like them to attain in sports?

*6. Have you encouraged your children to get involved in sports? If yes, in what way?

7. Do you and your children ever participate together in sport-related activities?

8. Do you ever have discussions with your children concerning sports? If yes, what do you talk about?

9. Is there anything you personally like about sports? If yes, what is it that you like?

10. Is there anything that you personally dislike about sports (for yourself)? If yes, what?

*11. Is there anything you like about organized sports for children? If yes, what do you like best?

*12. Is there anything you dislike about organized sports for children? If yes, what do you dislike most?

13. What do you think should be the purpose of kids' sports?

*14. Is there anything you would like to see changed in sports to make them better for children?

15. What could you do as a parent or coach to see that these changes come about?

*16. If there are things you dislike in organized sports for children, are you willing to do anything about them?

17. What types of activities would you like to see available in your community for the children (and for the adults)?

The adult interview questions can also be used with fellow coaches, fellow students, and so on, either in their present form or with slight adaptations. Likewise, coaches can interview kids with the children's interview questions.

What some kids feel

The child's perspective is one which is infrequently presented. For this reason we offer the following interview excerpts taken from children age seven to ten.

Case Studies—Children

Case 1: Age Ten

Q. What do you like about sports?

A. They're exciting . . . you get fun out of them . . . sometimes. They give you exercise and they give you a chance to run and breathe fresh air and have a bit of fun in your life.

Q. You said you get fun out of them *sometimes.* What do you mean?

A. Well sometimes when you're really losing badly, you really get sort of cranky and you say, "Oh, I'd like to quit" because you don't want to lose.

Q. What is it that bothers you about losing?

A. Losing isn't the end of the world . . . it's only a game . . . have a bit of fun in it . . . but you can't . . . *it's always win, win, win.* That's all the guys always think about . . . *we've got to win.* Sometimes a couple of the guys on the team say we've got to win this game . . . we've got to beat them! Everyone yells—yeah! And then if you lose, kids tease you. They say "hah" what a cinchy team, "hah hah" laugh their heads off . . . you guys are so lousy.

Losing bothers me most ... it just puts me off.

Q. Is there anything else you don't like about sports?

A. There's nothing I don't like about them 'cept for hockey and football 'cause you have to carry about 100 pounds of equipment all over you.... *I could probably play hockey better if I didn't wear equipment,* so that's how come I just don't like it and I don't play it. I just go out in little games they make up. I don't mind them.

Case 2: Age Eight

Q. Would you like to be a star on a team?

A. Well no, I'd like to be second star or something like that.

Q. Why wouldn't you want to be the star?

A. 'Cause everybody would be cheering for you ... then *you'd get all excited and you wouldn't play properly.*

Q. Do you think your mother or father would like you to take part in sports?

A. Yeah, that's why they joined me up.... I didn't want to go to hockey because it gets too cold and sometimes I don't want to go.

Q. Do you really want to go out for the team?

A. *I don't care as long as our team wins.*

Q. Do you think you will always want to go out for a sports team?

A. No, not that much. I'd rather play with my friends and all that.

Q. If you had your choice now would you go out for hockey or just play with your friends?

A. No. . . . I'd rather play with my friends and throw snowballs and all that.

Q. What's the main reason you're going out?

A. I don't know . . . my dad just joined me up.

Case 3: Age Nine

Q. Do you play any games or sports after school (like hockey, soccer, baseball, or others)?

A. No, I just go home and watch TV or read.

Q. What about in the summer?

A. I usually just lie on our hammock.

Q. What do you think it would be like for you if you went out for a team this year?

A. I'd be a little scared. I might get in everyone's way. People say I do. When we were playing football one time, Gerry [peer] always said I was in his way.

Q. How good do you think you could be in sports?

A. Not too good.

Q. Do you think you will ever want to go out for a sports team?

A. No.

Q. What do you like to do best?

A. "Kicking thistles," playing pool and ping-pong, reading books, and taking naps.

Case 4: Age Nine

Q. Why do you think you went out last year and you don't want to go out this year?

A. Pitching.

Q. What happened with the pitching?

A. I was lousy.

Q. What made you think you were lousy?

A. I could tell . . . 'cause my balls weren't going right.

Q. Were there other things you didn't like or that made you feel bad?

A. Trying to hit the ball they pitched to me.

Q. How often did you hit the ball?

A. Not too many times.

Q. How could they change a game like that so it would be more fun and you'd like it better?

A. *Make the bases smaller . . . make the bats bigger.*

Q. Is there some other sport you would want to try?

A. No, not really.

Q. Did you think it would be better than it was?

A. Yes.

Q. What do you think it would be like if you went out for a team this year?

A. Probably not make it.

Q. Do you think you will ever want to go out for a sports team again?

A. Not really.

Q. If you thought you'd surely make the team, would you go out?

A. Yes.

Case 5: Age Eight

Q. Why do you think you don't want to go out this year?

A. I won't go out if my mom makes me. I'm going to pick what I want.

Q. What happened before?

A. They signed it up and then told me. . . . I

didn't really want to go in the first place. But then I had to go.

Q. Did you stay with it all year?

A. I quit ... after about five weeks [baseball].

Q. What was it that you didn't like?

A. You never really got time to play against another team ... you just practiced up ... you just batted and some guys went out and caught.

Q. Did your parents try to sign you up this year?

A. They asked me if I wanted to go out. I just didn't want to go.

Additional Comments by Children
(age seven to ten)

These additional brief comments are presented to give you further insight into the child in sport.
Excerpt 1:

Q. What do you like least about sports?

A. Warm-ups and practices.

Q. What don't you like about them?

A. Well, sometimes you have to warm-up for the games and this I don't like ... and prac-tices ... *sometimes it's just a talk ... and it's a waste of time.*

Excerpt 2:

Q. How would you change sports so you would like them more?

A. Oh, *I wouldn't have so much practice,* you know like *there's so much practice just for one game.*

Q. Do you think you will always want to go out for a sports team?

A. No ... not really.... I have to have some
time for some other stuff instead of sports,
sports, sports.

Excerpt 3:

Q. What makes you think your dad would like
you to be good at sports?
A. Well, my dad was a good skater and he
learned to do lots of stuff ... and he'd like
me to be like that ... I guess.

Excerpt 4:

Q. Do you think your father or mother expects
you to be an athlete or expects you to take
part in sports?
A. They expect me to be an athlete.

Excerpt 5:

Q. Why do you think you didn't go out for a
team this year?
A. I don't play a lot of sports and I hardly play
any.
Q. Why don't you play much sports?
A. Some I don't like ... some I like a bit but *they
only have practicing ... not real games.*

Excerpt 6:

Q. What makes you think your dad would like
you to be really good at sports?
A. Oh, my dad said he wants me to play sports
'cause he wants me to win lots of money so
I could give it to him.

Excerpt 7:

> Q. Did you like playing hockey?
> A. Well, it wasn't as good as it was the year before that, just *for fun*.

Excerpt 8:

> Q. What don't you like about sports?
> A. I don't like hockey.
> Q. How come?
> A. 'Cause I can't skate. . . . Every time I get up on skates I just fall.
> Q. Do you think you would make the team if you went out for it?
> A. No.

Excerpt 9:

> Q. Would you like to play on any team?
> A. *No, I'd rather just play for fun* . . . and make up teams with other friends.
> Q. Why would that be better?
> A. *You won't have to rehearse so much.*

Excerpt 10:

> Q. Do you think it would make your father or mother happy if you were really good at sports?
> A. Yes . . . they'd be glad that I was really good at sports.
> Q. What makes you think that?
> A. Like *if* I come home and say *I got goals* . . . *he'll say it's good* and he says congratulations . . . it's nice!

Excerpt 11:

> Q. What do you think it will be like for you

when you go out for the team this year?

A. Cold.... I might not feel too good 'cause someone checks you ... and the whistle blows and you don't want to go back for those guys to come out [line change] ... *you just want to keep on playing* ... like you don't want to go into the gate ... 'cause I get warmer moving when I'm playing.

Excerpt 12:

Q. Do you think you will ever want to go out for a sports team?

A. No, I don't think so.

Excerpt 13:

Q. What don't you like about sport?

A. People don't play right ... they throw the bat and things like that ... *they don't play the game right and they argue a lot.*

Excerpt 14:

Q. How would you set up games so you'd have most fun?

A. I'd make even teams.

Excerpt 15:

Q. Why didn't you go out for hockey?

A. I seen some games where there were three or four fights in the game.

Excerpt 16:

Q. What don't you like about sports?

A. In baseball I could never hit the ball.... The

pitchers threw too fast. . . . For the new boys they should pitch a little slower.

Excerpt 17:

Q. Did you like baseball?
A. Not very much.
Q. What was it you didn't like?
A. I always go out and I always got hit with the ball.
Q. Are you going to go out for baseball this year?
A. No.

Excerpt 18:

Q. How could you change sports to make them better or more fun?
A. You could do it backwards.
Q. What do you mean?
A. Well, like if the other team gets a goal, then you get the points, and then if we get a goal . . . they get a goal. Like we're not really getting a goal . . . they are . . . we try to make a goal for them and they try to make a goal for us.
Q. Why do you think that would be better?
A. 'Cause *it would help them like each other.*

Excerpt 19:

Q. Do you think the kids would like you better if you were really good at sports?
A. Some of them would . . . but quite a few wouldn't because they're really good and they don't like kids kinda getting in their way.
Q. Do you think you will always want to go out for a sports team?

73

A. Not always.... I may not join next year.
Q. Why not?
A. Well, *if I like the team this year then I will join next year, and if I don't, I won't.*

What some parents feel

The parents' perspective is one that is probably not discussed or shared with others as much as it should be. Many parents who were interviewed made extremely insightful and relevant comments regarding the child in sport, some of which are outlined below.

Case 1:

Q. How do you think you've encouraged him to get involved in sports?
A. Probably by example ... you know we enjoy it and we participate with him ... you know skating and skiing. I'm sure this is why he likes it.
Q. Is there anything you dislike about sports?
A. I think some of this organized hockey gets a bit out of control. You know how they have the boys so terribly organized in their games and they're switching players ... they're trying to find the best players and I think *they kind of use the boys a bit.* This idea about one player not being able to join this team because he's not good enough to play on it ... you know.... I think team sports are really great for children and if they get too competitive it loses its point of it all ... really!

When Keith was playing hockey at six or seven he only got to play about five minutes in the whole game. The rest of the time he was just sitting there getting cold. *One day when he was only six or seven he came home and said he was giving up hockey.* He would have quit if we hadn't encouraged him to continue.

I think they should let everyone play for the enjoyment. Those who want to be competitive and get to the top will do so anyway. Everyone should be involved.

Q. What sorts of activities should be offered through the community?

A. They should have grass hockey 'cause not all little boys can skate. For the kids who can't skate ... they're way behind and there's really nothing for them in the winter. *They also have nothing for girls.* They should offer things through the school, but the school doesn't provide any leisure activities for the kids in grades 1-3. They can't play floor hockey at lunch, they can't play football. They should have skiing and skating and hockey for the kids. The rink and ski hills are right there. The kids aren't even allowed to change until grade 4. That's too late.

My boy who loves physical activity doesn't even like gym. The teacher wrote on his report card, "If Keith would learn to sit still and listen he would get much more out of gym." He's been sitting all day long!

There are lots of mothers in the neighborhood like myself who would gladly go in and help with a gym class so the kids have an hour of enjoyment.

Even in the school concert the kids must audition to be in it. So if you haven't had some training outside school you can't be involved. How can kids become enthused when they're not allowed to become involved!

Case 2:

Q. Were you ever active in sports or athletics?

A. I just did it for enjoyment; I knew I'd never get anywhere in competition. . . .

    . . . I tried to take the boys skiing but they weren't too interested because all their friends were so much more progressed.

Q. Are your children involved in sports?

A. No. *They're not good enough so they never get approached; they feel left out, I think.*

Q. Do you watch sports on television?

A. I'm not interested in watching . . . it bores me to tears. I'd rather do it myself . . . badly, but do it myself. The boys aren't so interested in watching it which makes me happy . . . I think they should *do* more.

    Scott [son] roots for the winners. . . . He always likes to be on the winning side . . . and he switches. He'll cheer for one team halfway and switch to the team that is winning.

Q. Would you like him to be involved in sports?

A. Yes, definitely. I think it would help him and I don't want him to be just involved, *I want him to succeed at something* . . . because he has his troubles in school; maybe if he got a bit of confidence in some sort of sport it would help him . . . his overall respect of himself, you know.

Q. What do you dislike about sports?

A. I don't like organized sports for kids because the grown-ups go in and manage it. . . . I remember playing ball with my friends without anybody telling me I have to do it this way and that way . . . and just plain old doing it for the fun of it. *I think there's very little fun in organized sports for children.* . . . There's too much pressure put on them. I wouldn't want to play under those conditions.

Q. Where do you think the pressure comes from?

A. From the grown-ups. . . . They want little Billy-boy to be just as good as his daddy used to be or as good as everybody wants to make him believe that daddy was. There's a hell of a lot of pressure put on these kids.

When I think of that little league crap . . . they take it all so very seriously, the parents and the kids. I think it would have been much better if they [the kids] would have had a rabble-rousing thing in some sand pit without any grown-ups . . . and just have fun.

All you need is an empty field and a ball. Let's face it; everybody is not meant to excel . . . there's so few who are tops in their field . . . why should all the others never get a chance to do it. Many never get a chance to do. . . . They stand on the side lines and watch when they'd be much better off going and getting a little group and doing it themselves . . . lousily, but somehow. *The ones who aren't good don't get a chance . . . they don't even make the team.*

There's a coach we know who's wandering around with great power talking about how he cut this kid and that kid. It's a big ego trip for him but how about 700,000 other kids? He does get a real sense of satisfaction from

77

hammering these kids who are twelve or thirteen.

I think this is where it is wrong . . . *it seems that kids' sports nowadays* aren't to exercise the body . . . *they are meant to eliminate the bad ones* so you finally get a fine good national team going, with lots of money behind it. That's organized sports which just gripes me to no end. That's what the Caesars used to say with their populace . . . give them bread and circuses . . . that's all it is . . . that's a social-ill. Keep the masses occupied and happy.

Case 3:

Q. What do you dislike about sports?

A. The organized sports . . . *the pressure is so bad* . . . we have to win. . . . I find the pressure in hockey is terrible . . . most of the pressure comes from the parents. . . . The emphasis should be on learning to play well and having a pleasant experience and learning to get along with kids. I think the fun comes from relaxing and enjoying it. . . . *Why would some little eight-year-old kid have to win? Let him play for fun* . . . and if he's really good he's going to win.

Three little boys along with my son told me there was a coach in the little league and he hit a little boy in the face. This team was very good and it was going to finish first apparently . . . the attitude was: "we're going to win?" and he hit that little boy so hard his nose bled. This was bad and my son was very upset over this and he didn't want to play for awhile . . . but I think he realized his coach wouldn't hit anyone. Now he will watch hockey as a spectator but he will not take part in it . . . he has in fact emphatically said he will not.

One day he came home and said: "I want to try out for baseball." About four weeks before it started . . . I said, "fine" . . . when it came down, the day I knew he had to go . . . he said, "I don't want to go." I said, "Oh, but you're going because you made a commitment and you're going." "Oh no, I'm not going, *I don't want to go. . . . I'll do everything wrong.*"

Case 4:

Q. Do you ever watch your boy play or practice sport related activities?

A. I've never missed a game in organized hockey. We never take them and drop them off and then go and pick them up again.

Q. What sorts of activities should be offered through the community?

A. I'd like to see flag football for young boys because I don't feel that there should be the body contact when they are young.

Q. What about for hockey?

A. If you've ever heard any of your NHL stars, Gordie Howe, for instance, feels that skating, handling the puck and shooting are far more valuable to the youngster than hitting. And after all the little guys are growing . . . and *my son* (eight years old) *had a broken collar bone from this last year from someone cross-checking him on the boards.* I don't feel that this is necessary. I think they can show their ability far better by skating and handling the puck than knocking the other kid over. My boy wasn't the only one . . . we had another boy in pee wee's who had a broken collar bone last year, too.

Q. Is there anything you dislike about sports?

A. There are so many coaches in hockey who perhaps were not good enough to make the Big-Time and so they are trying to push the kids they're coaching into that Big-Time, instead of giving them straight enjoyment and teaching them basics. And my boys are young and there's lots of time for the hitting and the body-contact in hockey . . . but *you have so many coaches now with even the six year olds saying "get out there and hit them . . . slow them down."* Instead of teaching them the basics and enjoyment of getting out there and learning and doing something and doing it well . . . but I don't think you should take it out on the kids because they made a bad play at that age.

Q. What do you mean?

A. Well, *they expect them to do too much. . . .*

I really think there's too much emphasis on winning at this age level . . . but nobody agrees with me . . . you ask my husband. And his brothers too . . . *they say, "Well, that's football" or "That's hockey . . . that's the way it is . . . they have to be pushed."*

Sometimes they do push these small kids . . . and on these outdoor rinks when the weather is 10° below and these poor little kids are freezing to death. The little boy down the street . . . he was crying at one of the games . . . his hands were just frozen off . . . they should have taken him in . . . not left him there. My own boy cried a few times last year . . . frozen feet and what have you.

Q. Where do you think the emphasis on winning comes from?

A. The fathers.

Q. Where do you think the emphasis should be?

A. Well, of course I've got a really square answer . . . they should just play to enjoy the game . . . but everybody laughs at me . . . even Tim [older son] used to laugh at me when I said that. . . . They say, *"What's the use of playing if you're not going to win."*. I think it's wonderful if they win but if they don't they shouldn't take it so badly. You should play for the joy of playing and if they win that's something extra . . . isn't it?

Q. Do you think that's common thinking?

A. No . . . nobody thinks that way except me. *I've always been shouted down when I've said things like this so usually I don't express my opinions anymore.*

I think it's such a pity, you know that here you have to be good at a sport to participate . . . you see in Europe, everybody plays. . . . You don't have to be good. When I played field hockey and net ball, I wasn't particularly good at either of those games but I played throughout my childhood and when I was a young person . . . but *I'm sure if I'd been playing in this country I wouldn't have been good enough to make the team* . . . therefore I probably wouldn't have played. They do emphasize

81

that too much here . . . you know you've got to be really good to make it. Isn't it a pity, really?

Case 5:

It's a pity that you have to be so good to be on a team. The little boy across the street is chubby and can't run very fast. In soccer they'd let him play a few minutes and take him off to let somebody better play. We asked him if he was going out this year and he said, "No, I don't think so." I'm sure it was because he didn't think he'd make the team. This was really sad. I'm sure it was because *he didn't think he was good enough.*

When my son (older) started playing football in high school his whole personality changed. *He started to think that winning was the only thing in the world.* He used to call me old-fashioned when I tried to tell him there were other things. He would say, "You've got to play to win."

I'm English, of course you know, and when the older boys started to play in organized sports in hockey I thought they were pretty brutal, you know . . . the only thing to do was to win and if you didn't win it was the end of the world for them. . . . It took me a long time to get used to that theory.

Couldn't they have a sort of a house league system in the schools so that everybody could be on a team and everybody could participate?

Q. When you watch the games [last three years] do you find that some kids don't play or do they let everybody play?

A. Yes, some of them don't get to play. . . . I've noticed that. I used to notice that in the soccer games in Vancouver . . . there were some little kids who were only out a few minutes in the whole game and I felt so sorry for them . . . they would stand there shivering in their little short soccer pants . . . and the best kids would be out there on the field.

I wish it could be that everyone could just go out and enjoy it. It seems a pity that so many of them get discouraged . . . because they're not first class . . . but that's the way it is over here.

Q. Would you like to see anything changed to make sports better?

A. There should be facilities for more children to play . . . it shouldn't be only for the best ones.

Q. Is there anything you dislike about sports?

A. Well, the only thing is that I do think some of the sports over here are a little bit brutal. . . . I think sometimes the hockey coaches push these little guys too hard.

Q. Just watching the games do you see that quite often? [Parent has three boys playing hockey and has never missed a game.]

A. Yes . . . you do . . . oh yes!

Q. Do you think the coaches are out there to win at that level?

A. Oh, the majority of them are, yes. Last year our boys were very active in flag football and we had a situation where our older boy (Peter) wasn't the top player and so when it came to the final games he sat on the bench

... whereas Rick in the junior league was quite good for his age so he played the whole time, offense and defense ... and then there were the other little fellows who sat on the bench. So we were in a situation where we felt badly to think that Peter didn't play and yet we had the same feeling for those other little fellows in Rick's league that sat on the bench.

Q. Are there a lot of kids sitting in the hockey?

A. Quite a few, yes. If it's a close game, they'll put in the best that they have and the other ones sit. I think for the tiny mites and pee wees ... the whole thing isn't to win. It's to get out there and teach the kids sportsmanship.

Q. Where do you think the pressure comes from?

A. In some cases it comes from both coach and parents ... but I wouldn't say that all coaches are this way. Our tiny mite hockey coach last year wasn't a pressure coach. He was there to give the boys the enjoyment and he would teach them what he knew ... the boys liked him real well.

Now Peter's football coach, there were two coaches and they were strictly to win and the coaches from the two teams argued more than the players did ... because no matter what they did they had to win and the boys felt this ... naturally. And so they pick out their outstanding stars and they're the ones that play ... and I think the other kids felt that too.

Case 6:

Q. Were you ever active in sports?

A. I never liked them very much ... mainly because I think I wasn't very good ... and I think this is the secret of it ... if you're successful at it then you're more likely to do it.

Q. What do you like about sports?

A. Well, I think the main thing really is to have fun and get this team spirit and enjoy yourself. But when it matters whether there are goals ... when there's a lot of pressure ... this is when I don't like it. Mainly ... probably because when I was a child playing on a team if I missed ... you see there were lots of "boo's" and things ... and this I think discourages people from playing.

Q. What do you dislike about sports?

A. I think with the children, they more or less had to play in these baseball matches at school and once my daughter was hit on the head with the ball ... she had a huge lump ... I'm sure this put her off an awful lot ... well I know it did. I think when they're small the game could be adapted a little ... and I really think the emphasis there should be on fun for them ... having lots of fun together and the pressure left out all together.... And there again she found this too; she just couldn't hit the ball ... and every time she missed they had some sort of rhyme that these boys would shout ... and this does upset a sensitive child. Well, she didn't go for one or two matches and the final one she did go back reluctantly and we had a little talk and she said she'd go for the last match.

I think when they are small everything should be done to encourage them to do their best and have little matches but I think these children [boys who ridicule others] should be discouraged by the staff if they hear them shouting these things at others.

Q. How would you adapt the sport for the children?

A. Well, I think they could have had a softer ball, and football goal posts could be little for kids ... and just make these games a little bit simpler for them.

Q. From your own experience how could your own first experiences have been positive?

A. When I went to secondary school we had all of the apparatus out immediately ... as soon as I got on top of that box. I felt quite sick ... you know to jump off ... and immediately we were left behind. And the teacher also wasn't very pleasant with us ... she classed us as just being lazy. When I was about fifteen, we had a new teacher and she was full of the new P.E. which was movement and expression ... for the first time I started to enjoy P.E. You see, *anyone could be successful* ... if we'd have started off like this, we would have developed much better, rather than being faced with this apparatus and commands such as leap-frog over the box, you know ... *we were failures before we'd started.*

I think I'm against organized sports ... I'm

against the idea. You know it's pressure all the time . . . if there's a lot of pressure put on it then I don't agree with it . . . but if they're just encouraged to do their best and put up a good fight, this is fine . . . if it's not carried to excess . . . it's all a matter of keeping it in perspective.

Additional Comments by Parents

Excerpt 1:

Q. Is there anything that you dislike about sports?

A. Yes. *The attitude is you must win . . . win . . . win. . . . That I don't like.* I don't like it when it's so competitive that it spoils it. The kids are made to feel that it's so darned important that nothing else exists . . . and that's not true . . . it's just for the fun of the game . . . and if they lose, well better-luck-next-time type deal. They shouldn't be forced to feel bad about it . . . or that they're not up to standard or that they're inadequate in some way.

Excerpt 2:

Q. Where would you like the emphasis?

A. Learning the game and the fun of it . . . *just having fun* . . . because they very quickly feel if their coach is disgusted because they didn't win . . . they very quickly feel this . . . and have occasionally come home and said, "I don't want to play anymore." Or if the coach runs down the referee, he can disagree

87

with the calls, but to actually run him down or call him out . . . they quickly pick this up, too.

Excerpt 3:

Q. Is there anything you dislike about sports?
A. I think they can overdo it a bit . . . too much time and *too much pressure*. . . . I think it's good if every child can play no matter what his ability is. I think a lot depends on the coaches . . . like in soccer this year . . . and it's happened a couple of years . . . the poorer boys . . . they haven't even played. Most men try to get them to play . . . but there's kids left out and it's really sad. It's too competitive that way.

Excerpt 4:

I really don't feel they're ready to be putting so much into an organized sport . . . it takes the fun out of it for them . . . it develops a drive that I don't think is healthy. They don't just go and have fun and enjoy it . . . it gets to be a real serious business . . . and it's just not right at that age. . . .

Q. Where do you think the push to win comes from?
A. The parents . . . *the kids have got nothing to do with it . . . their advice isn't asked in this.* . . . I mean they don't ask to have these things made up into teams . . . and organized like this. I mean they'd just as soon everybody got together and had a good game. It wouldn't occur to them to organize it like that.

I'd rather see it where the thing is just available and the kids are left to do it on their own.

Q. Why do you think they're playing?

A. I think they're playing because they've been encouraged to play by the parents ... the teams are there and available, it's what the other kids are doing ... parents feel, "Well, the kids should belong to something" ... and this is what's available ... *it isn't available to go and just play.*

Q. If it was up to you would you want him to play in an organized sport?

A. No, I'd sooner that he didn't.

Q. But your husband would rather that he did?

A. Yes, he feels that they learn more ... they learn to compete and to stand up for themselves as much as anything ... and maybe Jim needs this but I don't really think so ... and he feels they'll learn to skate better and just learn more about it ... that if he's left to do it on his own they'll have fun at it but they won't learn anything. But I don't think so ... *they'll acquire an interest which will eventually lead to their learning more.*

Excerpt 5:

I really think that everybody thinks their child is the greatest ... and they're really not ... and *I think they expect too much.* We've seen children in tears come off the ice because they haven't done things right, and I don't think that's right ... better to stay home and let him enjoy what he's doing than stand out there and yell at him.

89

The most important thing is just to do it and get the ice time . . . *just to play* . . . because at fifteen or fourteen they've all dropped off . . . only the real die-hards, the kids who are really interested in sport carry on . . . but not the rest.

Q. Why do you think they all drop off?
A. 'Cause they're not that good . . . or maybe they haven't had a chance to be that good.

Excerpt 6:

Down East you're supposed to give equal time to each player regardless of how he plays, which we thought was very fair for little guys . . . and it was surprising over the year how you'd see those kids improve . . . some of them could hardly stand up when they'd start the year . . . by the time the season rolled around they weren't doing too badly. But *some of the coaches would try to slip somebody in that they shouldn't have, and that's not fair play and that's not what you're trying to teach kids.*

Q. Where do you think the serious win-attitude comes from?
A. I think it's probably the coaches. . . . I think it's the people themselves . . . they'll treat life this way . . . if they cheat on something and get away with it. . . . *I would think a lot of people play sports as they live.*

Excerpt 7:

I think the swimming lessons are very good. They're not pushed . . . they go strictly at their own speed and they take a lot of time with them.

Excerpt 8:

Chris will not go to swimming lessons anymore. He went last year and we enrolled him this year but he wouldn't go . . . he will go to swim on a Sunday as long as it's not swimming lessons. . . . *He likes to go just for the fun of it,* but he doesn't like to go because it's lessons and he's got to go.

Excerpt 9:

My boys took swimming lessons and there was so much pressure on them that now I can't even mention the word swimming.

Note: Previous three excerpts show what a difference the quality of a program means to the child.

Excerpt 10:

Q. What do you like about sports personally?
A. Well, I don't like sports, I never have. . . . I don't know really why . . . it was probably the competition. . . . I didn't like to compete that well. . . . *I didn't like being a failure.*

Excerpt 11:

At the school they announced a Saturday morning calisthenics class for children and I asked Mike if he wouldn't be interested in going. . . . I said I'd be glad to sign him up . . . but he said he wasn't interested. *If he goes tobogganing, he's so happy and excited about it, he comes home and tells about his different experiences.*

91

Excerpt 12:

> Q. Do you think you would like him to partici-
> pate in organized sports?
> A. No, I don't think so, because I think they go
> overboard a little.
> Q. What do you mean by overboard?
> A. Like the hockey here, it's getting to the stage
> where it's not really a fun sport anymore . . .
> *it's just not a fun sport anymore* . . . it's too organ-
> ized . . . *it's drummed into the kids,* they have to
> be there, *you have to win.*
> Q. What else bothers you about sports?
> A. When it gets past a sport . . . when it turns
> into fighting or clobbering someone just for
> the sake of winning . . . *I think it's wrong to get
> the kids* so *determined to win that they're going to hit
> somebody with the stick on purpose or trip them up on
> purpose just for the sake of winning a game.*

Excerpt 13:

> If the parents don't know what goes on . . .
> and . . . sometimes there's a lot of pressure on
> the children . . . and I don't think that's too
> good for them. I think *if the parents get in there
> and see what's going on it would help quite a bit.*

Now that you have had a chance to think about
how you and your family feel (as well as how others
feel), you should be in a much better position to answer that vital question posed earlier: *what is best for kids?*

The remainder of this book should help you to
clarify your position further. Suggestions are provided
which we feel may be helpful to you in your attempt
to provide the best environment for children.

7

What Can We Expect from Kids?

Too often the minor league coach rationalizes his temper outburst at an official as protecting the rights of his kids or he suggests that pressuring a youngster pro-style is only preparing him for real life. "It is all for their own good that I do it." Despite the best of intentions we must ask, "Is it really in their best interest?" Isn't there a limit to how soon kids can handle adult situations and come out better?

If we begin to regain any comprehension of our own childhood we almost certainly begin to wonder, just as the prominent child psychologist has:

> almost no one seems to be thinking about children. . . . We are thinking about what these children will some day become. . . . We seem more

and more determined to get children to give up childhood and become little adults. It appears in all our efforts to provide "advantages" we have actually produced the busiest, most competitive, highly pressured, and over-organized generation of youngsters in our history—and possibly the unhappiest. We seem hell-bent on the elimination of much of childhood. (Le Shan, 1968:5-6)

It seems as though Jacques Plante, the famous NHL goaltender, was saying similar things when he spoke at the Kinsmen's Sportsman's Dinner in Edmonton in May, 1972. He talked of too much scheduling and organizing in many aspects of a kid's life and remarked on how little free-time even a five-year-old child often has today. He talked of the pressure and tension in organized minor league games—of kids being afraid to make mistakes. He mentioned the coach of a team of twelve-year-old boys criticizing their performance and declaring, "You guys play like a bunch of kids!" Plante, in effect, is pointing out the need for kids to explore, to discover, and to experience success in order to learn and be motivated to improve. We begin to realize that childhood is an important transitional phase of life that everyone must go through. Plante realizes the need to empathize with youngsters and to recognize their needs if we want to present them an environment of reasonable and helpful challenges.

Sportswriter Vince Leah, who has had extensive experience and involvement with kids in sport over the years, comments about the environment created:

I don't know exactly why, but everytime grown

men get seriously interested in kids' sports and
try to promote it and improve it, they end up
teaching the youngsters adult sins and adult
anxieties of the kind that make ulcers. (1964)

We believe a low-pressure, "fun-oriented" environment, without these adult problems, is necessary to
keep kids in sport. In an interview, Team Canada-
USSR hockey star Paul Henderson stated, "The kids
will shy away from hockey if you take all the fun out
of it."

The arbitrary relegation of fun to unimportant
play activity is utter nonsense. Learning can be a lot of
fun and fun can facilitate learning and provide incentive. The degree of seriousness of an act bears no relation whatever to whether or not it is a learning
experience. One is reminded of the seven-year-old in
Sunday School class who was asked to write his own
Ten Commandments. He headed the list with "Thou
shalt have fun!" He was right; the fun, the playfulness
of childhood is a legacy that reaps rich rewards forever
(Le Shan, 1968:333).

Similarly, some adults subscribe to the fallacy that
games have to be highly structured to be competitive.
Probably some of the most competitive games ever
played occurred spontaneously on sandlots and ponds;
but the competitive spirit did not prevent the break-
ing-up of crucial play to investigate the welfare of one
of the participants. Cooperation and competition, often of the best types and in the best proportion, seem
to occur naturally in youngsters' unstructured play.
They compete vigorously (with themselves, with others, or as groups), but frequently adjust rules and reor-

95

ganize teams or games. This can equalize competition, allow for cooperation, and keep the chances of success close to fifty-fifty for all.

Plante's testimonies, along with those of other hockey stars such as Gordie Howe and Jean Beliveau, reveal that these people achieved their phenomenal levels of achievement by getting confident beginnings in the kinds of games now referred to as scrub, shinny, street hockey, and others which occurred spontaneously in the backyards, ponds, and alleys of their communities. These facts and thoughts tend to make us wonder if there are things in those games which are vital to recapture. This will be kept in mind as we move to make suggestions for a more natural environment for kids' sport programs.

The key to learning is motivation. However, motivation in sport and play activity for youngsters should never be the problem it is made out to be by some adults. It becomes a problem only when it has been destroyed by an unsuitable play environment.

If you are developing suitable sports environments, it is important to consider the child's perspective. Probably the first thing a child would appreciate and benefit from would be an exposure to a relatively wide range of different kinds of desirable activities (e.g., individual sports, team sports, outdoor activities, etc.). Because initial exposures are so important, every community should take pride in the kind of beginners' experiences it provides. Beginners don't need uniforms, they don't need practices, and they don't need pro-style coaches. What they do need is a relaxed encouraging environment in which to try things.

The Research and Development Committee of the

Red Cross Water Safety Program has come to realize
the importance of appropriate beginning experiences
and has suggested changes in beginning activity terms
to avoid misleading connotations (Smith, 1972). They
have also recognized the need for realistic expectations
based on a careful series of progressions in skill,
maturity, and capability (beginner—junior—intermediate—senior). Each level contains new expectancies of performance, but an individual seldom moves

Outline of Community Hockey Program

Level	Level Title	Leader Title	Ages
I.	Beginning Ice Sessions	Counselor-Helper	5 to 7
			8 to 10
			11 to 13
			14 and over
II.	Advanced Ice Sessions	Supervisor	5 to 7
			8 to 10
			11 to 13
			14 and over
III.	Community Hockey	Leader or Game Director	9 to 10
			11 to 12
			13 to 14
			15 and over
IV.	Inter-Community Hockey	Coach	11 to 12
			13 to 14
			15 to 16
			17 and over

Note: A three-year age range within a group in the
beginners and advanced ice sessions is not a problem
when skill levels are similar and strong consideration
is given to maturity and capabilities.

up until he has satisfied both himself and his leaders as to his capabilities. Similar thoughts applied to other sports might make the environment for early experiences more appropriate and make the progressive challenges for kids more reasonable. For example, a hockey structure such as the one below, which involves careful progressions both in leadership roles and participant capabilities, could be applied to other sports and be a big asset in improving sport environments for kids.

When the terms "coach" and "practice" are designated, they tend to bring connotations of organization and formality to the situation which may be detrimental to initial experiences. Initial practices might be called "ice experience sessions"; the term "hockey" might be replaced with "ice activities"; and the "beginners' coach" might be more appropriately called a "counselor-helper," or something similar. The function of formal teaching or coaching at this stage is not anywhere near as important as creating an environment which allows the beginners to learn and discover on their own. Perhaps a session with parents prior to beginning would be highly useful in encouraging their participation and in outlining the fact that the major objective of the program is to provide an experience for the child that will leave him eager to return. Initial emphasis should be on numerous skating-type activities with guidance.

The complexity of activities attempted over the season will naturally increase as the participants seek new challenges and learning experiences. The role of the counselor-helper in these sessions might be described as:

1. developing and maintaining surroundings in which fear is reduced and kids are eager to try and to discover new things;
2. guiding the youngsters and making suggestions as to new challenges, fun activities, and things to try which develop and improve skill (particularly skating);
3. playing with the kids to provide a model of many different things to try;
4. encouraging youngsters and commenting positively on anything that resembles a step toward improvement, a new game or idea, or anything that appears like an effort or accomplishment.

The youngsters will gain confidence in themselves and their leader as they play together and get helpful suggestions and encouragement from the counselor-helper. The process of learning hockey skills (such as skating, puck handling, and shooting) will become one of discovery under guidance, and motivation will be self-sustaining. The "counselor-helper" would do well to observe kids playing spontaneous hockey-like games in backyards, streets, or on patches of ice and/or to recall similar situations in his/her own life. Being able to recognize and identify the needs, capabilities, and desires of children in those kinds of highly functional initial learning experiences, would be an extremely valuable asset to the leader who is trying to create the same kind of environment in a community facility. By the end of their beginning year, the participants will have enjoyed a wide variety of hockey-type activities, and skill development will be a rewarding side-effect. Age groupings for beginners' programs might include the following ranges: five to seven years, eight to ten years, eleven to thirteen years, and fourteen years and over. As is evident, the role of a leader in such a group is distinctly different from that of a competitive coach.

After his beginning season, the participant needs two to five years of hockey-type experiences in a relaxed, natural environment where guidance on fundamentals is available and the complexities of the game are introduced gradually.

It is usually some time before the young hockey player is able to develop sufficient personal skill, strength, endurance, understanding, and social awareness to experience much success or reinforcement in the complicated adult version of the game.

In these stages of development, as a child and a player, each individual should have a choice as to the type of hockey activity he or she participates in. Many children who have found the beginning season highly rewarding would choose a simple extension of that program in which a supervisor participates with the kids in a variety of spontaneous hockey-type games and activities (advanced ice sessions). For younger kids, cross-ice games for maximum use of facilities and more ice time would be suitable. Individuals should be encouraged to attempt and develop the skills for playing different positions. This insures that the child will develop an appreciation and understanding of all skills while finding out which he prefers or excels at. At this stage, as with beginners, scaled down and modified versions of the game are crucial to the experiencing of success. For a while, the whole end or side of the rink might be a goal.

After a season or so of these advanced ice experience sessions, the individual may choose a slightly
more advanced program where some of the sessions
involve a reasonable number of house league games in
the community. The games might be under the supervision of designated "game directors" or "leaders"
who would be responsible for both coaching and officiating. The sessions without a game scheduled would
involve slightly more organized skill development sessions, but the emphasis would still strongly be on play
activity. A low-anxiety climate should be maintained
throughout the different levels to facilitate children's
natural self-motivated learning.

When the child is over ten years old, if he begins
to find his major challenge and satisfaction lie in the
pursuit of excellence and competitive games, he should
have the opportunity to move on to inter-community
hockey programs. The opportunity for youngsters to
really find out how good they can be is an important
part of any community program. The crucial point lies
in insuring that the youngsters are capable of facing
inter-community competition. When they are ready,
inter-community leagues under the supervision of par-
ticipant-oriented coaches can provide valuable developmental experiences. (Note: Coaches should possibly
be required to experience leadership roles in all four
levels of activity.) The prime concern for the welfare of
all participants must remain paramount, even though
the child may move into a more competitive environment in order to find new skill challenges. The game is
still play and still fun.

The environment, leadership roles, and behavior
described in this model are considerably different from

what occurs in many community minor hockey programs. Far more people meet the requirements of the new leadership roles because the demands required are within many people's capabilities. For example, teenagers, students, mothers, fathers, and more elderly citizens have the potential to be highly valuable and efficient at one of the levels on the four-level leadership progression. This new approach to certification and registration of leaders, which involves philosophy and attitudes rather than only sports knowledge, is bound to have a positive effect on many present minor league programs for kids. Specific behavioral expectations and requirements might be presented so that regular leadership evaluations could be made for the good of the kids.

Poor communication itself is one of the blocks in providing good minor sports experiences. There often appears to be a lack of communication with the kids as well as between adults. Public awareness of the goals and objectives of programs does a great deal to insure their success. For example, communication to parents and interested people on "The Objectives of Beginners' Ice Sessions" and "Beginners' Needs" would serve to help recruit the kind of people necessary to make such a program a success. In addition, anyone associated with the program (parents, kids, counselor-helpers, observers, etc.) would all have a clearer image of the part they could play in presenting realistic expectations for participants. In most communities, publicity in local newsletters describing the *new* leadership roles and program objectives, along with a request for help from people really concerned with doing what is best for kids, will bring forth a host of new and genuine volunteer leaders. Remember, *you don't require specific sport knowledge to be a good leader!* Try to bring out some of the tremendous currently unused leadership potential in your area.

When you move to create suitable new community programs, make sure you consider the female as well as male child's perspective. Girls have often been short-changed in the presentation of opportunities for positive sport and play experiences. For most of childhood, the physical capabilities of boys and girls are similar, so there is really no reason to expect any less from little girls. They should expect equal opportunities for positive exposures and experiences in sports. A co-educational approach to activities is recommended.

We have presented an outline and description for one activity which we feel provide more reasonable expectations and suitable experiences for youngsters. Rather than just being critical about problems, we feel it is important to suggest and develop better alternatives.

The kinds of structures and environments presented to kids shape their expectations and behavior. Perhaps the best evidence available to show the tremendous importance of the *structural* arrangements for competition comes from research by social psychologist, Muzafer Sherif. He has shown that by making simple changes in the structure and environment for groups of youngsters, it is possible to direct their behavior toward either extreme interpersonal hostility and aggression or toward friendly, constructive interchange.

A system of competition was arranged for a group of boys in a camp setting whereby, despite being previously committed to sportsman-like conduct, the boys developed extremely self-centered attitudes. The result was bitter dislike for one another, hostility, aggression, and the development of "beat the other guy at any cost" attitudes.

Even attempts to provide pleasant social contact and interchange were futile until changes in the structure of the competitive environment were made. When structural changes were made so that it became important or necessary to cooperate with others from time to time, the behavior in the camp began to change completely. Before long the boys developed cooperative constructive attitudes and a genuine interest and concern in one another (M. Sherif et al., 1961).

It begins to become obvious that what kids feel, what they learn, and how they behave are dependent on the structure and environment presented to them. We can't expect "desirables" from kids if their environment doesn't encourage it.

Most sport programs for youngsters would benefit from a "child's-eye" analysis along with some ingenuity and foresight in follow-up. It is important to think about what we can realistically expect from kids prior to developing programs. Take a careful look at the structure and environment for kids' sport in your community!

8

It's Gotta Be Fun

When is the last time you heard kids laughing during structured minor league play? Compare what you hear to the joy-filled sounds from the games kids create themselves. Is something being repressed by organized play?

Many of sport's most skilled stars have developed their skills and acquired their tremendous desire and motivation to excel through early, spontaneous, fun-filled "child-oriented" play experiences. We have heard the same people make statements to the effect that kids will quit if the fun is taken out of sport. There seems to be a decreasing number of fun-filled childhood experiences which could even faintly compare with the "horse-apple-on-the-river" hockey of days gone by.

This, combined with the mounting evidence that child psychologists are beginning to provide, leaves us with one distinct impression—*it's gotta be fun!*—whether it is during practices, games, teaching of fundamentals, drills, exercises, scrimmages, or whatever. In order to achieve our goals and to get the impact we want out of these activities, we have to find creative, innovative, interesting, and different ways of presenting them.

Ironically, diverting the focus from winning to fun results in happier, more enthusiastic youngsters, who inevitably perform better and do more winning. It's usually much easier to do a good job if you enjoy doing it.

The participants themselves can often be an important source of ideas and suggestions. Kids are filled with creativity—we only need to give them the chance. Their reactions and responses are the vital feedback to which a good leader or observer responds. It is usually not too difficult to determine when kids are having fun, or when they are enjoying themselves. Learning can be fun, and spontaneously developed games can be extremely enjoyable as well as highly competitive. Sport should be fun, and for youngsters this is critical. In addition to the thoughts suggested in this book, Murray Smith (coach and teacher extraordinaire at the University of Alberta) outlines a few teaching principles which can be extremely helpful to anyone trying to put fun into kids' sport (1970):

Prepare through Planning

If, for example you are limited in terms of facility time, you should plan carefully in order to make the best use of what you have. You can often develop a helpful "off-field" or "off-ice" program—games and contests, or drills and exercises, whereby youngsters compete with themselves. Perhaps the best kind of competition for the child is often competition with oneself, for children and adults alike need to learn that the real competition in life is with oneself. A program of self-improvement with many intermediate, or short term, goals is usually motivating and highly satisfying.

Take time before and after your active practice time to get feedback from participants and pick up suggestions or ideas that they may have. Use this information to modify and improve your teaching. Utilize fun ways of learning skills, and eliminate or modify drills, games, or situations which the participants don't seem to enjoy or learn from. Such planning will undoubtedly make your teaching more effective and enjoyable, both for you and the kids.

Aim for Maximum Activity for Each Participant

We learn by doing and kids like to be active. They have unbelievable stamina, and in the games they play on their own, they will often perform continuously for hours on end. Try to eliminate a great deal of standing in lines and waiting for turns. You might provide every child with a ball or puck and perhaps have stations through which small groups rotate, doing something different at each station. It is often helpful to have teaching assistants (anyone interested can help and learn), or to develop leadership by appointing different group captains each time out. Kids thrive on responsibility! Be helpful in suggesting efficient ways to do things, but do not be overly concerned about young-sters "picking up bad skill habits." With enough prac-tice, kids will find efficient ways of doing things even though their method may be somewhat different from the way you were taught.

Plenty of activity and hustle makes things more fun and develops strength and endurance as well as skills. The kids can probably play you out!

Use Your Facility to the Fullest at All Times

If you make the best use of the area and equip-ment available, your kids will be provided with more room and more opportunities to learn and to have fun. For example, if you are involved in gymnastics, arrange the equipment so that the most activities possible can be carried on at the same time, or if you are involved in hockey, try to use as much of the ice as possible all the time, perhaps by utilizing different groups in different areas.

Try to Let Youngsters Use a Natural Way of Learning

As we mentioned under principle 2, do not hesi-tate to suggest or demonstrate what you feel is an efficient way to do something, but do not be afraid to select an end or goal, then let them use their own means within reason to reach that end. You can help guide and provide tips to those having the most difficulty while permitting the natural learning method of trial-error-correction. By utilizing this method you provide motivation and encourage creativity, which should always be a part of learning. (It is more fun and who knows when someone will find a better way?) This method also prevents the child from being overloaded with skill-description-information. Kids have limited capacities and cannot learn efficiently if presented with too many suggestions, or with advanced skills.

The beauty of the natural process, which is only beginning to be recognized, is that you don't have to be an "expert" to teach. We could involve hundreds of people (women, teenagers, pensioners, and others— many of whom would be excellent leaders) who are interested but do not feel "qualified." They certainly can help! They can accurately perceive if the learning experiences are effective and if the kids are having fun. Note: Don't hesitate to get involved or to involve someone new!

Innovative Games and Practice Drills Should Develop Fundamental Skills and Tactics

In every sport there are fundamental skills which should be developed before moving on to others. For example, reasonable skating ability is fundamental to success in the complex game of hockey. There are many examples of individuals whose development has been hampered by their attempting advanced adult skills and tactics before really knowing the basic fundamental skills.

Therefore, encourage and utilize game-like drills and activities which require and develop fundamental skills (e.g., games which involve turning and stopping both ways on skates). As kids improve their basic skills, they experience more success and often enjoy themselves more. In the past, basic skills have often been taught in terribly boring ways. Let's put "Fun in Fundamentals!" It's an important challenge which can make us more efficient and more popular leaders.

Keep the Child's Perspective in Mind

It is this principle with which we are most concerned in this book. It's important to recall how valuable encouragement and approval are for kids and to remember how stimulating to explore and to attempt things on your own can be. It's important to realize how refreshing change and variety are. Try not to forget how you loved responsibility as a child yet dreaded being expected to do more than you felt capable of doing. It's important to recall how you learned that success is possible but never certain, and how you became able to handle the consequences. Reflect back on why you tried things and how helpful good feedback was to skill development or achievement. Do you recall enjoying the execution of formal drills, high social pressure, or being chewed out in defeat?

It is important to think about all these things: to think about how you would like to be treated as a child in the different situations and to think of what could possibly be the best experience for each child. Watch the children's faces—*their smiles should be your victories!*

Your win-loss record may take a dynamic new perspective when it becomes evident that every kid can win.

Perhaps the ultimate we should strive for is games without "formal" officials or "formal" coaches. A great deal of enjoyment and learning takes place in kids' backyard and street games without people stereotyped in these positions or roles.

Peter Hopkins, the creative Director of Intramurals at the University of Waterloo, has shown that it is possible to run sports programs without officials. He has assessed the problems officials face and concluded that "there must be a better way!" He suggested the ideal of people "calling their own fouls" is not an impossibility, and that by insisting on officials we are only repressing our maturation and eliminating opportunities and situations which force us to discipline ourselves (1972). It makes us wonder if with "formal" officials we are only hindering the social objectives of play and discouraging self-discipline.

With these thoughts in mind, Hopkins established a voluntary, recreational intramural program at the University of Waterloo in a variety of sports (including many team activities which are contact in nature). Hopkins admits it has taken three years to develop this approach and a better attitude to activity; but it has now come to the point at which students request this type of game rather than the competitive one with formal officials. He makes some of the following conclusions about intramurals without officials:

> It reduces the "win at all cost," overcompetitive attitude to games.
> It teaches self-discipline.
> It is economical—saves money while involving more people.
> It reduces injury and fights in activity.

111

It creates a proper atmosphere for co-ed activities which are more social in nature.
It increases playing time—no delays for officials' decisions like foul shots or penalties.
It is a great area for faculty/staff involvement.
It tends to involve the "radical element" on campus—those who may have become disgusted with sport and often dropped out.
It makes you think—about yourself, your involvement, and creative adjustments or modifications.
It puts *fun* back into activity!

These would seem to be some pretty convincing and saleable conclusions. Although things do not change overnight, we suggest this innovation be kept in mind as we move toward better sport experiences for kids. However, youngsters accustomed to a traditional established minor program may have some difficulty adjusting to such a change without some intermediate steps.

Many kids, because of their past experiences, may have essentially forgotten how to play for fun or how to play without trying to beat the rules. It has taken considerable time and effort to produce kids who feel winning is everything and it will correspondingly require time and effort to convince these same kids that *winning isn't everything.* Don't expect instant changes, but the natural attitude and perspective of playing for fun can certainly be rekindled and reclaimed. As a start, when a youngster returns from a game, parents might first ask: "Did you have fun?" or, "Did you try the things you wanted?" rather than "Did you win?" or, "Did you score any goals?"

The appointment of game-directors rather than formal coaches and officials might be another important intermediate step.

The game-director situation eliminates any "ego" concerns, as the leader uses his guidance in the interest of all the kids on both teams. Learning while having fun and not offending others becomes the theme. You can begin to establish pride in calling your own fouls, playing by the rules, and having fun. There are many ways to move toward better minor sport experiences for youngsters. Your creative innovations and adjustments in your particular sport could be even more effective than the examples we present. However, think them over carefully to insure that you feel they will have the desired effect. In addition to innovations already mentioned, we have tried or observed some of the following ideas and feel they are interesting examples:

—the use of lighter balls or pucks (often sponge), to reduce injuries and increase opportunity for success.

—co-educational and girls' games. Both sexes should have equal opportunities. Co-educational games have been found to be highly successful for all ages (e.g., ice hockey with sponge puck, broomball, etc.).

—cross-field, cross-gym, cross-pool, or cross-ice games. Perhaps three games on one surface to have all youngsters active and to better utilize available area, usually only four to seven players per team. Everybody in the water, on the field, floor, or on the ice! (A shorter, but totally active game is more enjoyable.)

113

—when "picking" teams, have the appointed team captains choose the opposing team rather than their own. This helps eliminate the humiliating scene of the poor players being overlooked and really not feeling wanted. Give everyone a chance to be captain. Having the game-director select both teams is another way around the problem.

—changing of shifts on-the-go to make maximum use of pool, field, gym, or ice time, to give all players equal playing time and to keep players on the sidelines alert and involved in the game. The blast of a horn by the game-director every three minutes would mean players in the pool, on the floor, field, or ice, must leave for the sidelines instantly and not touch the ball or puck or interfere with the on-coming shift of players (infractions cost a penalty shot). The ball or puck is always in play unless the game director blows the whistle.

Note: If for any reason a player is playing on two shifts, he or she must go to the sidelines and then return to play.

—the use of penalty shots rather than penalties in certain games (e.g., hockey) to provide instant negative reinforcement, yet virtually no loss of playing time for the player as long as the child taking the shot is not subjected to high anxiety levels.

—the use of expulsion from the game for *any* deliberate attempt to injure.

—the use of penalties for potentially dangerous behavior (e.g., any stick blade higher than the waist, throwing the bat, etc.).

—the use of matched lines on opposing teams in order to balance play

—the use of the entire end of an area of play as the goal for beginners to increase opportunities for success.

—the use of a "goal-box" rather than a goal which can *not* be guarded (within the crease area). This results in everybody learning to swim, dribble, cradle, or skate, rather than having someone stay in goal—perhaps it also improves shooting ability.

—the rotation of players through different playing positions to insure that they get the opportunity to appreciate and try all skills. (Perhaps this may give them a chance to determine what they are best at or enjoy most.)

—full length games with as many as twenty participants per side and as many as four balls or sponge pucks in play. Sometimes two nets or baskets can be used at each end (side by side, or one in each corner). This game gets everybody active—there is always a challenge not far away. There is still the opportunity to go end-to-end with plenty of swimming, dribbling, running, or skating. It may sound chaotic, but the kids love it because there is plenty of action, which results in skill development, more opportunity to score, and more motivation. As game-director, they may want you to keep score and it will keep you hopping! Note: "Multi-ball" and "Multi-goal" approaches are excellent in basketball, soccer, field hockey, ice hockey, water-polo, etc.

—dry land training (e.g., "tennis ball" hockey games on a field, or floor hockey in the gym to develop skills and conditioning when ice is not available).

—similar programs can be set up in dry land training for cross-country skiing or diving (e.g., use of skate boards and trampoline respectively).

—games without heavy contact padding and equipment allow better agility, are less expensive, don't eliminate those without equipment, and discourage over emphasis on hitting.

—coaches and game-directors who stay "on the floor," "on the field," or "on the ice" with kids during games are able to offer more encouragement and guidance on fundamentals as well as team play. Suggestions and opportunities to try things on the spot are often valuable.

—the use of different team captains and leaders for each game to develop leadership, respect, and responsibility. (Arm bands might signify "captains".)

—games without sticks to develop balance and ability to handle the ball or puck with feet (e.g., ice hockey, field hockey, lacrosse).

—games of tag to improve swimming, dribbling, running, skiing, or skating ability.

—games of "scoro" to see how many times you can hit a target—improves shooting.

—games of ball or puck control—everybody dribbling, swimming, cradling, skating, and handling a ball or puck in a congested area. Keep head up and do as much with the puck or ball as you can (turning, stopping, "dekeing," faking, etc.).

—games of "keep-away" to develop ball or puck handling, and passing.

—relay races or contests which involve agility or speed, running, swimming, skating, volleying, passing, ball or puck handling, throwing, shooting, or any combination thereof (e.g., for water polo, soccer, ice hockey, baseball, lacrosse, volleyball, basketball, football, etc.).

—games of passing keep-away. One or two players inside a circle and three outside. Object of players on outside is to pass the ball or puck through the circle safely, to move for passes, and to receive passes. Players inside try to intercept. If they do so they trade places with the players who made the pass.

—balance contests to see who can improve their own performance most. For example, glide as far as you can on one ski or skate, or on two skiis or skates sitting down on haunches.

—power contests—pushing or pulling a resisting player going forward or backward.

—crocodile simulations—little guys love this one! Tell them a good player (e.g., soccer, basketball, or hockey) is constantly aware of everything around him, just like a crocodile, with his head up and eyes protruding just above water. Demonstrate with your best "crocodile eyes" and have them practice this while handling a ball or a puck.

—games where every child must touch the ball or puck at least once, in any order, before a teammate can take a shot (e.g., European handball, floor hockey, pinball, ringette, soccer, etc.).

—games where every child must score in order for a team to win (i.e., the first team to have everyone score wins). This sets up a cooperative situation where every child is important, learns the skills, and eventually makes a point because his teammates help him or her (e.g., European handball, basketball, etc.).

—keeping score on something other than baskets

made or goals scored. Try counting the number of times one child helps another, or the number of smiles you see.

Keep in mind that any or all of these suggestions may be adapted to your particular sport or interest. Think of your own situation!

If you want self-motivated learning and healthy individual growth and development for youngsters, *it's gotta be fun.* Smiling, relaxed, and happy kids who are eager to return to an activity should be the aim. We have provided only a few examples of the countless ways we can make sport more *fun* for youngsters. We hope you think about your sport and your situation and proudly come up with more smiles and chuckles. It's hard to label a happy child a loser!

9

What about Girls?

A highly regarded twelve-year-old baseball player, Marie Pepe, was dropped from the team because National Little League, Inc., threatened to cancel the team's charter if the coach let her play. Abigail Hoffman, track and field Olympian, was one of many young girls who had to disguise herself as a boy in order to get on a hockey team: "The season was three-fourths over before I was discovered. I was never allowed to play again. I was eight years old at the time." Two high school girls decided to try out for the baseball team (the only ball team, baseball or softball, in the school). Three weeks after practice began the director of athletics forced them out. He said, "It is illegal under the N.J. State Interscholastic Athletics Association rules for girls to play. They're nice girls and they are very involved in sports but we can't violate the rules."

There are many similar cases of discrimination against young girls in a variety of sports which have gone unchecked and unchallenged. However, recently in New Jersey, the Essex County chapter of the National Organization for Women decided to test the validity of some of these boys-only "rules," specifically with reference to little league baseball. The case of Marie Pepe being expelled from little league solely because she was a girl was taken to court. The state hearing examiner for the N.J. Division of Civil Rights ruled that little league was violating the state anti-discrimination law while getting public financial support and using parks and playgrounds supported by public funds. The ruling meant that little league of New Jersey had to allow eight- to twelve-year-old girls the opportunity to play.

There were mixed reactions to this ruling, some of which were highly emotional. The man who coached Marie Pepe's team was pleased with the ruling and was hopeful that it would set a precedent for other sports. However, state little league officers appealed the decision and voted to suspend all play in the state (for the 1974 season) rather than let girls play. Much to the dismay of little league officials, the appellate division of the superior court and the state assembly upheld the original ruling.

At the local level some communities quickly and willingly changed their discriminatory policy to include all children, while others disbanded rather than abide by the new "rules." In one community where little league was cancelled, the parks and recreation commission took steps to replace those coaches and organizers who resigned over the issue. Interestingly enough they ended up with more volunteer coaches and supervisors than they had had before, including, for the first time, a woman. In another New Jersey community the mother of a nine-year-old girl went to register her daughter, Susan. "The adult registrar spent thirty minutes trying to convince me that girls should not play baseball." However, Susan "had assured me that the boys she knew were not against her playing with them."

Susan summed up the situation perceptively when she said, "But it isn't the boys who don't want me to play and little league is for kids. It's only the grown-ups who made the mess. Well, when I grow up I won't be like them because I know how it feels."

Maybe we won't have to wait until nine-year-old Susan grows up. Maybe we can begin to change things right now.

As Laura Sabia said in her keynote address at the national conference on women in sport, there are three factors which are vital for girls' and women's total development: "Equal Opportunity, equal responsibility and choice." Unfortunately many girls and women have found the opportunities of sports involvement closed to them solely on the basis of sex. Many others have been made to feel that they must choose between being an active sports participant and being a desirable teenager or woman. It is time to introduce real choice to girls and women with respect to sport. This includes the choice to be involved in sport or not to be involved, the choice to play the sports that boys play or not to play, and, perhaps most important, the choice to be involved in stimulating activities that are new and different and that are totally beneficial for girls' social and psychological development. As Marion Lay, a concerned, forward thinking leader from Sport Canada expressed it, "Our task is to make sport a beautiful and meaningful dimension of the female."

It is time for little girls to stop wishing and wondering—wishing they could play and wondering why they can't. It is time for girls to move from the sideline to the center of the field, but on their own terms. It is time to enter a new era of beneficial and active involvement for girls in sport and physical recreation. It is time to turn the tide, to have sport serve women and to have women play a more active role in sport at all levels.

When we look at the social environments to which most young girls are exposed it becomes apparent that they generally have neither the models nor the reinforcements necessary for long term sports involvement. This appears to hold true for most girls during childhood and becomes even more pronounced during adolescence (as girlhood fuses with womanhood). If we wish to modify this situation, we must again look to the environment. It is only by rearranging the environment and rewards within the environment that behavioral alterations can be made.

Former Olympian Marion Lay stated in the rationale for the National Conference on Women in Sport, "Women are interested in developing viable sporting environments in which they can exist first as women and second as athletes." This kind of approach is particularly important in children's sport, where the foundations for active sporting lives are being established. It is vitally important that children have positive initial exposures to sports and physical recreation. Attitudes toward sport are born out of experience (real or perceived).

Girls and women have the same kinds of needs for positive activity experiences as do boys and can greatly benefit from them if they are properly constructed and operated. However, neither the opportunities nor the social sanctions for these kinds of experience presently exist. One need only examine their own community league or their own schools to verify this statement. Because the opportunities for girls in sport have been relatively nonexistent, women's sports are in many respects far behind, and yet, in other respects are far ahead. One advantage of setting up programs to benefit large numbers of young girls at this time revolves around the fact that it is not necessary to first move backward before moving forward. Women are in a position to capitalize on the misdirections of the boys' programs and to consequently devise and implement much superior programs for girls. Women have the capacity to construct and operate children's sports programs which could serve as a model for all sports programs.

After interviewing the parents of many children (participants, nonparticipants, and drop-outs) we became aware that most mothers (as well as some fathers) knew of the problems, were sensitive to the child's needs, and were very concerned with the child's getting a positive exposure in sports. Perhaps this was because many of these people had negative experiences of their own to draw upon which helped them to empathize with the child, or because the child tended to confide in them, or because they were very perceptive people. At any rate, from a human development view-point, as a group women appear to be extremely well qualified to work with children. Mothers seem to be primarily concerned with the outcome of the child, whereas fathers often tend to be less empathetic and more interested in the outcome of the game.

At least three studies indicate that mothers should be taking a much more active role in organizing and actually running children's activity experiences. Higgs (1974) found that what mothers liked best about kids' sport was the stress on comradeship while the fathers liked the competition. In the same study he found that while many fathers responded negatively to their children after a losing game, mothers generally responded more positively both after a winning or losing game (e.g. good boy, you tried your best, etc.)

These findings support those of an earlier study (Orlick, 1972a) which showed that mothers were extremely sensitive to the needs of the children. When mothers were asked if there was anything they disliked about organized sports for children, they responded in the following manner:

Mothers of Participants		Mothers of Nonparticipants	
Response	Percent	Response	Percent
Too much emphasis on winning	68.8	Too much emphasis on winning	62.5
Too competitive	37.5	Too much pressure	31.3
Not letting all kids play equally	37.5	Too competitive	25.0
Too much pressure	25.0	Not letting all kids play equally	25.0
Too organized	12.5	Too organized	18.8
Too serious	12.5	Too dangerous	18.8

Mothers of both participant children (87.5 percent) and nonparticipant children (75 percent) expressed a dislike for the winning emphasis, the pressure, the competitiveness or some combination thereof.

Each mother was asked if there was anything she would like to see changed in sports to make them better, or to make it a better experience for the children. The mothers responded with the following suggestions:

Mothers of Participants		Mothers of Nonparticipants	
Response	Percent	Response	Percent
Equal opportunities for all	62.5	Emphasize fun (enjoyment)	62.5
Emphasize fun (enjoyment)	43.8	Less winning stress	18.8
Emphasize good sportsmanship	12.5	Less competitiveness	18.8
Less organization so early	6.2	Less pressure	12.5
		Equal opportunity for all	12.5
		Prevent injuries	6.2

Recent work by Rosenthal (1974) has also shown that females are more sensitive to nonverbal cues. Women appear to be more capable of reading signals such as facial expressions, body position, body movement, and verbal tone, especially when these cues imply some negative feeling. This kind of perceptive skill is important in an activity setting where often a child will not tell you that he is cold, or that she feels left out, or that he feels embarrassed, but may communicate it in nonverbal ways. It was further found that those who were more sensitive to nonverbal communication tended to be more democratic (less autocratic) in teaching situations, perhaps because they understood the child better.

If more of these perceptive people (women as well as men) were to become involved in kids' sport, many problems could probably be quickly eliminated. For example, no kids would be left out, the children's needs and interests would be paramount, there would be no overemphasis on winning, no unnecessary stress would be put on the child, and in all probability the kids would have very positive fun-filled exposures to sports. We personally feel that there are tremendously valuable human resources, in the form of mothers who are presently not being utilized in children's sport. If these people would become more involved, not only would the kids have positive models and more fun, but so would they.

Although we have great respect and faith in women's capacity to draw upon their strengths to right their situation with respect to sport, we also have some real fears with respect to the replication of negative aspects of men's programs. This fear is legitimized by the following three initial inquiries at three different educational levels.

A survey was recently taken to assess the amount of ice time each elementary school age girl was receiving in a recently formed Ottawa township girls ringette league. (Ringette is a rapidly growing organized sport similar to floor hockey but played on ice with skates.) The survey indicated that during a forty minute game some girls were getting as much as thirty-five minutes of ice time while others were getting less than four minutes. The effects of this kind of approach are predictable: a high percentage of dissatisfaction, and dropping out. One father already indicated that his little girl came home in tears one night saying that she only got on the ice once and that she wanted to quit.

In a similar vein, McNally (1974a) recently found in a pilot study that such things as not being good enough to play, being made to feel inferior or unacceptable and unsportsmanlike conduct were listed by high school girls as definite reasons for not playing more sports. Likewise Schmitter (1974) in a pilot investigation concerned with why only 150 females out of a possible 4,000 participated in a university intramural program found that most girls interviewed felt that if you did not have a good background in the game you might as well forget it. This is precisely what the masses of women seem to be doing—forgetting it. (It is interesting to note that at the same university half of the male population participated in intramurals over the same one year time period.)

The winning thing was fairly prominent in this women's intramural program with physical education majors reportedly most win oriented and nursing students least win oriented. When nurses were asked what they thought about their competitors (in basketball), they replied with comments such as: they are poor sports, they always want to win, they are too aggressive, they always cry to the refs (particularly with reference to physical education). When physical education majors were asked about playing against the nurses they responded with comments like: nurses are a joke, we don't even have to try, it's just hacky basketball.

Many of the women interviewed who came out "for fun, to goof around, for laughs, to learn the sport, for exercise, to get to know other people," felt their reasons for wanting to participate had not been fulfilled, and they were doubtful about returning next year. Unfortunately some of the most win oriented students are the ones who will eventually be drawing from their own past experience to provide an example and to set up programs for young women.

It is vital that all young girls receive equal exposure in the form of playing time and that they are exposed to successful and rewarding experiences. Both sitting on the bench and the absence of rewarding experiences in general lead to feelings of inadequacy, rejection, unworthiness and unfun, which in turn leads to a rejection of sport as a viable alternative.

If sport makes a girl feel like a reject either in the sports environment (e.g., failure) or outside of it (e.g., socially), she may either devalue and drop the sport or begin to question her own self-worth, neither of which is desirable. When you are trying to create a desire to be involved in sports and a sense of personal worth, it is difficult to surpass the positive impact of a good experience and equally difficult to reverse the effects of a bad experience. The manner in which the child perceives sport, in relation to her concept of self, greatly influences her behavior in relation to it. Sports environments should be designed to develop and enhance a girl's positive image of herself and not to detract from it.

People tend to behave in ways which are consistent with their perceptions of what others expect from them. As Betty Friedan has pointed out, the dilemma of women is the continued acceptance of an inferior self-concept which is no longer valid or necessary in today's environment. Laura Sabia, chairperson of the Ontario Status of Women Council, concurred when she said, "We must change the thinking about ourselves, the women, that is the problem."

Perhaps sports environments can be constructed to help solve this problem, this dilemma, by developing and reinforcing girls' resourcefulness, independence, self-reliance, and positive self-perceptions. Perhaps girls can learn through sport that the pursuit of self-actualization in any domain can be a satisfying and rewarding endeavor.

After conducting over 1,000 interviews with both men and women, Steinman and Fox (1966) discovered a discrepancy between men's concept of the ideal woman and women's perception of men's concept. Women predicted incorrectly that men would prefer a woman with little self-assertion or self-achievement who had a permissive, subordinate role in the family setting.

Perhaps some similar misconceptions are operational in sports. In a recent pilot study Yeoman (1974) found that high school males did not in fact feel that it was unfeminine for girls to be involved in sports. Yet many females, particularly around adolescence, seem to feel that males will perceive them as unfeminine if they participate in sports, and they act according to this expectation (even though it appears to be unsupported in reality).

Boslooper and Hayes in their book the *Femininity Game* mention several instances of this occurring in sport. They speak of a fourteen-year-old girl who stopped playing street games and sports because she started liking boys and wanted to be accepted. One night after a dance she got into a snowball fight with the boys. The girls took her aside and said "boys don't like that." That's when she gave it up. She quit to become a "lady."

Micki McGee, track coach at Oberlin College, tells a similar tale. "As a young girl I enjoyed playing sports even though I wasn't particularly talented . . . and for my thirteenth birthday my father gave me what I dearly wanted, a new baseball glove. And then my mother took me aside and said, 'I want you to know that gift isn't from me. I am concerned that you're still a tom boy. At your age you should be a young lady.' That frightened me enough to hang up my glove and I didn't participate in sports again until I was eighteen when I began to pick up the remnants of my love for sport."

Unfortunately some people fail to realize that a "lady" can become a more complete person and a girl a more complete child if she is a physically active, healthy, and self-reliant individual. She can feel better and look better and can have the option of sharing in a variety of experiences (outdoor, recreational or competitive) with other people (males or females). This is one important message which must be transmitted to girls and young women.

Whether we are interested in girls participating for the sheer pleasure of the activity or for self-actualization, a general climate of acceptance and interpersonal warmth should permeate the sports environment. All those who come out should feel this overall warmth. For example, an equally warm greeting should be extended to all girls, even the ones who are not highly skilled. As a result they will feel more acceptable as people and happier about being in the sports setting.

Good behavior or improved performance should be pointed out in an especially warm way to all girls. Even the less skilled or less socially adept will then feel good about what they have done. Try to give an equal amount of instruction, help, and attention to all girls—not just those expected to perform better. Give all girls an equal opportunity to play, to practice, to question, to demonstrate, and to do things they like to do. In this way all the girls will feel good about physical activities and good about themselves.

Acceptance is extremely important for girls and young women. They need to feel totally socially acceptable both in the sports environment and outside the sports environment in order to function best in both. Initially, a child needs to know that sports will be fun, that she can compete at her own level, and that she will be accepted, without any fear of rejection. As she approaches adolescence, she needs to know that an active leisure life will add to, rather than detract from her acceptability and social development as well as to her physical development. She also needs to know that she can pursue excellence through sport if she so desires, or can play for fun, relaxation or social interaction, if so desired. A woman needs to know that sports and physical recreation can be a source of great satisfaction and enjoyment as well as many healthful benefits. Physical activities can serve as an excellent deviation from the stress of the day or can provide some much needed excitement in what may have otherwise been a dull day. Participation must be viewed as the asset that it can be and not as the liability that it has sometimes been.

We have ahead of us the challenging task of introducing and promoting sport for girls with a renewed emphasis, one which avoids the major pitfalls which are so evident in boys' organized sport programs (e.g., destructive competition, destructive aggression, destructive elimination).

Fortunately we seem to have both the knowledge and human resources necessary to meet this challenge successfully. However, if positive change is to take place, women have to bring it about and women have to support each other in the process. Men who are aware of the problems and are prepared to do something about them will help.

If you have a little girl or are important to a little girl you can have a great effect upon her future development. The best way of ensuring that she will have an opportunity to enjoy healthy physical activities as a part of her life is to get involved yourself. Take her cycling or hiking or cross-country skiing or whatever you and she decide to do. (You'll have fun too.) Make sure she has the opportunity to participate in a variety of activities in your school and community. Get involved yourself, as a participant, an activity supervisor, an organizer, a supporter for others who are getting involved, or as someone who openly expresses concern for equal opportunities within the community league and school programs.

In conclusion, it can be said that in developing viable sporting alternatives for young girls, it is extremely important that (a) we begin to tap the tremendously valuable and powerful human resource in the form of mothers (and other female models) and (b) we benefit from, rather than replicate, the mistakes that have been so rampant in the boys' programs.

In order to meet our challenge:

Opportunities must be made available for all young girls to participate in and benefit from the activities of their choice (competitive and noncompetitive).

Programs must be created which provide positive fun-filled activity experiences and feelings of acceptance for every girl (regardless of skill level).

Programs must be run by humanly qualified people who are intent upon operating in the girl's best interest (the first priority being the girls, not the game).

Modeling techniques must be utilized to promote girls' participation—to promote the desirability of sport for girls and girls in sport (e.g., films, advertisements, human models).

If the children can be exposed to the right kinds of environments, the rest will follow as a matter of course. Our ultimate goal is to develop well adjusted girls who are eager to join, eager to return, proud for being, and better for having been.

10

Making Sport a Better Place for Kids

"Our policy is about people ... the greatest number possible ... increasing their participation in sports and recreational activities, and improving the benefits they can enjoy from such participation" (Munro, 1970:1).

The proposals of the Canadian Minister of National Health and Welfare for a strong movement towards participatory sport are an excellent beginning for a world of far better sporting experiences for children. A new manifesto has been proposed for sport: mass-participation and the most fun for the most people! There is a need for sport for fun as well as for achievement.

However, the nature, behavior, and lifestyle of

people will not change just because government leaders make these kinds of statements which, incidentally, appear highly desirable and promise attractive results. Government-stated philosophies and policies will not do any good unless *you* (those people at the roots of society) act in accordance with them.

Similarly, you are the most important people in achieving everybody's aim of doing what is best for kids. As we discuss making sport a better place for kids our prime concern remains with what you can do for kids.

Regardless of your role (coach, parent, fan, or whatever), we feel there are six important basic processes in which you can actively involve yourself in order to do what is best for kids! You can:

Establish a base and determine the kinds of behavior you truly consider desirable. Do so specifically with definite examples in mind.

Insure that you are, or that you project, an example of desirable behavior.

Provide opportunities for the child to determine the kinds of behavior he or she truly considers desirable.

Directly reinforce or acknowledge "anything that looks like" or approximates the kind of behavior considered desirable.

Directly discourage, or fail to acknowledge and accept, "anything that looks like" or approximates behavior considered undesirable.

Seek out and pursue indirect ways of insuring the promotion of desirable values and behavior.

Establishing a base and determining the kinds of behavior you truly consider desirable does not merely involve concluding things like: I believe in sportsmanship, I believe in fair play, I believe in mass-participation, I believe in equal opportunities for all, or I believe in winning. You must finalize in your own mind what these things really mean in terms of specific behavior and situations. To determine what you really value and to recognize it in situational terms are important. Examples might include:

Emotional and physical outbursts toward officials should not be tolerated.

Every child on a team should get an equal opportunity to play despite his or her ability level. Everyone deserves an equal chance.

Kids under ten years of age should play cross-ice or cross-field games (or other variations) to give more youngsters more opportunities to play and learn. Kids should not sit on benches for large parts of games.

Every child on a team should be given opportunities to play all positions and develop different skills.

Kids should be expected to shake hands after a contest.

Kids should never intentionally take penalties or be encouraged or allowed to bend or break any rule in pursuit of victory.

Individual penalties should not be announced over public address systems because the attention may be reinforcing.

Kids should be encouraged to pursue improvement and/or excellence in the true fundamental (game) skills (e.g., in hockey—skating, shooting, stickhandling, passing, and checking).

All strategies in kids' sport should be based on

improvement of one's own skilled performance rather than the degrading of an opponent's.

Girls should have every opportunity to play games that boys have and should also be encouraged to create new games.

All behavior which endangers the welfare of participants should be discouraged (e.g., in hockey—carrying a stick blade above the waist; in baseball—wearing of metal cleats by youngsters).

Early exposures and experiences for youngsters should take place in a relaxed, encouraging situation with plenty of opportunity for success.

All in all, the process of determining specific desirable behavior is a crucial one in your movement toward "doing what is best for kids." Your situational behavior values and perceptions are the *base* from which you operate. (Appendix D illustrates some situational behavior values on "Sportsmanship.")

Insuring that you are, or that you project, an example of desirable behavior may often involve a bit of introspection or self-analysis, along with some frank personal discussions with those around you in whom you can confide. It is not uncommon to find inconsistencies between what you say you believe and your observable behavior, perhaps due to oversight, excitement, or whatever—for we are all human. For example:

You may advocate self-discipline, yet you may become visibly upset or outraged over a close call by an official, rather than concentrating on overcoming it.

You may say you believe in equal opportunities

137

for all, yet only encourage sport for boys, or give the better players more opportunity to play in games.

You may recommend sportsmanship, yet accept a youngster's bending of rules to win a game; or refuse to shake hands with an opposing coach after a game, instead of using the opportunity (for the kids' sake) to rationally discuss any problems that may have arisen during the game. You may advocate healthy initial experiences for youngsters, yet become impatient with one who shows little initial ability.

Perhaps there is no way every person can be the perfect model of the ideals he believes desirable, but any person can do a great deal to reduce these inconsistencies and to insure that what is projected to youngsters is a genuine example. We have already emphasized the importance of modeling for youngsters, and you, as one of the significant people in the lives of the children around you, can do a great deal. If you are someone who easily gets emotionally involved in the games kids play, this step or process may be a critically important one for you and the kids you care about.

Provide opportunities for the child to determine the kinds of behavior he or she truly considers desirable.

Regardless of whether you are the best example or not, you can make a tremendous contribution here. Your relationship and discussions with the child can often be the key. Because it helps them gain direction and a feeling of worth, kids thrive on "philosophical discussions," "think sessions," and above all, "being confided in." Youngsters have more ability to comprehend and capably direct themselves than they are often given credit for. They like to be able to explain and justify their behavior, and to personally discuss what to believe in, what is really important, and how to behave and why.

Do not be afraid to express confidence in a child's ability to make the right choice. A. S. Neill in his widely known book *Summerhill* shows that given *conditional* "freedom to choose," a child is quite capable of determining for himself or herself the types of behavior which are *truly* desirable. The key condition to this "freedom" is that it does not mean "license." That is, the freedom does not involve the "license" to infringe on the rights of others. With this simple condition a child's basic needs will direct him or her toward desirable forms of behavior.

In a classroom at Summerhill, this means freedom to do as you want as long as you don't interfere with anyone else's opportunity to learn. Inevitably, the child eventually finds something worthwhile and constructive to do or to learn. Similarly, on a sports field, a child can be free to do as he chooses as long as he doesn't infringe on anyone else's rights. He will inevitably come up with creative-directed behavior "within the rules" because the rules were developed to protect the "rights" of the participants. In such an environment you are free to do all kinds of creative things, but *not* free to cheat, to be violent, or to take advantage of an opponent in any unfair way. As a result, to gain approval (which kids need) the child directs himself toward desirable constructive behavior.

These fair opportunities to choose his own behavior can be tremendously important to the child. However, if the child's environment involves license (where others are permitted to cheat, to be overaggressive, etc.), then attention should be drawn to the potential consequences of different kinds of behavior, perhaps through discussion and by using examples.

If you feel that you sometimes behave questionably or you see a point-of-view or behavior in others which you feel is questionable, do not be afraid to explain and discuss it with the child you care about. It is important that a youngster come to realize that no one, adults included, is perfect. He or she then has a clearer picture of reality and can become much more self-determining and selective about the models chosen and the behavior emulated. A mature relationship with a child, which includes "openness" (the complete confidence of the other), can be extremely meaningful to both parties. As in any relationship you can help one another to know yourselves and others better. Therefore, it is important not to talk "down" to kids or to assume that they have little to offer. A child may not develop to his fullest if he is made to feel unworthy of your confidence or unimportant. Children are often overlooked in seemingly simple ways like not being introduced among adults, being by-passed in team selection, or not being involved in decision-making processes.

We think contributing to opportunities for, and discussions about, *freedom without license* can be an extremely valuable and meaningful process.

Directly reinforcing or acknowledging anything that looks like or approximates the behavior considered desirable has a great impact on the people in your environment, particularly kids. Whether you are a leader, a parent, an official, or just an interested observer, your communication and reinforcement are crucial to moving towards better behavior and better things for kids. You can verbally and physically express appreciation of *anything that looks like* an improved skill, a good effort, a concern for others, a creative or novel approach, a cooperative team effort, self-control or self-discipline, and so forth. With your encouragement and that of others like you, a child can begin to feel success and achievement in these desirables and move on with enthusiasm to better things. You will begin to see that Every Kid Can Win!

When you pursue this positive course you really begin to analyze and appreciate the finer parts of sports, and realize their tremendous value and potential. As you become better at identifying the beginnings of desirable behavior and skills, you will find yourself a more objective, busy, and significant person, who is able to "weigh" reinforcement. That is, an individual's best efforts (performance or behavior) will be recognized and strongly reinforced, while lesser efforts are still recognized and encouraged. Remember the lesser efforts may be the beginnings of something big for a youngster. Let him know you like it! He will probably do even better next time. (Note: The more immediately reinforcement follows behavior, the more effective it tends to be.) Here are some examples of what you can do.

You can communicate approval to a youngster who can hardly skate but makes a valiant effort to reach the puck. *You* may be the key as to whether he tries again or quits.

You can acknowledge the sacrifice of an opportunity for the benefit of the team or another player. *You* may determine whether he becomes a cooperative team player or a selfish egotist.

You can cheer a beautifully executed skill or play and be part of the reason a child seeks excellence or improvement.

You can praise and vocalize satisfaction at a child's self-control and desire to overcome, rather than retaliate to frustration. You can develop that pride in succeeding with "integrity" despite "adversity."

You can accept and attempt to implement unique suggestions from youngsters regarding adjustments in games, rules, and so forth. By doing so, you can often improve a game and youngsters' experiences while reinforcing "creativity."

You can direct compliments toward the kid who loans his equipment to an opponent, or who stops in the middle of play to help a player who might have been hurt. *You* can be the key to a genuine concern for others.

The important thing to realize is that you can do nearly all these things regardless of your role in kids' sports. This kind of exercise can make an official an important positive as well as negative reinforcer; and there is no reason on earth why he should not be! The official who talks to kids, communicates, and acknowledges good play, as well as penalizing bad, has much more impact in guiding and directing the behavior of children. Likewise, clear, concise reasoning concerning a penalty or infraction can be tremendously effective in increasing one's respect and/or significance as a leader or guide (whose aim should be improving all behavior and performance). In sports such as gymnastics, diving, and synchronized swimming, officials can be helpful to the athletes by taking a few minutes after the meet to make positive suggestions. If the athletes were to get some constructive feedback on where they need work to improve their scores, it could be a great asset toward their future performance as well as to athlete/official relationships.

Perhaps one of the finest experiences for anyone involved in minor sport is to be the official in a game (or meet) as well as the coach for both teams (perhaps small teams). At first this will seem difficult, but you will begin to develop objectivity and skill in guiding and directing behavior based on a genuine concern for all involved (what is best for everyone). This is the kind of experience which we have suggested for leaders involved in early sports exposures and experiences for children. Through these experiences, leaders will usually develop the kind of rational ability and leadership skills which are needed by those involved in kids' activities. These kinds of people need to develop the skill to reject polarization toward questionable aims and to maintain a more accurate and objective perspective of what is best for kids—*all of them.*

At any rate, regardless of your role in kids' sport and play, try to refine your ability to identify the beginning of desirable things and utilize some of the tremendous potential *every* person has to encourage and promote the desirable.

Directly discourage or fail to acknowledge or accept anything that looks like or approximates behavior considered undesirable.

We first have to develop our ability to recognize "anything that looks like" behavior which might become undesirable. Just as we nurtured the *beginnings* of desirable behavior, it is equally important to discourage the *beginnings* of behavior which could be undesirable and possibly dangerous.

You can contribute tremendously to this process regardless of your role, but we will choose to make an example of its effectiveness in the key role as an official. Officials today (due to crowd pressure, heckling, etc.) often seem hesitant, and more concerned with "appearing fair to both sides" than concentrating on and identifying *anything* that looks like the beginnings of undesirable behavior. We look at hockey for an example. A study by psychology-of-sport students in London, Ontario (Bentley and Hunter, 1973), revealed that a group of forty hockey players, eight and nine years old, responded to the question, "Why do you think fights start?" in the following way:

Responses Classified As:	Number	Percentage
Retaliation	31	77.5
Frustration	6	15.0
Rough Play	1	2.5
Bad Sportsmanship	2	5.0

Responses like, "When they hack, you fight" were prevalent. Most fighting seems to occur when the boys themselves feel they have to control an opponent's

144

behavior rather than relying on the official to do so.

The official, therefore, is the preventative key if he develops his skill at identifying and instantly calling (penalizing) anything that looks like undesirable behavior or bending of the rules. As he calls even the minutest interference, or a stick accidentally higher than necessary, or a follow-through to a check that might even faintly resemble an elbow, or any slight approximation of an attempt to injure someone or physically retaliate, he concisely tells them what he sees and lets them know it is not desirable. Calling it close, *real close,* can be the key to preventing molehills from becoming mountains. He may initially be chastised with comments such as, "Let them play the game," but in the process, he is presenting a clear and distinct picture of what is desirable and why. The irony is that he truly is "letting them play the game," rather than letting undesirable behavior destroy the experience. At any rate, if he follows this course, his respect as a game-director grows, and the game progresses to the kind of clean, beautiful, fun-filled experience it should be.

The coauthor himself has made this theory a reality by officiating the games kids play. He has changed "clutch and grab," interfering, overaggressive, dangerous behavior to fast skating, effort-demanding, clean, cooperative, and disciplined behavior within the duration of a period or two of play. By concentrating on calling every tiny undesirable offense, rather than being overconcerned about one's justification and appearing fair to both sides, the official or game-director can do more for kids and make his own role more enjoyable.

Therefore, regardless of your role, be *constructive,* but be critical. Your opinion counts, as a fan, a coach, a community leader, or whatever. We all have some idea of what is desirable and undesirable. The least we can do is offer our best to the succeeding generation if we feel it can possibly contribute to happiness and an improved quality of life. You may not be outspoken but you can still achieve a great deal by expressing your feelings in other ways (e.g., a smile, a frown, a wink, a letter, a nod, a pat on the back). The key is first to decide and know what is most desirable and then let your feelings be known in a helpful way. It is obvious that the entire world today is suffering from lack of communication. We all have the ability to communicate; learning to use it may be critical!

Seeking out and pursuing indirect ways of insuring the promotion of desirable values and behavior are the final important processes you can develop. The possibilities in this area are essentially unlimited and the action may sometimes seem to you to be direct. What we mean by "indirect" is that you can affect other people and organizations who in turn have an influence on kids. You can also affect kids' environments which, in turn, has an impact on them. This process can involve such widely ranging actions as writing a letter to your national government representative, or talking to the other kids with whom a child plays. Following is a partial list of change-agents that influence sport and behavior. Through such channels you may find an opportunity (or person who will help you) to promote and create what is really best for kids. The list is broken into levels of hierarchy for discussion purposes, and you may notice the importance of the media (channels of communication) at every level. Once again, after you identify a channel of influence, communication is the key!

	Level	Change-Agent
I.	Immediate	Parents — family Coaches Officials Teachers Players Peers — other kids Spectators Media (newspapers, radio, television, newsletters, magazines, books, etc.)
II.	Community	Sports clubs — administrators; Community clubs — supervisors; Recreation departments — leaders; Schools — principals, etc.; Media....
III.	District	Municipal government (departments); District sports associations; School boards or systems; Private or business sponsors; Universities or colleges — departments of education, physical education, medicine, recreation, etc. Media....
IV.	Provincial (or State)	Provincial amateur sports bodies and federations; Provincial coaching and officiating bodies;

		Provincial government (particularly departments of youth, health, recreation, education, etc.); Media....
V.	National	Federal governments (particularly departments of youth, recreation, education, etc.); National sports and recreation associations and federations; National coaching and officiating bodies; Professional sport.

You begin to realize that indeed what you can do is almost unlimited. At the lower levels of indirect contact, you will probably receive some fairly immediate, specific feedback which may motivate you on to much greater things. However, on the higher levels of contact you may often find feedback at ground-level painfully slow, or sometimes nonexistent. This can be tremendously discouraging, but remember, if you reach someone in the smallest way at a high level, and that may be extremely difficult, you eventually may have done an immeasurable amount for the kids of a country or of a world.

We will now proceed to describe a few examples of the indirect ways of promoting desirable values and behavior. You will note that these methods often involve directly reinforcing someone who in turn influences the kids. In other situations you will be attempting to adjust the environment to improve the situation.

Level I

1. You may reinforce and encourage a member of the family, a friend, or acquaintance (perhaps another child) who influences the child concerned. It can be extremely effective to talk to that person about how he can contribute.

2. You can reinforce and encourage teachers, coaches, and officials when their behavior has a desirable effect on the kids and, correspondingly, talk to them (under control) and suggest through constructive criticism things that seem to have a negative effect. Pointing out such things and suggesting "why" can be helpful to the young teacher, coach, and official. If these people do not seem to appreciate constructive feedback, their genuine interest in kids would have to be termed questionable.

Level II

1. You might contact the different administrators, supervisors, and leaders of the community and make suggestions as to how to improve programs and behavior and explain how it would work. For example, you might suggest cross-field or cross-ice games to provide more opportunities for more youngsters, or you might encourage or suggest the distribution of information similar to what is found in this book for all coaches, officials, parents, and others concerned.

2. You could voice your support of any community suggestion, policy, program or action which results in improved experiences for youngsters. Similarly, you could make important suggestions as to modifications

in a game, rule changes, or other things which would make it more enjoyable and rewarding for the participants.

3. You might start a group of concerned mothers, fathers, or people who have feelings similar to yours. There are more than you think! Such groups can discuss concerns and perhaps take action to insure positive experiences for youngsters.

Level III

1. You can suggest to the head of your district hockey association that community clubs should only recruit and certify leaders who meet the criteria of being a positive influence on kids, rather than just having a knowledge of game skills. Current professional and former Canadian National Team goalie and teacher, Ken Broderick, mentions the almost complete lack of control over the types of people coaching kids:

> We've got a P.T.A. to check schools and parents get up-tight over the qualifications of a math teacher who might see their boy, say two hours in a week. But the coach has the same boy for games, for practices, and is in a position to be a far more influential figure. Yet almost anybody can be a coach. (Frayne, 1972:37)

Potential coaches might be interviewed or given fairly specific guidelines and behavioral expectations at a preseason clinic. Community leagues should determine the specific kinds of behavior they expect from leaders and coaches. This information should be written into a code, or a set of rules and requirements, which is presented to the leader and insisted upon (e.g., the Metro Toronto Hockey System, Rule #10, requires that coaches give all players equal playing time). The supervisor then has a required behavioral base to compare reports to and is in a position to take necessary action. Note: Despite these people being volunteers, having to "move one out" does not pose the problem many people anticipate. There are currently many excellent people outside kids' sport who would willingly become involved *if* they saw evidence that the values and behavior in such activities were improving by such stands. George Harvie, president of the Alberta Amateur Hockey Association, reveals that it has been shown that for each person who is forced to withdraw because he would not conform for the good of all, there are usually several more sensitive, empathetic, and qualified individuals anxious to take part in a program based on desirable values. This was also reportedly true in New Jersey communities which had to replace little league baseball coaches who chose to resign rather than let young girls play.

2. You could approach universities for the latest information which could be applied to the administration of a positive-oriented minor sport program. Or you could possibly seek guidance and leadership help from concerned physical education-recreation students (perhaps get involved yourself). You might let local sportswriters know about a book like this. They can be a tremendous help to you in promoting ideas. They are usually receptive to any contribution to sport.

You might write an article for, or letter to, the local paper or newsletter which expresses your current concerns and makes positive suggestions. You could possibly just write to agree with or disagree with an article that was written. Such feedback is a learning experience for the publisher, writer, and sometimes the public.

Level IV

1. You might suggest that your provincial (or state) sports governing body compile and distribute pertinent information to volunteer coaches. The Ontario Ministry of Community and Social Services-Sports and Recreation Branch (400 University Avenue, Toronto, Ontario) has begun working on a coaching certification program and a coaching resource package which could ultimately be extremely beneficial to hundreds of thousands of coaches and kids. You might express your support for this forward-looking step and/or suggest that similar certification opportunities and child-oriented resource packages be made available for coaches in your province or state.

2. You might contact your provincial body for your sport and suggest a change. A specific example for hockey might be that clinics for officials pay special attention to controlling the beginnings of undesirable behavior in front of the nets. (Is there any reason the defending team should have divine rights and advantages to interfere in this zone?) Suggest that anything that even looks like interference be called in this zone. A great deal of retaliation and violence could be thus avoided.

You might encourage your provincial body for a sport to take a stand on professional influence in terms of values, attitudes, and behavior for kids (e.g., active stands like the Alberta Amateur Hockey Association's withdrawal from their national body in 1972 to protest the professional-amateur agreement).

3. You might suggest or encourage the provincial sports federation to develop quizzes or contests to be distributed through the various sports. They could be multiple choice contests on what is the most desirable behavior in different sport situations, or what kinds of behavior and situations will be most valuable to youngsters at different stages of development. The answers, along with the reasoning behind them (determined by a panel of people who should know), could be publicly announced at games, over the radio, in the newspaper, or on television. Sponsors could be found for such contests and prizes given to people who really seem to know what is best for the kids in sport.

Level V

1. You could suggest that national amateur sports bodies produce and distribute films or film clips of professional sports stars and coaches reinforcing and suggesting *desirable* behavior in different situations for the young player or coach.

In addition, film clips showing innovative kids' sports programs and desirable kinds of behavior could be suggested for coaches' clinics, sport shows, and for intermissions of pro-games on TV (e.g., NFL or CFL football, Hockey Night in Canada, Wide World of Sports).

2. You might encourage nationally prominent people to take stands on the importance of healthy play experiences, mass-participation in sport, and fun in

kids' lives. Suggest government-funded marketing on the saleable "desirables" in participant sport. There should also be some control over the promotion of undesirable behavior.

3. You could make suggestions to large national corporations as to constructive projects which could benefit both them (tax write-off) and the kids of the world.

4. You might make people aware of some revealing authors on sport such as Scott, Meggessy, Bouton, Shaw, and others, by buying their books or discussing their topics. These people can play an important role in reducing the distorted "ivory tower" views and fallacies of big time sport, so that young people have a more realistic perception of sport and life on which to base their direction.

As well known sport commentator Howard Cosell testifies:

> Through the years, the legend that owners have fostered, that the various sports commissioners have endorsed and that even my own industry has seen fit to perpetuate is a fairy tale in three parts: first, that every athlete is a shining example of noble young manhood; second, that every athletic competition is inherently pure; and third, that every owner is a selfless, dedicated public servant concerned only with the public entertainment and utterly unconcerned with profit. That's been the myth of American sport and a lot of people have been indoctrinated by it. (Cosell, 1972:76)

Making sport a better place for kids is a big job,

but there are many ways to improve things and *you* can be the key. *Your* action in one of the several ways we have suggested could be crucial.

11

Every Kid Can Win

Our aim in this book has been to do something for kids and to encourage you to contribute. We find, as we are sure you do, that kids are beautiful. Their honesty, their enthusiasm, their frankness, their creativity, their energy, and above all, their empathy and sensitivity are like a breath of fresh air! These natural assets themselves can be invaluable to future generations—think of their potential in improving our quality of life or solving world problems. We are concerned that these assets not be destroyed, but rather be encouraged and developed, in the games they play. Our children hold our future!

With this in mind we have attempted to divert the attention of people in our world from the scoreboard to the child. We feel that the potential for victory in each youngster is almost unlimited, yet sometimes hardly discovered. We feel it is important and possible that each day be full of victories. The games kids play present countless opportunities for winning friends, developing confidence, helping others, exploring personal limits, being trusted, knowing reality, winning respect, discovering abilities, maintaining health, gaining satisfaction, learning things, and knowing joy and happiness.

There are many things we value. Our concern is that kids win more than "ball games." We feel every kid can win in terms of having a fun-filled experience, in terms of the values he learns, and in terms of the individual improvements he makes. We want the different roads to victory left open to the child. We feel it is easy to identify strongly with the unique victories shared and revealed by parents such as Catherine and Loren Broadus in their book, *Laughing and Crying with Little League*:

> "It's not fair," my 10-year-old son said. Barry was angry and sounded a little hurt.... "I've been to three practices and the coach hasn't let me practice batting yet."
>
> Barry batted very well the year before and this new coach was not even giving him a chance to show what he could do. Condemned without trial—my son! ...
>
> Finally, I suggested to Barry that he tell the coach before practice that he had not batted. He did and the coach told him, at the end of practice—after he had not permitted my son to bat —that he could bat at the next practice....
>
> Obviously, the coach had his team picked and

everyone else was insignificant. After several games, the expected event occurred. "Mother, I'd like to quit Little League and play ... for fun."

... He really wanted to play baseball for fun. He was tired of watching the other dancers at the ball, even though he was dressed for the occasion and listed as an honorable guest. He would rather dance in the honky-tonk than watch at the ballroom.

... It was not an easy decision for a 10-year-old boy to make in a competitive world, but he and I cheered inwardly as much as I cheered when my other son was chosen for the All-Star team.

Seeing your 10-year-old son make a decision against the tide of personal prestige and public opinion ("Nobody quits Little League," people had told him) is a glorious event. It is a great way of winning in Little League.

There is something biblical about turning defeat into victory. (Broadus and Broadus, 1972: 26–29)

... The less spectacular and more subtle victories have been the most joyous and satisfying aspects of the activity for us. Barry's "I want to play for fun" and Philip's capacity to enjoy a team victory when he had a bad day on the pitcher's mound evoked feelings of tenderness and joy in us toward them.

Or the silent thrill that Mark gave us in one game. The previous batter had struck out, slammed his bat on home plate, stomped toward the dugout, and in total self-disgust had thrown the bat against the fence as hard as he could. He was thrown out of the game.

Mark came to bat. The score was 3-2 in favor of the other team. One man was on base with one out. Mark was batting cleanup (fourth in order) and the pressure was on him. Mark swung and missed. The count finally reached three balls and two strikes. Catherine and I were really tense, sitting erect in our lawn chairs as if they were electric chairs. I turned to her and said, "I never could resist striking on a full count. I would swing at the ball if I had to leap for it."

"Thanks," she sarcastically replied.

Mark swung. I jerked like the executioner had thrown the switch.

"Out!"

Our fans groaned. The other team's fans cheered.

Mark turned, threw both hands up in the air with an "I surrender" motion, smiled and said, "Ohhh! Did he get me! He waved congratulations to the pitcher, trotted to the dugout, and commented to the next batter, "I took my eye off of it, it was a beautiful pitch. I just goofed."

We want our boys to play hard at the game, but always to play and not make sports a life-or-death issue. We also want them to learn how to lose and use failure as a stepping-stone to greater maturity and a more satisfying life. As Mark said later, "It wasn't a big deal, I struck out. I will be at bat a lot this year. Next time I will watch the ball all the way in."

We have always thought that if we do not take the game too seriously, maybe the boys will enjoy it more. The reverse is just as true. When they do not consider a strike-out a matter of life-or-death, we do not have to either.

To get back to the point. As Mark entered the dugout, my hand touched Catherine's. We looked at each other and exchanged a victory smile. Suddenly the grass seemed greener, the sky bluer, her touch tenderer, and the suited gladiators looked more like healthy boys having fun playing baseball. Now that was a peak experience.

The less spectacular and more subtle victories of character give us much joy and satisfaction.

We, like these parents, feel that:

the competitive spirit looms large in the hearts of North Americans. This spirit can be helpful but it can also be very destructive to children with small egos who are beginning to test and be tested by this win-lose concept. The pressure to win, to be perfect, to please, to improve, to produce, and to achieve glorious things can be harmful to a person when it is applied too early and too often in life. This pressure is applied too often in children's organized activities. It happens in Little League when the emphasis is upon winning. When this occurs, the individual (child) is often overlooked in the excitement. (Broadus and Broadus, 1972: 82–84)

We wrote this book because we feel kids should have more fun with sports and because we feel we have positive suggestions for putting children above the competition. We hope that our effort helps and that you will help too. We can all play the game so that *every kid can win.*

Appendix A

The Child in Sport

Recommendations

The first national conference on "The Child in Sport and Physical Activity" was held in Kingston, Ontario, at Queen's University in May 1973. Specialists working with children came from every province, as well as from other countries, to put forth the following major recommendations:

—All persons and agencies who are involved with competitive sport programs for children should recognize that such programs have the potential *to benefit* the growth and development of the total child, *or to be detrimental* to the growth and development of the total child.

—Opportunity for all children to participate must be the first priority in programming. That is, there should be opportunities for all to experiment, to make mistakes, and to succeed without fear or pressure.

—Level of ability or sex should have no bearing on the opportunity to participate.

—Each child in a competitive situation should have equal participation time.

—Fun and enjoyment should be emphasized in the program.

—There should be structured opportunity for unorganized participation (e.g., scheduled facility time for spontaneous activity).

—Respect and cooperation with reference to team members, opponents, and officials should be actively encouraged.

—Violent behavior and cheating behavior should be actively discouraged, by rules or other means, in children's sport.

—The child's interest should be kept above the winning interest.

—There should be active encouragement for the development of cooperative skills.

—Awards, trophies, all-star competitions, most valuable player awards, provincial and national championships, and other secondary incentives, should be de-emphasized in favor of benefits intrinsic to the activities which foster inclusion, rather than exclusion, of young children in physical activity.

—Physical educators, volunteer leaders, recreation departments, and sports governing bodies should be urged to involve children in the planning, leadership, and evaluation of the activity.

—Researchers should be encouraged to conduct studies on the possible positive and negative effects of competition.

—With more and more leisure time becoming available, children should have opportunities for using their free-time creatively.

—Support should be given to the growing movement in which *all* children might be related in active ways to the out-of-doors, particularly the natural physical environment.

—Equipment, facilities, and rules should, whenever possible, be designed in such a way as to be adaptable to the maturity and size of the child to insure greater success and security.

—Employment of physical activity personnel should be on the basis of their teaching ability, attitudes, and values rather than upon their personal athletic accomplishments, coaching success, or specialization in one sport.

—There should be an emphasis in physical education programs away from formalization, drill, and competition to experimentation, discovery, and cooperation.

—Sensitivity, mutual respect, positive self-images, and social skills should be encouraged through voluntary participation.

—Early adult intervention should not be permitted to destroy the benefits of self-organized child play.

Appendix B

Minor Hockey
Recommendations

The following recommendations came out of the City of Edmonton Parks and Recreation Department Investigation of the Edmonton Minor Hockey Association (E.M.H.A.). (We might mention that the Province of Alberta seems to be fortunate in having numerous creative, innovative, child-oriented leaders.)

—That each Community League and Athletic Club recruit coaches whose first interest is the well-being of the boy, and whose secondary interest is the game of hockey.
—That the E.M.H.A. require every coach to have taken and passed a coaching clinic (this clinic should be designed to emphasize the philosophy of hockey coaching), and that each coach be required to upgrade his training periodically.

—That the Federation incorporate a rule which requires coaches to give each player on his team equal ice-time throughout the game.

—That the E.M.H.A. institute a public information program to educate the adult community as to the true purpose of the minor hockey program, and to what constitutes proper behavior while attending a minor hockey game.

—That the E.M.H.A., with the assistance of the Alberta Referee's Association, continue its efforts to overcome the violence in the minor hockey program.

—That the style of National Hockey League play be recognized as a negative influence on the Edmonton minor hockey program.

—That opposition be expressed to the teams of the Western Canada Junior Hockey League for the use of fighting and violence as a drawing card for the games of the Western Canada Junior Hockey League.

—That opposition be expressed to the present Canadian Amateur Hockey Association—National Hockey League agreement, that by the payment of funds to the Canadian Amateur Hockey Association and its members encourages the development of highly skilled players to the exclusion of the average player.

Appendix C

Desirable Athletic Competition

Recommendations

A Special Joint Committee on "The Desirability of Athletic Competition for Children of Elementary School Age" in the United States made the following points:

—Children at this age are not miniature adults; they are boys and girls in the process of maturation into adults. They seek and can profit from suitable play opportunities but the benefits are not automatic.

—Perhaps one of the strongest arguments against the varsity type program for young children is the tendency to start sports specialization too early. The elementary school years should be the time when the basic skills are learned, when children have the opportunity to engage in a

broad range of skills. They are not yet ready for specialization.
—One cannot ignore the possibility that varsity type athletics school age children may give youth a distorted sense of values.
—Sports with varying degrees of collision risk include such sports as baseball, basketball, football, hockey, soccer, softball, and wrestling. The hazards of such competition are debatable. The risks are usually associated with the conditions under which practice and play are conducted, and the quality of supervision affecting the participants.

The same group recommends:

—modification of rules, game equipment and facilities to suit the maturity level of the participants.
—activities limited to a neighborhood or community basis without play-offs, bowl contests, or all-star contests.
—avoidance of undesirable corollaries to organized, competitive athletics, such as excessive publicity, pep squads, commercial promoting, victory celebrations, elaborate recognition ceremonies, paid admission, inappropriate spectator behavior, high pressure public contests, and exploitation of children in any form.

Appendix D

What About Sportsmanship?

These pages constitute a revised guideline, containing a few situational behavior values, on "sportsmanship" which was developed at the University of Alberta for distribution to youngsters at sports camps, to parents of children, to intercollegiate teams, and sometimes to the general public. It is an attempt to help people become aware of the kinds of behavior which can truly be considered "sportsmanlike." It might be of some assistance to you as you attempt to determine the kinds of specific situational behavior which you consider desirable and/or undesirable. Highly successful Golden Bear Hockey Coach, Clare Drake, has found it a helpful teaching aid.

Introduction

Every contest is based on certain rules or laws and it is only by abiding by those rules, both in spirit and letter, that the game is best played and enjoyed.

Good sportsmanship is nothing more than the "Golden Rule" (treating others as you yourself would like to be treated) applied to sports. This results in not only better played contests but also larger dividends in sportsmanship and good fellowship.

Conduct of Players

Toward team-mates

1. Team-work and cooperation are absolutely essential for success in any group endeavor. Group spirit, unselfishness, a concern for others, and self-sacrifice are all necessary for the best team performance.
2. Criticism and sarcasm seldom accomplish anything beneficial. The end-result nearly always is less relaxation, more tension, and a corresponding decrease in skill.
3. The destructive "beefer" has no place, either on the team, on the bench, or in the stands.

Toward opponents

1. The other team members are guests and should be treated accordingly.
2. Uncomplimentary remarks toward or concerning the visiting team, should never be made.
3. Competition would not be possible without

169

the cooperation (i.e., the appearance and participation) of the visiting team.

4. TREAT YOUR OPPONENTS AS YOU YOURSELF WOULD LIKE TO BE TREATED!

Toward officials

1. The official's task at best, is a difficult one and respect, rather than antagonism, should be the attitude of all players.
2. Their decisions must be respected in order that the players and the spectators will receive the greatest benefit from the game.
3. Officials are attempting to handle a difficult job to the best of their ability and players have a great responsibility in establishing patterns of conduct for the spectators by the way they accept decisions.

Conduct of Parents and Spectators

Toward the players

1. "Kidding" players on the home team may soon resolve itself into "riding" and, as a result, upset the spirit and team-play of players.
2. No encouragement should be given to the destructive "critic" who continually finds fault with everything and everybody.
3. Players should be encouraged to play according to the rules regardless of the "tide" of victory or defeat.
4. A team does not always play the best brand

of hockey, does not always score the most goals, and does not always win. At least the members should be encouraged to play their best within the rules and "win, lose, or draw" they should still be accepted as people.

Toward opponents

1. Fair-mindedness and an appreciation of excellent play and desirable behavior, whether by the home team or the visiting team should be the ideal to strive toward.
2. The same type of courteous and considerate treatment should be given the guests, as you would like your team to receive on out-of-town trips.

Toward officials

1. The official's goal and intent are admirable ones—"To guide and control behavior according to a pre-established set of rules and insure that no one gets an unfair advantage over others." He deserves fair treatment and encouragement.
2. Let them know about their good calls—like anybody, they perform better with encouragement and feedback through the proper channels. Officials *do care* and will usually respond positively to constructive criticism that is reasonably presented.
3. Officials are human and thus subject to error, but they are close to the rules and their interpretations, and are nearly always in a better position than others to judge what is happening on the ice. Like anyone they will usu-

171

ally perform better if their job is made enjoyable.

4. Continual "booing" and derogatory remarks are generally the poor sportsman's way of displaying feelings in a group which he usually lacks courage to express directly as an individual.

5. "Booing" decisions will not change them or improve the situation in any way. The officials are honestly trying to do their best.

Good sportsmanship does not just happen, but it is the result of a definite program of education. It must be a continuing process, resulting through the years in the establishment of traditions of behavior. New players and fans are soon initiated into such tradition and the pattern continues. If the players and the spectators really want good sportsmanship and desirable behavior, it can be reinforced and would soon be accepted as "socially approved conduct" at every game.

Appendix E

Girls in Sport, Children's Attitudes

Recommendations

The First National Conference on Women in Sport was held in Toronto, Ontario, on May 24–26, 1974. The Canadian government invited over 100 specialists from Canada and the United States to confer and make proposals for the future of girls' and womens' sport. The conference was conceived and organized by Marion Lay, a sports consultant from *Sport Canada* (Journal Building, 365 Laurier Ave. W. Ottawa, Ontario).

In the workshop which focused on the development of children's attitudes towards sport, the following major recommendations were put forth:

—that equal opportunity be given to girls to participate in existing facilities (e.g., playing fields, ice rinks, pools, etc.);

—that we stress a participation philosophy rather than a performance philosophy;

—that a sincere attempt be made to attract more women (particularly mothers) to be actively involved in children's sport at all levels (e.g., supervisory, administrative, coaching, etc.);

—that within local sport settings children play an active role in deciding the rules for their own sport;

—that modifications in games, facilities, equipment, rules, and structures be proposed and tested to enable increased enjoyment and success;

—that children ten and under be involved at an intramural or community level only and not in an organized league with a winning hierarchy;

—that "all win" sport structures be developed for girls (e.g., based on fun, individual improvement, self-actualization, etc.);

—that the teaching and playing of games be encouraged rather than the highly organized professional type adult sports;

—that a wide variety of team and individual sports, competitive and noncompetitive be developed and promoted at many different levels for girls, so that more girls can have positive activity experiences;

—that more emphasis be given to the intrinsic values of participating in sport (e.g., for the fun of it, for the good of it) rather than for extrinsic rewards (e.g., money, trophies, etc.);

—that programs be instituted to develop competent leaders who are interested in the participant first and foremost;

—that volunteer coaches attend clinics on children's sport which focus not only on skill development but also on the potential of sport for the social, psychological, moral and physiological development of all children (girls and boys);

—that workers at day care centers and nursery schools be given training in movement education for preschool children;

—that pre- and post-natal classes be used to promote awareness of movement patterns and the importance of physical activity for total child development;

—that parent–tot programs be implemented in all activity areas (e.g., community and school programs);

—that violence in sport be banned from TV at times when children may be watching; and

—that pressure be applied to the media to provide good models of sports activities and sports behavior (e.g., expose positive innovative children programs; show models of desirable sport behavior).

Appendix F

Girls in Sport, Elementary Curriculum

Recommendations

At the National Conference on Women in Sport, the curriculum development committee for elementary school physical education expressed the following:

All girls (and boys) should be given a wide experience of physical activities on a daily basis. All children should be encouraged to explore a variety of movements in different media (on land, in the air, in water, on ice, and in snow) and become skillful in many of these. The curriculum should include activities of a creative and objective nature. The programs should provide both individual and team experiences of a cooperative and competitive nature. In this way children may enjoy activity and make it part of their lifestyle and the experience may also help to develop loving, caring, empathetic, and vital citizens.

With specific reference to elementary school curriculum they recommended:

—that daily instructional classes in physical education at all grade levels for all children be taught by an interested teacher knowledgeable in the developmental needs of children;

—that the curriculum from K-13 reflect a continuing progressive program that is appropriate for the developmental level of students;

—that use of facilities and equipment in all educational, recreational and community centers be equally available in terms of time, space and leadership for boys and girls and that an effort be made to make the public aware of their use through adequate coverage by the media;

—that equal opportunity free from excessive competitive pressures be provided for participation in activities of special interest to all individuals regardless of sex.

Bibliography

American Association for Health, Physical Education, and Recreation Report. *Desirable Athletic Competition for Children of Elementary School Age.* Washington: NEA Publication Sales, 1968.

Bandura, Alberta. *Principles of Behavior Modification.* Toronto: Holt, Rinehart and Winston, 1969.

Bentley, Brian, and Bill Hunter. "Aggression in Minor League Hockey." Unpublished pilot study (Psychology of Sport project). University of Western Ontario, 1973.

Boslooper, Thomas, and Marie Hayes. *The Femininity Game.* Briarcliff Manor, N. Y.: Stein and Day, 1973.

Botterill, Calvin B. "Minor Hockey Environment and Behavior: An Analysis With Proposals For

Change." Unpublished Master's thesis, University of Alberta, 1972.

Bouton, Jim. *Ball Four*. New York: Dell, 1970.

———. *I'm Glad You Didn't Take It Personally*. New York: Dell, 1971.

Broadus, Catherine, and Loren Broadus. *Laughing and Crying With Little League*. New York: Harper and Row, 1972.

Bronfenbrenner, Urie. *Two Worlds of Childhood: U.S. and U.S.S.R.* New York: Russell Sage Foundation, 1970.

Canadian Amateur Hockey Association. "Minutes of the 54th, 55th, 56th and 57th Annual Meetings." Issued from CAHA National Office, Vanier, Ontario, 1970, 71, 72, 73.

Child in Sport and Physical Activity Conference. "A Summary of Resolutions" (a preliminary report). Queen's University, Kingston, Ontario: May 1973.

———. Recommendations from Workshop on "Competition." Queen's University, Kingston, Ontario, May 1973.

———. Recommendations from Workshop on "The Effect of our Value Systems on Children's Sports and Physical Activity Programs." Queen's University, Kingston, Ontario, May 1973.

Cosell, Howard. "A Candid Conversation with the Fustian Oracle of Sport." *Playboy*, May 1972.

Crichton, A. "No Wins—No Losses." *Sports Illustrated*, March 18, 1974.

Deakin, Michael. *The Children on the Hill*. London: Quartet Books, 1973.

Department of National Health and Welfare. "Task Force on Sports for Canadians." Ottawa, 1969.

Daily Register. Red Bank/Middletown, New Jersey (Girls and Little League Controversy). November 8, 15, 1973; March 12, 13, 18, 21, 26, 29, 1974; April 1, 2, 4, 5, 1974.

Department of Parks and Recreation. "City of Edmonton Report on Investigation of the Edmonton Minor Hockey Association." Edmonton, 1972.

Frayne, Trent. "Parents, Pressure, and the Puck." *Quest Magazine.* November 1972, pp. 41–43.

Glassford, R. G.; T. D. Orlick; and H. A. Scott. "Territorial Experimental Ski Training Program." Unpublished research paper, University of Alberta, December 1973.

Globe and Mail. "Neel to have eye removed—hopes to continue hockey." December 19, 1973, p. 39.

——. "Mississauga youth guilty in fight death after hockey game." April 23, 1974, p. 1.

Hall, Julian, ed. *Children's Rights.* London: Panther Books, 1972.

Hansen, Hal C. J. "Plea to Save Thousands of Hockey Players Who Want to Enjoy the Sport." *Canadian Coach.* July 1972, p. 7.

——. "Minor Hockey in Canada—Observations, Problems, Solutions." Unpublished paper, University of Ottawa, September 1973.

Higgs, James R. "Anxiety as a Function of Participation in Boys' Minor League Hockey." Unpublished Master's thesis, University of Western Ontario, 1974.

Holt, John. *How Children Fail.* New York: Dell, 1970.

Hopkins, Peter D. "Intramurals Without Officials."

Paper presented at the Twenty-third Annual National Intramural Association Conference, University of Illinois, April 1972.

Kramer, Jerry, ed. *Lombardi—Winning Is The Only Thing.* Richmond Hill, Ontario: Simon and Schuster of Canada, 1971.

Leah, Vince. "The Case for Abolishing Hockey Leagues for Youngsters." *Mcleans Magazine,* April 1964, pp. 62–65.

Leith, Larry, and T. D. Orlick. "Aggression and Minor League Hockey." Unpublished study, University of Western Ontario, 1973.

Le Shan, Eda J. *The Conspiracy Against Childhood.* New York: Atheneum, 1968.

Madsen, Charles H., et al. "Rules, Praise, and Ignoring: Elements of Elementary Classroom Control." In *Operant Conditioning in the Classroom,* ed. Carl E. Pitts. New York: Crowell Co., 1971.

McNally, Jane F. "High School Girls' Attitudes Towards Sports." Unpublished pilot study, University of Ottawa, Ottawa, Ontario, 1974a.

_____. "Perceptions of Female Athletes by High School Girls." Unpublished research project, University of Ottawa, Ontario, 1974b.

Meggyesy, Dave. *Out of Their League.* New York: Ramparts Press, 1971.

Munro, John. "A Proposed Sports Policy for Canadians." Report presented by Minister of National Health and Welfare, March 20, 1970.

Neili, A. S. *Summerhill: A Radical Approach to Child Rearing.* London: Hart Publishing Co., 1966.

"No-Win Hockey." *Time* (Canada), January 14, 1974, p. 10.

Orlick, T. D. "A Socio-Psychological Analysis of Early Sports Participation." Unpublished Ph.D. thesis, University of Alberta, 1972 *a*.

———. "Family Sports Environment and Early Sports Participation." Paper presented at the Fourth Canadian Psycho-Motor Learning and Sports Psychology Symposium, University of Waterloo, Waterloo, Ontario, October 1972 *b*.

———. "Children's Sport—A Revolution is Coming." *Journal of the Canadian Association for Health, Physical Education and Recreation.* January/February 1973 *a*.

———. "An Analysis of Expectancy as a Motivational Factor Influencing Sport Participation." Paper presented at the Third World Congress on Sports Psychology, Madrid, Spain, June 1973 *b*.

———. "Development of Children's Attitudes Toward Sport." Paper presented and workshop conducted at the National Conference on Women in Sport, Toronto, Ontario, May 24–26, 1974.

———. "The Athletic Drop Out—a High Price for Inefficiency." *CAHPER Journal.* September/October, 1974.

Ottawa Citizen. "Injuries and threats halt junior B playoff struggle." April 18, 1974, p. 32.

Rosenthal, Robert. *The Pygmalion Effect—What You Expect is What You Get.* Chicago: Ziff-Davis Publishing Co., 1974.

Schmitter, Peggy. "Evaluation of a University Intramural Program." Pilot project, University of Ottawa, Ottawa, Ontario, 1974.

Scott, Jack. *The Athletic Revolution.* New York: Free Press, 1971.

Shaw, Gary. *Meat on the Hoof.* New York: Dell, 1973.

Shecter, Leonard. *The Jocks.* Indianapolis: Bobbs-Merrill Co., 1969.

Sherif, Carolyn W., and Gillian D. Rattray. "Psychosocial Development and Activity in Middle Childhood" (5–12 years). Paper presented at the First National Conference and Workshop on the Child in Sport and Physical Activity, Queen's University, Kingston, Ontario, May 13–18, 1973.

Sherif, Muzafer, et al. *Intergroup Conflict and Cooperation. The Robber's Cave Experiment.* Norman, Okla.: University of Oklahoma, 1961.

Skinner, B. F. *Beyond Freedom and Dignity.* New York: Alfred A. Knopf, 1971.

Smith, Murray F. "A Summary of Teaching Methods for The Community Hockey Coach." Unpublished paper, University of Alberta, 1970.

——. "Coaching Methods: Some Psychological Implications." Paper presented at the International Symposium on the Art and Science of Coaching, Toronto, October 1971 *a.*

——. "Adults in Kids' Sports." Paper presented at the International Symposium on the Art and Science of Coaching, Toronto, October 1971 *b.*

——. "Age Pre-requisites in the Red Cross Water Safety Program." A report of the Research and Development Committee, University of Alberta, 1972.

Steinman, A., and D. Fox. "Male-Female Perceptions of the Female Role in the United States." *Journal of Psychology* 64 (1966): 265–276.

Tharp, Roland G., and Ralph J. Wetzel. *Behavior Modification in the Natural Environment.* New York: Academic Press, 1969.

Wankel, Leonard M. "The Interaction of Competition

and Ability Levels in the Performance and Learning of a Motor Task." Unpublished Master's thesis, University of Alberta, 1969.

_____. "Competition in Motor Performance: An Experimental Analysis of Motivational Components." Unpublished Ph.D. thesis, University of Alberta, 1971.

Webb, H. "Professionalization of Attitudes toward Play among Adolescents." In *Sociology of Sport,* ed. G. S. Kenyon. Chicago: Athletic Institute, 1969.

Yeoman, Patty. "High School Students and Sport Involvement." Pilot project, University of Ottawa, Ottawa, Ontario, 1974.

Index

Adults, role of, 1-14, 135, 140-41, 146-47, 149-55

Behavior, undesirable, 4, 28, 34-37, 45-46, 49, 143-45
Beliveau, J., 96
Bentley, B., 45, 144
Boslooper, T., 129
Bouton, J., 154
Broadus, C., 157-60
Broadus, L., 157-60
Broderick, K., 150

Case studies
    of adults, 74-92
    of children, 65-73
Cosell, H., 154
Cosentino, F., 54

Drake, C., 169
Duthie, J., 52

Eliminating children from sports, 15-18, 20, 21, 30
Expectations, unrealistic and unreasonable, 31-34

Facilities and equipment, 39-40, 100
Fear of failure, 8-9, 19, 25, 42-43
Fox, D., 129
Friedan, B., 128
Frayne, T., 150
Fun, importance of, 37, 39, 49-50, 110-18

INDEX

Fundamental skills, development of, 49-50, 109-10

Glassford, G., 41
Goals, establishing, 8-10, 19

Hansen, H., 49, 51
Harvie, G., 151
Hayes, M., 129
Henderson, P., 95
Higgs, J., 44, 124
Hoffman, A., 119
Holt, J., 43
Hopkins, P., 111
Howe, G., 96
Hunter, B., 45, 144

Interviews, 57-60
    with children re dropping out, 21-25
    with children re making the team, 19-20
    with mothers, 14, 124
Interview questions
    for adults, 63-64
    for children, 60-62
Intramurals without officials, 111-12

Kingston, G., 49

Lay, M., 122, 173
Leah, V., 94
Leith, L., 46
LeShan, E., 34, 94, 95

McGee, M., 130
McNally, J., 127

Meggessy, D., 154
Munro, J., 134

Negative control, 43-47
Neill, A.S., 139

Orlick, T., 15, 18, 20, 38, 41, 46, 124

Pepe, M., 119, 120
Plante, J., 94
Participation, restricted and inappropriate, 29-31
Positive reinforcement 3-5, 9-10, 20, 41-42, 47-48, 50, 53-55, 140-42, 146

Sabia, L., 121, 129
Schmitter, P., 127
Scott, H., 49
Scott, J., 154
Self-worth
    importance of, 41
    developing, 41-43
Sendak, M., 34
Shaw, G., 154
Sherif, M., 103, 104
Smith, M. F., 97, 106
Sportsmanship, 168-72
Steinman, A., 129

Unstructured play, 40-41, 105

Wankel, L., 13
Way, A., 49

Yeoman, P., 129

ABOUT THE AUTHORS

TERRY ORLICK is a professor and researcher in sports psychology, School of Physical Education and Recreation, University of Ottawa. Previously he was a teacher and coach at Montclair State College and the University of Western Ontario.

Dr. Orlick received his B.A. degree in physical education and recreation at Syracuse University; his M.Ed. in guidance and counseling at the College of William and Mary; and his Ph.D. in sports psychology at the University of Alberta.

A former Eastern Intercollegiate and N.C.A.A. regional gymnastic champion, Dr. Orlick is active in sports-related organizations. He is a member of the International Society of Sports Psychology and the North American Society for the Psychology of Sports and Physical Activity.

His articles have been published in many magazines, including the *International Journal of Sports Psychology*, *Human Factors Journal*, and the *Canadian Journal of Health, Physical Education, and Recreation*. He has presented many research lectures before international groups.

CAL BOTTERILL is a teacher, high school coach, manager of the Dutton Memorial Arena, and director of the sports program at St. John's-Ravencourt Private School, Winnipeg.

A former member of Canadian national hockey teams, he also was team captain of the University of Manitoba hockey club, directed the youth department of the Winnipeg Central Y.M.C.A., and served as recreation director for the Manitoba provincial government.

He earned his B.A. degree in physical education at the University of Manitoba and his M.A. in sports psychology at the University of Alberta.